Rogers is Burgess Professor of Public Law and Government (Emeritus) at Columbia. Avery Leiserson is Professor of Political Science and Chairman of the Department at Vanderbilt University. Edgar H. Brookes is Professor of Political Science at the University of Natal in South Africa and during the year 1962-1963 was Visiting Professor at Duke University. William Anderson is Professor of Political Science (Emeritus) at the University of Minnesota and a past president of the American Political Science Association. William S. Livingston is Professor of Government at the University of Texas. Earl Latham is Joseph B. Eastman Professor of Political Science and Chairman of the Department at Amherst College. M. Margaret Ball is Professor of Political Science and Dean of the Woman's College, Duke University. Charles S. Hyneman is Professor of Government at Indiana University and past president of the American Political Science Association. John M. Gaus is Professor of Government (Emeritus) at Harvard and past president of the American Political Science Association. The editor, Robert H. Connery, is a Professor of Political Science at Duke University. J. Peter Meekison, who prepared the Bibliographical Essay, is a graduate student at Duke University.

Teaching political science

WILLIAM ANDERSON

M. MARGARET BALL

EDGAR H. BROOKES

ROBERT H. CONNERY

JOHN M. GAUS

CHARLES S. HYNEMAN

EARL LATHAM

AVERY LEISERSON

WILLIAM S. LIVINGSTON

LINDSAY ROGERS

Teaching political science

A challenge to higher education

Edited by ROBERT H. CONNERY

with a bibliographical essay by

J. PETER MEEKISON

DUKE *University Press*

Durham, N. C. 1965

© 1965, Duke University Press

Library of Congress Catalogue Card number 65-13653

*Printed in the United States of America
by the Seeman Printery, Durham, N. C.*

Acknowledgment is made of permission to re-
print passages from the following books: from
Rationalism in Politics by Michael Oakeshott
(Basic Books, New York, 1962 and Metheuen
and Company, London, 1962); from *A Fourth
of a Nation* by Paul Woodring (Copyright ©
1957 McGraw-Hill Book Company: used by
permission of McGraw-Hill Book Company);
from *The American College* edited by Nevitt
Sanford (John Wiley and Sons, New York,
1962).

Preface

In 1957 the Department of Political Science at Duke University received a grant from the Public Affairs division of the Ford Foundation to be used to encourage research and demonstration projects in public affairs. The Foundation intended "to provide a source of relatively free funds" to be used in some imaginative way not only to push forward the frontiers of the discipline in whatever areas political scientists themselves felt were most important, but to bring to bear what knowledge that might exist in the hope of stimulating further expansion of this knowledge. This was a challenging assignment, and over a period of some five years various projects involving both faculty and graduate students have been supported by this grant. In the spring of 1963 the committee administering the grant decided to sponsor a conference on teaching political science at the college and university level. The committee felt that the conference itself would stimulate interest in this important subject and that publication of the papers presented at the conference would be of service to the profession generally. Certainly, the problems of college teaching are matters of national concern and clearly fall within the scope of public affairs. To bring existing knowledge to bear in this area might well stimulate the further growth of knowledge.

It has been widely predicted that college enrollments in the next two or three decades will increase greatly. As more and more young Americans attend institutions of "higher learning," much more attention should be given not only to what they are taught, but also to how effectively they are taught. Already public-school men, colleges of education, and professional educators have been showing increased interest in all phases of college teaching. Admittedly, political scientists are amateurs in the somewhat involved language that educators use when they talk about teaching; but if they are not willing to examine the problems they themselves face as college teachers and to find solutions for them, they must not object if professional educators dictate the answers. Moreover, historians have been exploring the rise of American colleges and universities as an historical phenomenon; sociologists have been wondering about their impact on American culture; and economists have been studying the financing of higher education. In the past, political scientists have been principally concerned with the research aspects of their discipline. Now more attention should be given to their role in the college community as college teachers.

These papers are a series of thoughtful essays by men and women who have had a great deal of experience in teaching political science. Some of them are persons who have long been regarded as great teachers; others are in the mid-stream of their teaching careers. Each was asked to comment upon what he regarded as most important to successful teaching. All of the papers are intentionally autobiographical.

Both the conference and this volume were a project of political scientists and primarily for political scientists. The whole project might have been called "Operation Bootstrap." This is the most effective way, one might argue, to bridge the gap between those in education who study teaching for teaching's sake and those in the arts and sciences who practice the art of teaching. Although the political scientists who prepared these papers examined much of the current writing on college teaching, this volume is neither based on quantitative research nor is it an exposition of the "science of teaching" in the sense that phrase is understood in schools of education. There has been an increasing amount of "scientific research" in the last decade regarding college teaching, principally by professors of education. Some of it is pertinent to teaching political science at the college level. However useful this research may be, it will not be widely accepted by political scientists until it is put in the context of the discipline and in understandable language. This can best be done by political scientists, and this is what has been attempted in this volume.

The individuals whose papers appear in this volume are well known to the profession and, consequently, are briefly identified here. Lindsay Rogers is Burgess Professor of Public Law and Government (Emeritus) at Columbia University. Avery Leiserson is Professor of Political Science and Chairman of the Department at Vanderbilt University. Edgar H. Brookes is Professor of Political Science at the University of Natal in South Africa and during the year 1962-1963 was Visiting Professor at Duke University. William Anderson is Professor of Political Science (Emeritus) at the University of Minnesota and a past president of the American Political Science Association. William S. Livingston is Professor of Government at the University of Texas. Earl Latham is Joseph B. Eastman Professor of Political Science and Chairman of the Department at Amherst College. M. Margaret Ball was Ralph Emerson Professor of Political Science at Wellesley College; at present she is Professor of Political Science and Dean of the Woman's College, Duke University. Charles S. Hyneman is Professor of Government at Indiana University and past president of the American Political Science Association. John M. Gaus is Professor of Government (Emeritus) at Harvard and past president of the American Political Science Association. J. Peter Meekison, who prepared the Bibliographical Essay, is a graduate student at Duke University.

While there has been no attempt to appraise the techniques of all of the famous teachers in the profession, the methods of those with whom the authors had personal contact are occasionally described.[1] As the titles of the various essays indicate, the viewpoint from which each author considers college teaching differs somewhat from that of any other, thereby including a wide range of views. Each author, however, was at liberty to comment generally upon what he regarded as the most pressing problems of college teaching and to add such remedial suggestions as he might care to offer. As one might expect, there was considerably less agreement upon solutions than upon problems.

Lindsay Rogers thinks that too many courses in political science are offered in colleges and that there is too much featherbedding. ". . . few courses in our field of study can honestly be said to be a necessary prerequisite for the profitable taking of another course." Political science has become an academic discipline which has little to do with the literary life of the country as a whole or with political life. Much of the best writing and thinking is being done, not in the cloistered halls of academia by political scientists, but by

1. For a description of the methods of two score American college professors see, Houston Peterson (ed.), *Great Teachers* (New Brunswick, 1946). Only one political scientist, Woodrow Wilson, is included.

literary men and politicians. Political science should be made more humane since its usefulness lies in the education of laymen. Failure on the part of graduate schools to test the ability to teach may result in considerable damage to college students. Lack of exposure to broad cultural courses and more consideration of teaching ability are seen as the major problems.

The continuing cleavage in political science between the empirical theorist who seeks more satisfying models for explaining behavior and normative philosophers who pursue a more traditional course, Avery Leiserson thinks, presents the college teacher with a difficult problem. To be successful he must formulate in his mind and transmit to his students a sense "of the vital balance between political philosophy, his scientific theory of politics, and personal participation." A good teacher of politics requires knowledge of the methods of scientific inquiry for he must develop in his students the ability to analyze. It is not sufficient simply to weigh policies and institutions in terms of moral ends. These are the goals of good teaching, and much remains to be done before they can be achieved. Moreover, the survival of political science is dependent upon high professional standards in recruiting replacements.

Commenting not only on teaching political science, but on the American college scene in general, Edgar H. Brookes agrees with Rogers that there are too many courses, and too much specialization. American students lack broad vision. Too much time is taken up in college with lecturing and research, too little given to personal contacts with the students. There is too much departmentalization. The goal of college education should be "to see life steadily and to see it whole." He is concerned with the way in which college teachers are educated and about the tyranny of the Ph.D. However, he believes involvement of the professors in the political life of the nation is good both for the professor and for the nation.

William Anderson is not so much concerned with present-day problems of college teaching as he is with emphasizing the opportunities. From his survey of the ancient Greeks and of the period since, he concludes that on only a few occasions in the history of the Western world has it been possible to make an objective study of political behavior. He maintains that conditions for the scientific study of politics exist in modern America to a degree that was rare in the past.

The challenge of numbers was William S. Livingston's assignment. He thinks that political scientists have failed to take full advantage either of their own experience in teaching or of the research which is being conducted in other disciplines. In the future, increasing numbers of students will force a re-examination of teaching methods. Large lecture classes, perhaps television and mechanical aids for the mass of students, independent study for superior students, and much better use of faculty time are among the possible changes Livingston discusses.

Earl Latham argues that there are a great many misconceptions about faculty-student relations. The whole college environment and its relation to teaching needs re-examination. The college has much less impact on the student than is commonly thought. On the other hand some of the more recent attempts to develop new techniques through honors programs, comprehensive examinations, independent study, internships, and the like have both good and bad aspects. The extent to which they are used should be determined on the basis of the goals of a college program.

To what extent do differences between men and women in personality and other characteristics pose a special problem for college teachers? More and more women are going to college today. What they should be taught and how they should be taught are important questions. M. Margaret Ball considers these problems along with the question of who should teach women.

Charles S. Hyneman is worried about the emphasis upon facts in college courses. He argues that the enlargement of knowledge is only part of what a young man should acquire at college. Too little attention is given to fixing new working habits and developing new know-how for getting evidence. More attention should be given to forcing students to think through problems. Courses are so crowded with factual knowledge that students have no time to analyze and understand. Students are not given a sufficient number of analytical jobs to do. Even most term papers require a very low level type of analysis. He wonders whether students in college political science classes have an opportunity to study critically a great book, to have face-to-face confrontations with other human beings, or to analyze a newspaper. In setting up the college program in political science, how much attention is consciously given to the realization of what Hyneman calls "learning experiences"?

The task of the political scientist, as John M. Gaus sees it, is to analyze and interpret the need for government beyond the family and face-to-face groups. While he must draw upon the resources of history, literature, and the social sciences as a teacher of political science, his focus will be on the sector of the problem which might be termed public housekeeping. Too much of the study of politics is devoted to a narrow course approach. Experiments in general education have a therapeutic value. Graduate instruction leaves much to be desired. We are endeavoring to substitute methodology for sober judgment, and offering more and more courses covering less and less.

In the last essay in the series the editor, Robert H. Connery, considers what is involved in good teaching, whether it is an art or a science, and various teaching methods that may prove useful to political scientists.

Discussants of the various papers at the Conference on the Teaching of Political Science, April 18-20, 1963, on the Duke University campus were Professors Ralph Braibanti, Roma Cheek, R. Taylor Cole, J. Woodford Howard, Richard H. Leach, Robert S. Rankin, William Simpson, Allan P. Sindler, and Robert R. Wilson of the Duke University Department of Political Science; Professors James W. Prothro, Shepard Jones, Andrew Scott, and Frederick Cleaveland of the University of North Carolina; Joseph Taylor of North Carolina College; Warner Moss of the College of William and Mary; Chester Bain of the University of South Carolina; Wiley Hodges of The Citadel; William Block of North Carolina State College; C. H. Richards, Wake Forest College; and Herman Walker, Visiting Professor, Duke University. The editor wishes to thank them for generously giving of their time and effort. Their comments have been incorporated by the authors of these papers in their respective essays.

William Simpson of Duke University, who served with the editor as Co-Chairman at the Conference, did much to make it a pleasant occasion for all of the participants in handling the administrative arrangements. John Morgan assisted in editing this volume.

The conference and the publication of these papers was made possible by the Ford Foundation. To Dr. Paul N. Ylvisaker and Matthew J. Cullen, Jr., of the Foundation's Public Affairs Programs and to his colleagues on the Duke University Public Affairs Grant Committee, Robert S. Rankin (Chairman), Ralph Braibanti, John H. Hallowell, R. Taylor Cole, Robert R. Wilson, Robert Smith, and A. S. Brower, thanks are especially due.

The editor cannot conclude this preface without expressing his personal appreciation to two men whose sympathetic interest and sage counsel prompted him over the years to experiment with various teaching methods. Alvin C. Eurich some fifteen years ago, while he was Vice-President of Stanford University, first aroused the editor's interest in college teaching methods. Frank Bowles, a friend of many years, formerly President of the College Entrance Examination Board and now with the Ford Foundation, not only advised the editor upon a Duke project for better utilization of college teaching resources, but over the years has given many hours of his time to broad-ranging discussions of college teaching. From these discussions came encouragement to undertake an examination of the problems political scientists face in this area.

This is the background for "Operation Bootstrap." May it be a means by which political scientists can strengthen and deepen their interest in what must always be the major function of the profession— college teaching.

ROBERT H. CONNERY

Contents

Teaching political science

ROBERT H. CONNERY

"Gladly ... lerne and gladly teche"

Chaucer's Clerk of Oxenford, with a horse lean as a rake, cloak threadbare, cheeks hollow, and manner sober, was too unworldly a man to seek a benefice. At the head of his bed he would rather have twenty books of Aristotle and philosophy than rich robes, a fiddle, or a gay harp. What little gold he obtained he spent on books and learning, praying for the souls of those who gave him the wherewithal to study. His speech was full of meaning and resonant with moral virtue. Gladly would he learn and gladly teach.

Does the modern clerk gladly teach? Certainly when he does he has recurring doubts as to his success. What real impact does he have on his students? He has moments of concern about what he teaches. Aristotle and his philosophy alone no longer seem enough. He is frequently worried about the metes and bounds of his "discipline," and its relation to other areas of knowledge. Sometimes he asks himself what education is all about, what colleges and universities really intend to accomplish.

No one who examines the recent outpouring of books and magazine articles dealing with higher education can doubt that there is grave dissatisfaction with universities not only in the United States but around the world. To be sure, the criticisms vary from country to country and are much more intense in Western Europe and the United States than in Latin America and Asia. In the United States the principal concern seems to be what to teach and how to teach it. This in turn raises the larger question of the purpose and goals of higher education. In other countries access to collegiate institutions is the major problem. In many of them facilities have not kept pace with the rising population or access is restricted on the basis of social class or educational requirements which have little to do with intellectual ability. More and more frequently a university degree is the passport to higher positions in the business world as well as in government service, since the management of a modern technological society requires a large range of skills obtainable only through extensive education. Small wonder then that since World War II the demand for higher education has increased by leaps and bounds and the problems of answering this need have multiplied.

As the recent UNESCO study directed by Frank Bowles explains,[1] "Throughout the world today, education is being remoulded by the action of powerful forces which are impinging on the whole of modern life and radically changing its patterns as well as its urges. Among these forces mention may be made of the population growth, the spread and intensification of industrialization, technology and specialization, the explosion of knowledge (particularly in science), the 'revolution of rising aspirations' leading to a greater democratization of society, and the growing interdependence of the nations and regions of the world."

French students have rioted in the streets of Paris and the expansion of college facilities has become a major political issue. According to the *New York Times,* the opening of the academic year of 1963 was called a catastrophe for French universities. Although the present Sorbonne buildings were built to house not more than 2,000 or 3,000 students, some 33,000 registered that year. Since the library seats only 500, "Studying goes on in crowded noisy cafes where mimeographed copies of the lecture are passed from student to student."[2]

Drop-outs in French universities have ranged as high as 64 per cent in some departments, and much of this is attributed to a teaching system which is confined to large lecture groups with no opportunity for discussion in smaller units and seminars. The whole university problem in France has deeper significance since the distribution of university students is lopsided in favor of young men and women from the upper middle classes. It stems from the secondary school system, where children of rural and working-class families, because of economic pressures, are not able to pursue courses of study that lead to higher learning. Thus, improving the university product involves

1. Frank Bowles, *Access to Higher Education* (The International Study of University Admissions) (New York, 1963), p. 19. This report has been drawn upon freely in describing barriers to higher education in various countries.
2. Henry Giniger, "Paris Students Defiantly Demonstrate on Crowding," *New York Times,* Jan. 16, 1964, p. 79.

democratizing the whole educational system, which, because of the limited facilities available, amounts to a major political headache.

In the last decade the number of persons studying at German institutions of higher learning has increased by 100 per cent. West German authorities have recently approved the establishment of five new universities. These are still in the planning stage, but are expected to begin operations within the next two or three years. The older schools have also enlarged their student bodies, but, as in France, the number of low-income families represented at the universities is still very small, though larger than before the war.[3] It might be noted that even in the United States, the land of opportunity, the same situation exists, although not to the same extent as in many other countries. In 1960 eight times as many youths from the upper social and economic quarter of the population went to college as did youths from the lowest quarter.

Since the war Britain has seen the rise of the "red brick" universities which are in many ways much like municipal colleges found in some of the larger American cities. While this development helped relieve some of the demand for higher education, it was quite inadequate. In the summer of 1963 it was announced that the government at long last had decided to sponsor several new universities. These will be organized more on the pattern of the American university than on the traditional British system of Oxford and Cambridge.

In Latin America highly selective secondary schools privately owned and privately financed act as a barrier to the expansion of university student bodies. Admission to the university rests upon completion of the secondary school, and this closes higher education to all but a small percentage of the population. Asian institutions have had the largest numerical increase in the number of students recorded for any region in the past decade. The number of new universities established in the larger Asian countries, particularly in India and Japan, has been impressive but demand for admission has risen even more rapidly. Consequently university requirements for admission have been more rigid and frequently are quite unrelated to actual programs of higher education.

"Asian education systems characteristically employ long series of

3. Gerd Wilcki, "Germany Plans More Colleges," *New York Times,* Jan. 16, 1964, p. 79.

examinations, each of which takes its toll of candidates in their movement from primary education to the completion of higher education.
The final examinations which determine admission to higher education are the most difficult of all, and in two countries—India and
Japan—repetition of the examination is commonplace. In both countries the examinations are regarded as hurdles rather than as tests
of educational development, and intensive coaching on previous
examination questions is the accepted method of preparation."[4]

The American phenomenon of hundreds of new community colleges, new state university branches, and new private institutions offering increased opportunity for higher education seems to be unique.
To be sure, as James B. Conant points out, there are major difficulties in making accurate statements comparing education in different
countries and even in different states within the union. The word
"university" has a different meaning in Europe than in the United
States. But even in the United States there is no assurance
that two institutions carrying the name "university" have much in
common. They may differ enormously in standards and the range of
subjects they offer for study. Some may not offer graduate work at
all and the output of significant research may be small. "Yet the
opportunity for research and independent study leading to a Doctor's
degree is the hallmark of a university in the eyes of most Europeans."[5]
One example of the difficulty in making comparisons which Conant
cites is between German gymnasiums and American high schools and
colleges. It is quite frequently claimed that the last two years of a
German gymnasium are comparable to the freshman and perhaps the
sophomore years of American college. Yet the facts do not support
this comparison, according to Conant. The level of knowledge for
teachers in a German gymnasium is higher than that of most American high school teachers, but much lower than that required for an
American college professor with a doctorate. These are some of the
difficulties which plague comparisons between the United States and
Western Europe.

Even between states there is such a degree of disorder in the
American system of higher education that comparisons frequently
have little meaning. The state government and primarily the state

4. Bowles, op. cit., p. 128.
5. James B. Conant, "Conant Looks to Europe for Ideas Useful to U.S.," New
York Times, Jan. 16, 1964, p. 78.

legislature has determined the pattern of higher education in each of the fifty states. Political rather than educational considerations have determined the location, size, and, to an extent, the curriculum of state institutions. Generally the system has been divided among a number of more or less separate institutions. Sometimes it has been splintered to an alarming degree. Conant is disturbed about this situation.

American colleges have expanded rapidly in recent years and probably will expand to an even greater degree in the future. This in itself has given rise to much of the recent criticism of American college education. Even the most severe critic, however, has not charged that the physical structure of American universities is inadequate. Certainly American students are the best housed and best fed in the world. Libraries, laboratories, and sports facilities are superb. Millions upon hundreds of millions of dollars have been spent during the last decade for physical plants. Critics object to the sheer size of the campus, the tendency toward curriculum uniformity, and the large numbers of students which make close association with the faculty difficult. Their principal criticisms, however, are directed toward what takes place in the classroom.

What is wrong with American colleges? A recent English visitor thinks there are too many courses and too much splintering of subject matter and that consequently each professor's courses are "closed, self-contained, not subject to competition, comparison or criticism from students attending other courses on the same subject."[6] Each course has its own examination where the student regurgitates the opinions of his instructor. A broad, comprehensive examination covering the whole college experience, he argues, might overcome this difficulty, but the sheer number of students makes this impossible. Moreover, each professor prefers his own ivory tower, so comprehensive examinations are not widely used.

The compactness of the American academic year, with grades regularly assessed in one course after another in clearly defined steps towards the baccalaureate degree, leads students to approach each piece of knowledge as something to be mastered and then forgotten. ". . . the American undergraduate expects to be taught efficiently,

6. T. R. Henn, "Some American Universities as Seen through British eyes," *Harvard Educational Review,* XXIV (Summer, 1954), 203.

clearly, economically as his right."[7] The dominance of the "course" has an annoying by-product in that it encourages cribbing, which would be impossible if the student were examined instead by a board and if the examination covered all of his college career.

American observers have been equally critical about chopped courses and narrow departmentalization, which they feel causes confusion and unnecessary pressures. Paul Goodman in a recent article in *Harper's* not only objects to these characteristics of American education but goes further, asserting that "the great question is not what subjects 'ought' to be taught, but whether the teaching and learning of them make any difference to the student."[8] Oscar Handlin complains that American colleges are becoming "more formal, more bureaucratic, and more rigidly organized."[9] He wants to know, "Why are many of our more sensitive youngsters simply throwing up their hands?" Many of the most able students turn their backs on the whole process and leave before graduation.

Tests, Goodman thinks, should be used essentially to find out what the teacher is failing to get across. When they are tested but not graded, "students are eager to learn the right answers and they ask how to solve the problem."[10] Whether or not one agrees with Goodman, most professors would accept the idea that tests and grades as used in the American college system need to be re-examined. What do tests test and what is the significance of grades?

Too much emphasis, Goodman says, is placed upon pouring more and more facts into students' heads rather than upon developing better working habits and the ability to analyze. Indeed, the distinction between a good college and a poor one lies in whether it emphasizes the collection of facts or the ability to analyze. Goodman complains about the growth in the number of administrators in proportion to the number of teachers, and that deans and their staffs are taking over more and more the direction of student affairs once subject to faculty control. "If the college machine is run shrewdly and aggressively, it may produce bales of diplomas and scholarly publications,

7. *Ibid.,* p. 210.
8. Paul Goodman, "For A Reactionary Experiment in Education," *Harper's Magazine,* CCXXV (Nov., 1962), 69.
9. Oscar Handlin, "Are the Colleges Killing Education?" *Atlantic Monthly,* CCIX (May, 1962), 45.
10. Goodman, *op. cit.,* p. 63.

as well as bigger buildings, endowments, grants, subsidized research, athletic events, and classes of well-employed alumni. But the personal relations of the colleges have less and less to do with teaching and learning, and more and more with every kind of communication, policing, grading, regulation and motivation that is relevant to successful administration."

Although college administrators multiply like hamsters, too many faculty committees are charged with administrative tasks that might properly be handled by clerical staffs. There is too much paper work and not enough time left for contact with students. As Henn puts it, "Courses, curricula, 'integration,' and so forth, are in the long run less important than the relation between the teacher and the taught."[11]

Nor is Henn alone in this position. "Too many college teachers don't teach," says John Q. Academesis, reportedly a college professor of many years' standing, in an article in the *New York Times Magazine*.[12] The young instructor who wishes to climb the promotional ladder in his narrowly specialized department must impress his senior colleagues with his ability to do research. A good research man "does not have to teach. His research activity is the key to academic advancement. One year's research outweighs ten years of teaching, one published research article or book jumps him over many deserving candidates for promotion, whose chief asset has been good teaching. Often the more obscure the research, the further the jump."

"The modern teacher flees to the library and cries 'research' as the medieval thief fled to the church and cried 'sanctuary'. Thereafter, both are untouchable by law or society," says Jacques Barzun, Dean of the Graduate School at Columbia University.[13] Moreover, Barzun maintains that the emphasis upon research develops a contempt for teaching. "Today, it is no longer forbidden to parade oneself as 'a research scholar' and to look down on those fallen creatures who 'do not publish'; it is no longer improper for university departments to boast of their greatness, due to So-and-so and So-and-so, mighty 'pro-ducers' in the sight of men."[14]

11. Henn, *op. cit.*, p. 221.
12. John Q. Academesis, "Too Many College Teachers Don't Teach," *New York Times Magazine*, Feb. 21, 1960, p. 14.
13. Jacques Barzun, "The Cults of 'Research' and 'Creativity,'" *Harper's Magazine*, CCXXI (Oct., 1960), 71.
14. *Ibid.*, p. 70.

Even the very name of "teacher" is no longer respectable in university circles. John Diekhoff in a report of the Ford Foundation says: "The Professor's calling, the calling he hears and heeds, is usually to scholarship, not teaching. He sees himself as historian, or physicist, or critic, or economist. For his biography in *Who's Who* he may call himself 'educator,' but he seldom sees himself and very seldom refers to himself as a 'teacher.' Indeed, he is likely to resent identification with teachers, for teacher is the title and occupation of those who toil in elementary schools and secondary schools rather than in colleges and universities. Only the youngest neophyte, the 'teaching assistant' or 'teaching fellow,' has any form of the word 'teach' in his college or university title. For everyone else there are euphemisms —lecturer, instructor, and the several grades of the more august term, professor, which is reserved for higher education, circuses, and medicine shows."[15]

These are just a few of the complaints about American university education. Some of them are so broadly drawn that they are really criticisms of American society. But for whatever they are worth, they could be summed up in this single statement of Nevitt Sanford, "Indeed, a close look at the college-educated people in the United States is enough to dispel any notion that our institutions of higher learning are doing a good job of liberal education."[16] Sanford believes that while the public is told that the college experience will liberate the mind, build the capacity to make valuable judgments, and inculcate the attitudes and values of democracy, little evidence is offered to show that these noble ends are achieved.

He quite readily admits that colleges are in a position to bring about profound changes in students. A youth entering college frequently has a narrow, prejudiced outlook on life with shallow, transitory interests. He is wanting in discipline and replete with values derived solely from his childhood experiences. What a college can do is to "nationalize" the student, taking him out of his ethnic, religious, geographic, and social parish, and exposing him to a more cosmopolitan world in which the imagination is less restricted by preconceptions and ignorance. The question is, how well American colleges

15. John S. Diekoff, *Tomorrow's Professors* (Fund for the Advancement of Education, New York, 1959), p. 7.
16. Nevitt Sanford, "Higher Education as a Social Problem," in Nevitt Sanford (ed.), *The American College* (New York, 1962), p. 10.

succeed in accomplishing that goal, and to what extent is the college simply an initiation rite for separating the upper middle from the lower middle class? In our society one of the great cultural cleavages is between those who have been to college and those who have not. To go to college is to join what commencement orators call the "fellowship of man" and what Vance Packard more skeptically dubs the "diploma elite."

Jules Henry, an anthropologist and sociologist who has given considerable attention to the cultural background of American schools, charges that

Contemporary American educators think they want creative children, yet it is an open question as to what they want these children to create. . . . American classrooms, like educational institutions anywhere, express the values, preoccupations, and fears found in the culture as a whole. . . . School can give training in skills; it cannot teach creativity. . . . Schools have therefore never been places for the stimulation of young minds; they are the central conserving force of the culture. . . .[17]

The contemporary educational system emphasizes the importance of success and develops a great fear of failure. Because a human being has an inordinate capacity to learn more than one thing at a time, the net result of a class in any subject is frequently to activate the student's drives towards competition, achievement, and dominance. Instead of learning to love knowledge for its own sake, children become embroiled in a nightmare. "The contemporary school is a place where children are drilled in very general cultural orientations and where subject matter becomes, to a very considerable extent, the instrument for instilling them."[18] Could not the same thing also be said for the system of higher education?

Nor is this the only anthropological interpretation of American education. Riesman and Jenks, in a recent study comparing colleges with other American institutions, have this to say: "Looked at in terms of a theory of the labor force, one might describe colleges primarily as personnel offices, feeding properly certified employees into business and the professions. Some colleges supplement these general efforts by direct tie-ins between their education division and

17. Jules Henry, "American Schoolrooms: Learning the Nightmare," *Columbia University Forum,* VI (Spring, 1963), 25.
18. *Ibid.,* p. 30.

local schools, their engineering division and local industry, or their business division and local commerce."[19]

Apart from the technical skills they impart, the colleges also provide a place for inculcating those social and personal skills on which employers are putting increased emphasis. For this purpose, Riesman thinks the curriculum may be of less importance than are the dining halls, the fraternities, and the student-to-student relationships. From this perspective the college might be viewed as "a human relocation project that removes a student from parents, community, and employment, to submerge him in the 'student culture' of his adolescent peers."[20] In one sense, "the American college exists as a vast WPA project, which gives promising adolescents work to do while keeping them out of the job market, and also keeping several hundred thousand faculty members off the streets."[21] Many of the students in many of the preprofessional programs are actually not committed to a career, but are still shopping around.

There may be some truth in these charges, sweeping as they are, but colleges serve many masters, and even political science, as the last Association-sponsored study indicates, has multiple goals. One of the motives that led to the founding of American colleges was to serve a particular occupation. Hundreds of colleges have been founded to provide theologically orthodox clergymen for some sect or other. During the last century, however, the need for ministers has inspired fewer new colleges than the need for teachers, engineers, and other professional men. While training for the public service may not have inspired new colleges, certainly it inspired a number of schools within colleges. All of these vocational colleges have been under considerable pressure to liberalize their curriculum. Indeed, it is probable that if one examined the academic training of influential Americans in 1900 and 1960, today's elite would have spent far more time studying nominal liberal arts subjects than did their grandfathers.

The increasingly national scope of college recruiting is having a profound effect on college provincialism. Half a century ago, most students who went to college would automatically attend the nearest denominational institution, their parents' school, or the state universi-

19. David Riesman and Christopher Jenks, "The Viability of the American College," in Nevitt Sanford (ed.), *The American College,* p. 75.
20. *Ibid.,* p. 77.
21. *Ibid.,* p. 76.

ty. This is no longer true. Not only have the large Eastern colleges developed national recruiting systems, but Mid-Western and Southern institutions draw increasing numbers of students from outside their region. The effect has been to broaden the horizons of choice for college-bound students. In the long run this will undoubtedly have a marked effect on the college environment in which students find themselves.

One of the major difficulties facing a college teacher lies in the realm of communication. As Marjorie Nicholson said recently, ". . . the majority of college students do not read, write or speak English well." The root of the problem may be a failure to understand the nature of the communication process. Human beings communicate with each other by artifical means. Whether by hieroglyphics, or verbal symbols produced when the air is expelled from the chest across the vocal cords, or physical signs indicated by posture and body movements, in each case it is a symbol representing an idea which is broadcast. The whole process is in code. One individual encodes an idea in a written, vocal, or physical symbol which he broadcasts to other individuals who pick it up and decode it. This is the means by which thoughts are passed from one person to another. Poor encoding and decoding facilities lead to a great deal of confusion, especially when one is dealing with the complicated ideas of a highly sophisticated civilization such as ours.

Moreover, the code symbols are not the same for different social classes. The range of symbols for the lower class is much more limited and frequently the symbols do not convey the same meaning for other groups. A professor tends to be much more at home with students from middle or upper class backgrounds than with students from lower class backgrounds. Age differences create another problem of the same order. Although both the student and the professor can enlarge their codes, still both frequently suffer from inability to manipulate them properly.

Some students, of course, do not want to put anything into college, and when they get little out of their college experience, they are critical because, as they put it, college failed "to give" them an education. The whole approach of the college professor to intellectual life is so remote from some students' previous experience that it seems unreal to them. These students feel that they are living in the real world of people and that the professors' world is unreal and remote. Political science may have an advantage here over the humanities in that it is dealing with politics. Even a cursory examination of the daily newspaper should convince a student that the professor's concerns are practical. To be sure, politics may not seem very real to a woman student and some aspects of political theory, as it is sometimes presented, may seem remote to most students.

Running through all of this comment on the American college is a strong current of concern about the professor himself. What manner of man is the modern professor? How much has he changed from his prototype, the Clerk of Oxenford? Certainly the milieu in which the modern professor works is markedly different. Spencer Klaw in an article entitled "The Affluent Professors" says:

The professor is always being asked to fly somewhere: to 'cross-fertilize' a conference on city planning, to advise a government agency on how to cope with inflation or with Africa, to help an oil company teach its foreman how to get along with the men. In sophisticated business circles, to retain a consultant—or a team of consultants—from Columbia, say, or M.I.T. is becoming a recognized status symbol, like owning a big electronic computer. In politics, no man seeks high public office these days without a suite of academic advisers, including, if possible, at least one from Harvard.[22]

The professor's research and consulting assignments need not be limited to his own backyard. More than a thousand faculty members are abroad, participating in hundreds of programs now being operated in foreign countries by American colleges and universities. Some of these programs are financed by the American government, others by the United Nations. Moreover, hundreds of professors go overseas each year as Fulbright Scholars and under grants from various foundations—Ford, Carnegie, or Rockefeller, to mention only three.

The label "research professor" does not necessarily denote a man skilled in research; the term may mean nothing more than an expert in drumming up research funds. While this type of promoter may be only a small minority in the academic community, his existence breeds competition for foundation grants, consulting assignments, overseas junkets, and think-tank conferences. This may compel many a scholar

22. Spencer Klaw, "The Affluent Professors," *The Reporter,* XXII (June 23, 1960), 16.

to spend time and energy lining up financial support for his work and for the work of his colleagues and students in order that his area of interest may survive.

It is undoubtedly true that low academic salaries are one of the reasons that professors are willing to take these assignments. One suspects, however, that even if academic salaries were much higher, many of these same professors would be doing just what they are doing today. Consulting can be exciting and intellectually stimulating as well as financially beneficial. Nevertheless, as Klaw points out, "the mounting traffic between the university and the world outside is raising serious questions. Everybody wants the professor to be mobile, well heeled, and well armed in negotiations with his dean. But if he is always holed up in his laboratory or flying somewhere, what is to become of his students?"

Research and consulting, however, are not the only competitors with teaching. Every since the beginning of the Republic, as Raymond Moley says, there has been some "mingling of academic learning with the practical business of statesmanship."[23] George Wythe at William and Mary had a profound influence on Thomas Jefferson, John Marshall, and Henry Clay. Since Franklin Roosevelt's time, however, more academic men have entered politics. Some have renounced the campus entirely, but many more of them simply participate occasionally in political campaigns either as candidates or as workers in the party organization. These individuals are quite distinct from the scientists and technicians who take leave to serve in the administrative agencies of the government and are concerned primarily with administration, not politics.

Moley thinks that the academic man can learn a great deal from experience in practical politics.

He will learn, if he is perceptive, that high intelligence is just as plentiful among practical politicians as it is in academic life. Men whom hitherto he may have regarded as a lesser breed will rise in his appraisal. Political figures of the past and present will emerge from the books and newspapers and take on lineaments that he can know and respect and explain in his lectures and writings.

But these occasional forays pose a severe test to the teacher when he returns to the campus, Moley maintains.

23. Raymond Moley, "The Academic Man in Politics," *Columbia University Forum,* VI (Fall, 1963), 7.

In political life his expressions are designed to persuade. But ex parte, prejudiced exhortations carried into the classroom become indoctrination. And indoctrination is not good teaching; indeed, it is not teaching at all. It creates discipleship in some students and begets resentment in others. Restraint, moderation, fairness, characterize good teaching. The teacher should beware of the danger of wisecracks and obiter dicta. They may lodge in a student's mind and assume the character of conviction. The sorcerer's apprentices may enlarge offhand remarks to the exclusion of the central truth.

Dissatisfaction with the American college system would exist even if institutions of higher learning were not faced with the vast increase in enrollment in the decade ahead. But numbers in themselves present a challenge. As colleges double and triple their enrollment in the years ahead, can new teaching methods stretch faculty capabilities to teach more students? As the proportion of men to women attending college continues to increase, what effect will it have on curriculum, teaching methods, and college environment in general? Certainly these are factors which must be seriously considered if planning for the years ahead is soundly conceived.

Political scientists not only express many of the general dissatisfactions with colleges, but have a few of their own particular complaints. The nature of political science and its relation to other disciplines trouble some members of the profession, but many more of them are concerned about the way political science is taught. These are some of the problems that this collection of essays intends to examine. Since the series is not an exercise in induction nor designed as an example of detective fiction, the plan of the book does not demand that the plot unfold chapter by chapter. On the contrary, the reader will be better able to follow the detail if he has a foretaste of what the essays contain.

The major purpose is to set forth what a group of political scientists, all of whom have had years of experience in teaching college classes, believe to be important in teaching. It also proposes to fill a wish, at least to some extent, that an eminent political scientist, Frederic A. Ogg, expressed. Nearly two decades ago Professor Ogg said:

I wish that somebody would interest himself in assembling, digesting, and preparing for publication the data that might conceivably be gathered (chiefly from past students) throwing light on the approaches, methods, techniques, innovations, successes, and failures of a representative group of men who have contributed, or are today contributing, most significantly to fruitful teaching in some portion of our field. They would not all be necessarily best known men, or older men, or great writers, or famous scholars. Much fine teaching goes on obscurely. But, a small book could be prepared that would convey the most worthwhile information, breadth of view, and inspiration to all of us, and particularly to those coming along as new teachers in our field.[24]

While deeply concerned about lack of interest in preparing young political scientists to teach, Ogg did not favor "sending off our students to the courses offered by the professional educationalists. . . ." He thought that at some place in the course of graduate work attention ought to be given by the political science staff itself to the problems, methods, and techniques of undergraduate study in the profession.[25] In this position he was far from alone.

In recent days there has been much discussion of the role education must play in the war against poverty. Unquestionably illiteracy and lack of elementary technical skills are major causes of poverty. But the kind of world in which man finds himself demands much more than knowledge of these bare minimums. In a larger sense, the abolition of poverty depends upon a stable political system and one which is responsive to changing social needs. To manage such a system will require a high order of statesmanship. What is the role of the university in meeting this challenge and how can political science best make its contribution? To be sure, some argue that the primary goal of education is personal satisfaction. As Sir Francis Bacon remarked some four hundred years ago, "Knowledge is not a courtesan for pleasure or for vanity nor a bondswoman to acquire gain for her master's use but a spouse for generation, for fruit and for comfort."

Whether the purpose of education is to reform man or to reform the system within which he lives is an old dispute. But one wonders whether it is not a matter of emphasis and whether the two can be separated. Perhaps the task of the "modern clerk" is to achieve both goals. Just as learning and teaching are opposite sides of the same coin, so may development of the individual and the social system be inseparable parts of the same purpose. But there are even more

24. Frederic A. Ogg, "Political Science as a Profession: From the Standpoint of Teaching," *Journal of Politics,* III (1941), 511.
25. *Ibid.,* p. 512.

important problems. To what extent will we change the structure of our society to secure equality of opportunities in education? "Education for responsible citizenship" may well be not merely a cliché but an increasingly difficult and important task, too important to leave to the mass media or solely to the professional educators. The nation needs educated men aware of complex political and social realities of the times. Certainly political science, one of the oldest intellectual concerns of man, has much to offer in solving these problems.

LINDSAY ROGERS

"This is where I came in"—an autobiographical indiscretion

I

In this galaxy of participants in our symposium on the teaching of political science, I am, I think, the *doyen d'age* in respect of the year I received my trade union card—my Ph.D. degree—and I therefore claim the privilege of being discursively autobiographical. During the last forty-eight years I have had political science students at nine colleges and universities. Unhappily, if any student became a brilliant investment counselor, he failed to keep in touch with me, but a good many students have had modest success in other, although less lucrative, fields. One student, my friend over the years, became Secretary of State of the United States. (At the time of his appointment *Time* investigated his academic record and found that I had failed him.) I can call to mind a governor, two congressmen, a federal circuit court judge, several ambassadors (for three countries), half a dozen college presidents, and a good many deans, professors, journalists, and civil servants. (Several of the last category perch on top rungs of the executive and congressional bureaucratic ladders.) Moreover, from 1942 to 1962 I was a sort of employer of holders of trade union cards. As a member of the Superior Council of Education of Puerto Rico (whose principal duties are to act as a board of trustees for the university) I sorrowfully watched a political science department become elephantine and the flowering of a graduate school of public administration in which every single course was required.

Thus, in respect of the teaching of political science, I have had opportunities for an "input" and an "output" which are considerable —terms which I have never seen clearly defined but which I understand are admired by colleagues in esoteric sections of our "discipline."

If you think that my "output" today is too autobiographical, I ask
your forgiveness. "I may omit or transpose facts," says Rousseau in
his *Confessions,* "but I cannot go wrong about what I have built or
about what my feelings have led me to do." Some of the things that
I shall say may at first seem irrelevant, but when I finish I hope you
will agree that they relate to issues within the terms of reference of
this symposium. If some of my views seem to you extreme, I shall
be glad to argue; but if, as T. S. Eliot once said to an audience, "You
convict me of uttering nonsense, I ask for no quarter at all."[1]

II

In the autumn of 1912 I became a graduate student at the Johns
Hopkins University and in the late spring of 1915 I obtained a doc-
torate. On the state of political science and its teaching at Johns
Hopkins as of that period I venture several observations.

1. I began graduate work without having had any undergraduate
courses in political science—none was offered at Johns Hopkins—
and I never felt the lack of them. For nearly forty years I dealt with
hundreds of graduate students at Columbia University and never both-
ered to ask them what their undergraduate work, if any, had been.
What I spotted as literacy or illiteracy, I attributed to reading or lack
of it—not to certain courses rather than other courses.

I recall no instance of a graduate student's telling me about his
college courses and saying that, because of them, he felt it unnecessary
to take a certain graduate course. As I shall say later, in another
connection, graduate students in political science are advantaged if,
as undergraduates, they have drawn on a common fund of relevant
knowledge. History, literature, "great books" are useful—almost essential. Undergraduates who do not neglect them find that as graduate
students they have had good preparation and that their common background facilitates that "conversation" which is a vital factor in the
educational process. I recall two very good students who were handicapped because they had specialized in fields quite foreign to their
later interests and had big gaps to fill. One student had been a mathe-

---

1. Some years ago *The Times Literary Supplement* damned me with faint praise
by admiring the "facility with which he thinks in quotations." It will be noted
that age has not withered my propensity to quote.

matics major at Dartmouth; the other came from the Sheffield Scientific School at Yale. The former abandoned political science to save a lucrative family business; the latter, on the faculty of a major university, has an important book in press. The regret of these two students was that they had not had enough history and literature but I do not recall that either said anything about having had little or no political science.

Hence a question: Are undergraduate courses in political science of any real help to graduate majors in the subject? If the answer is that students become acquainted with some of the "literature" then I ask whether this literature is ephemeral and textbookish ("anti-cultural" as Henry M. Wriston calls it), or whether it "belongs to the ages." This phrase I leave undefined, but I think that the difference between the two categories is plain, and I add that the categories may be just as relevant in respect of students who do only undergraduate work in our "discipline."

Is it possible to make a distinction between teaching undergraduate and graduate students, save that, for the former, we should make the subject more "humane"? How can there be a real distinction when any intelligent young man (or woman), who has had no courses in political science, can take any one of the courses we call "advanced" and can do well? I notice in some curricula that completion of certain courses is prerequisite to admission to other courses. The explanation may be that certain influential professors insist that they have captive audiences. But the only proper excuse for such requirements must rest on the ground that what is initially required is more cultural than what can only be taken later; that, in other words, there must be some political literacy before entrance on what G. M. Young has called the Waste Lands of Experts and Specialists where each knows "so much about so little that he can neither be contradicted nor is worth contradicting."[2]

2. "The flesh of animals who feed excursively," Doctor Johnson told us, "is allowed to have a higher flavour than that of those who

---

2. When I was in college it took me two-and-one-half years to pass an elementary course in physics. (Later, my professor, then president of the university, dined with me and said that most of what he had failed to teach me had subsequently proved to be wrong). In physics one must go from the elementary course to more advanced courses, but is this true of political science? Many curricula seem to suggest that it is.

are cooped up." May there not be the same difference between men who read as their taste prompts and men who are confined in cells and colleges to stated tasks? Our stated tasks at Hopkins were not many. There were courses (for the most part staggered over three years) on American constitutional law, comparative constitutional law, the legal aspects of economic and industrial relations, ethical theories of law, and analytical political jurisprudence. It was almost undiluted John Austin: certainly unexciting and at times some of it did not seem worthwhile.[3]

A half-century ago graduate students at the Johns Hopkins could sit at the feet of only one professor of political science—Westel Woodbury Willoughby. As of his day he was eminent. His books on *The Nature of the State* and *Social Justice* had to be reprinted. My friend John Dickinson (who knew about such matters) used to say that Willoughby's "Political Theories of the Ancient World" was more satisfactory than William A. Dunning's volume on the same period which was long the standard textbook. "Willoughby," said Dickinson, "went to the best secondary authorities and relied on them. Dunning attempted to make an original contribution."[4]

Do political science students of the present generation ever hear of Willoughby? How long is it since he had what William James called the immortality of a footnote? If I am correct in thinking that he has faded into oblivion, we should be rather modest in our estimates of ourselves, for most of us have strutted on our academic

3. I revised this opinion somewhat when I read Walter Bagehot's "Essay on Sir George Cornewall Lewis." What Bagehot said in discussing John Austin applied to Willoughby who was Austin's disciple: "He gave politics not an interesting aspect but a new aspect; for by giving men a steady view of what political communities must be, he nipped in the bud many questions as to what they ought to be or ought not to be. As a gymnastic of the intellect and as a purifier, Mr. Austin's philosophy is to this day admirable, even in its imperfect remains: a young man who will study it will find that he has gained something which he wanted but something which he did not *know* that he wanted; he has clarified a part of his mind which he did not know needed clarifying." Later I thought that my mind had been clarified, but I did not realize it at the time.

4. This is how Dunning happened to write three volumes on political theory. John W. Burgess, the senior professor at Columbia, called him in one day and said: "Dunning, we have no course in the history of political theory. I want you to give one."

Dunning replied that his chief interests were in American history—in the Reconstruction period—and that he still had work to do in that field. "I do not know much political theory," he told Burgess.

"Well," said Burgess, "you read French. You know Paul Janet's *Histoire de la Science Politique dans ses Rapports avec la Morale.* The students won't know about this book. You use it for lecture notes until you can publish your own histories."

Dunning did exactly that. How many of us have done much the same thing?

stages less prominently and less influentially than Willoughby strutted on the Johns Hopkins stage. Moreover, it should be noted that he himself was not confined in a "cell"—in an ivory tower. He served as constitutional advisor to the Republic of China (while he was in Peking he was not asked for much advice) and later was for a time Counsel to the Chinese Embassy in Washington.

From time to time occasional lecturers appeared. One year James Brown Scott, Director of the Division of International Law of the Carnegie Endowment for International Peace, came over from Washington weekly and addressed those of us who turned up. His "method" (in days when "method" was not much discussed) was to read a paragraph from Rouvier's *Principes du Droit des Gens,* first in French (he thought his French excellent, but since we could understand him we knew that it was pretty American), translate the passage, and then discourse on whatever came into his mind. During a second year he reminisced weekly on "international relations." This was a time when nobody thought it worthwhile to argue whether "international relations" were, or could, by the "structuring of the subject," become a "discipline." No one worried about a "body of theory" for international relations. Washington, as a diplomatic capital, was less important than Constantinople or Brussels. To be sure, even then, Russia was something of an enigma wrapped in a mystery, but the actions of the Tsar were more predictable than those of the men in the Kremlin came to be.[5] Occasionally, there were short-order cooks who gave a few lectures on their specialties. I recall one (later a president of the American Political Science Association), who puzzled me by pronouncing the final syllable of plebiscite as if it were two syllables—"see tea," and sent me posthaste to a dictionary.

5. When the subject of international relations found its way into the Oxford curriculum—because of the endowment of the Montague Burton Professorship rather than by professorial pressure—Sir Alfred Zimmern's inaugural lecture sounded a defensive note. "Amid the group of studies devoted to the interpretation of modern society, International Relations is only one, and a late comer in the field. It is indeed legitimate to inquire whether, in an academic sense, it is a subject at all." Sir Alfred did not have to apologize for himself because a quarter of a century before a volume entitled "The Greek Commonwealth" had established his scholarly reputation. Now, however, mindful of the writers on politics, the economists, the political theorists, the historians, the geographers, the international lawyers, and the psychologists, he wondered whether the teacher of international relations could find a place among his colleagues. Unless he trespassed on these domains, he would be left "with a painful choice between the preaching of high sounding sentimentalities and the retailing of current events." Now the international relations scholars poach at will on other domains and maintain that they have a *terra* that is *incognita* to lesser mortals.

Constitutional law and jurisprudence, international law and relations—such was our diet in political science. For the doctor of philosophy degree two minor subjects were required, and here fortune
blessed some of those who made political science their major: one
minor could be satisfied by a bachelor of laws degree, and the University of Maryland's law school (in Baltimore) offered late afternoon
and evening courses. My second minor subject was political economy;
the requirements went little beyond the contents of Frank W. Taussig's
recently published two-volume textbook.

Several years ago at the Northwestern University Conference
on what should be in the graduate political science curriculum, I
remarked to Mr. Pendleton Herring, President of the Social Science
Research Council (which had spent millions endeavoring to live up
to its name), that we at the Johns Hopkins, on a meager instructional
kitchen budget, had eaten about as well as the latest generation of
graduate students who, offered courses galore, risked ruining their
digestions.[6] Mr. Herring did not disagree, but at that conference,
where the "discussants" (horrible word!) were considering (and for
the most part rather adversely) the curricular claims of Plato, Aristotle, Machiavelli, Rousseau, and John C. Calhoun as against those
adventurers who "measure" public opinion and argue that successful
public administrators are scientists rather than artists, there was no
opportunity to elaborate what was in both of our minds.[7]

3. But at Hopkins, half a century ago, students could profit from
a sesame that was more open than any I have seen at any other
university. There was a seminar room which housed a good working
library and which, just as importantly, displayed the current issues
of every weekly, monthly, bi-monthly, quarterly, and annual publication that might contain something of interest to young men who
thought they wanted to learn more about public law, government,

6. After Willoughby retired, the Hopkins acquired such a galaxy in the political
science department (now ten professors, two of them former students) that, unhappily, I think, there is no longer the bachelor of laws degree as an option for a
"minor" subject.

7. It is worthy of note that Willoughby, whose interests were narrow, had had
as a student the first president of the Social Science Research Council, Robert T.
Crane. Hopkins courses, largely based on analytical political jurisprudence, did not
prevent Crane and Herring from plumping for "cross-disciplinary" approaches and
the greater (excessive?) use of statistics in the study of political phenomena, and
giving aid and comfort to students of "behaviorism."

and politics. In a far corner of that room Willoughby had a desk at which he spent several hours each day, occasionally reading, but for the most part writing, undisturbed by the discussions of students elsewhere in the room. He was always willing to be interrupted and to reply to questions. There were no dormitories at Hopkins, but in that seminar room we had a good deal of communal life which is, I think, of vital importance in the maturing of graduate students as well as of undergraduates.

Weekly in that room the students foregathered with Willoughby, occasionally in a "journal club" where we discussed something interesting that had recently appeared in print, and more frequently in a "seminar." This was not a seminar in the specialty of the savant who chaired it (the prevailing practice of the present?) but a "seminar in political science."[8] Its primary purpose was to provide an outlet for the members to report on the progress of their dissertations. These we began to prepare soon after we began graduate work. The theory was that anyone opting for work in political science must have some interests; if not, that one had better go elsewhere. The theory also was that work on a manuscript that had to be good enough to be published would profit the worker as greatly as attendance on courses. The result was that, within three years, those of us who did not fall by the wayside finished the manuscript of an acceptable dissertation. We made a deposit to defray the costs of publication and could take a few months to do some polishing and repolishing before dealing with a printer.[9]

So in June, 1915, after three years, I finished my graduate work and in September went on the faculty of the University of Virginia. I was struck by the fact that Willoughby must have recommended me as probably being a good teacher when he did not have the faintest idea whether I could handle myself in front of undergraduates. He

8. If it be said that most universities now have too many graduate students for one such seminar, the answer is to have several such groups and not to proliferate the students under a feudal regime so that their knight service means, as Anatole France put it, that they learn more and more about less and less.

9. There is documentary evidence that what I have said does not glamorize "the good old days." Department heads at Johns Hopkins reported annually to the president of the university on what happened in their seminars. The reports listed the authors and the titles of the papers that were read, and the president included these listings in his annual report, which was published. As I look at the printed evidence (1913-1916), I see that one or two of my colleagues made false starts on dissertations and chose new subjects. In the first year of residence some of us, and by the second year all of us, were working on our dissertations.

knew me as an irregular attendant on his lectures; as a member of his seminar; as a possessor of a certain number of facts; as the holder of opinions he must have thought half-baked; as the author of a few articles that had appeared in American law reviews and in American and English journals for lay readers; and of an accepted dissertation. I was so impressed by his indifference to my jejuneness that I wrote a short article entitled "A Neglected Aspect of Graduate Instruction" (*The Nation,* September 9, 1915).

I pointed out that medical schools gave clinical training; that law schools had moot courts; and that at divinity schools the "seminoles" practiced the preparation of manuscripts, which would be kept in a barrel, and tried them out when pastors were vacationing away from their flocks. I boldly announced that "this analogy is closest, for both the clergyman and the teacher give the public not what it demands but what is good for it." I suggested that in the graduate school there should be some practice in "oral and extemporaneous discussion of elementary problems," so that the professors might discover "whether the student is able to teach," and his fellow students might report on whether they profited or suffered. I bolstered this proposal by quoting from one of Nicholas Murray Butler's reports to the trustees of Columbia University: "The youngest of instructors," he said, "is shut up in the classroom with a company of students and left to his own devices. The damage he may do in learning what teaching is all about is frequently irreparable but no older or more experienced head is at hand to counsel and direct him." So far as I know Nicholas Murray Butler never tried to do anything about this. Nor did any of his graduate departments.

4. At the University of Virginia I was the only person giving instruction in political science and the "introductory" course was the only one that mattered much. It was titled "American Government and Politics" and I promptly made its content cover the government of England. When I went to the first meeting I found 250 unfortunates who were to endure what a Trollope character described as "the verdure and malleability of pupildom."[10] I was to lecture to them, and I began by telling them that, while lecturing had been the

10. There was a course on municipal government, which, happily, interested only a handful of students. I met it quite irregularly and never offered it again. There were a few students in a seminar and we made it a journal club.

only possible means of teaching when universities were founded in the Middle Ages, it should have long since become obsolete. In the Middle Ages no printed books were available, so students had to listen to lecturers reading to them from Latin manuscripts. If the readers were precocious enough, they endeavored to make some comments of their own. The lecture system is still with us, even though the invention of printing made the lecture system's rationale evaporate —that is if rationales can evaporate.[11]

What should the students read? Well, even then I was allergic to textbooks. Beard's textbook and his *Readings* had appeared, but I cannot recall that I was familiar with them. I had read some of James W. Garner's *Introduction to Political Science,* and I had seen Ogg's *European Governments.* I used the word "seen" in the precise sense: Willoughby had held it in his hand and had read a few passages when he was lecturing on European constitutional law.[12] I made my 250 victims read Bryce's *The American Commonwealth,* Bagehot's *The English Constitution,* Dicey's *The Law of the Constitution,* Wilson's *Congressional Government,* some of De Tocqueville, and some of *The Federalist* papers. I asked them to read some biography, and since in the case of English statesmen biographies were usually on too ample a scale, during my time at the University of Virginia there was, I am afraid, much rough handling of what Trevelyan was later to call the "best record of a nation's past that any civilization has produced"—*The Dictionary of National Biography.* I do not know how successful it all was, but several of the students survived and are among those of whom I boasted in my first paragraph.

III

The addresses of the presidents of the American Political Science Association have rarely lent themselves to quotation; they have been

11. Several years later I came on the definition of a lecturer by F. M. Cornford: "A lecturer is a sound scholar who has been chosen to teach on the ground that he was once able to learn. Eloquence is not permitted in a lecturer; it is a privilege reserved by statute for the university orator."

12. My chief acquaintance with textbooks has come from reading manuscripts that have been submitted to publishers. I recall two incidents. One publisher said that he would not transmit all of my criticisms; they would so discourage the authors that they might abandon their project. The book appeared and was a best

delivered and then potted to blush unseen in the *American Political Science Review*. More than half a century ago, however, A. Lawrence Lowell (then a professor of government at, and not yet President of, Harvard) told his colleagues at least two things that merited future pondering and that are currently pertinent. His first point was that political science had not yet become a "science" because it had not developed a terminology that was incomprehensible to a man with no more than a good general education. To me, for at least the last fifteen years, a good deal of writing on political science has been completely incomprehensible. Some writers use a jargon worse than Jeremy Bentham's, which, Hazlitt complained, was "a language of his own that darkens knowledge."[13]

In the second place, Mr. Lowell said, our subject had "suffered because of imperfect development of the means of self-expansion." The natural sciences had been able to "grow by segmentation, each division, like the severed fragments of an earthworm, having a vitality of its own. Thus in zoology and botany we hear of cytology, histology, morphology, and physiology, expressions which correspond, perhaps, with aspects of our own ancient, yet infantile, branch of learning." Mr. Lowell did not specify the aspects, and I have always wondered whether he spoke with his tongue in his cheek.

Certainly, if he were able to view the present scene, he would say that the self-expansion—the segmentation—had been extreme, if not idiotic. When I joined the Columbia faculty of political science in 1921, I had thirty-six colleagues—six from my own department of public law and government and the other thirty from history, economics, and sociology. Thirty-six members of the department of public law now have seats on the faculty of political science. In 1921 the department offered thirteen general and research courses; in 1959-1960 the courses numbered seventy-four.

I take at random the political science offering at a small but quite respectable state university in the West. The student can choose between (rather he is compelled to select from) Government Control of Business; Legislature and Legislation; Political Parties and Pres-

---

seller. In the other case the publisher doubled my fee because I reported plagiarism and he could therefore cancel his contract.

13. "Therefore doth Job open his mouth in vain; he multiplieth words without knowledge" (Job XXXV, 10).

"Who is this that darkeneth counsel by words without *knowledge?*" (Job XXXVIII, 2).

sure Groups; Governments of Southeast Asia; Goverments of China and Japan; Governments of Western Asia; Eastern European Communism; Municipal Administration; Public Personnel Administration; Public Administration; Administration of Natural Resources; Intergovernmental Relations; Problems in Local Administration; Problems in Federal Administration; Public Financial Administration; Administrative Organization and Management; Government Planning; Administrative Theory; State Government and Administration; Problems in Local Government; and Problems in State Government. There is a condemnation of students without trial to serve sentences of confinement within the walls of specialized vocational minutiae.[14] Should one recall "Alice in Wonderland": "That's the reason they are called lessons, because they lessen every day"?

> Bell, book and candle shall not drive me back,
> When gold and silver becks me to come on.

But where are the gold and silver? Surely not in courses on "Congress and Latin American Policy," or on "The Strategy of Conflict: Deterrents in the Cold War."

Can it not be said that insofar as the teaching of political science is concerned our colleges are becoming more and more like technical schools? Even if the answer is only a qualified affirmative we should keep in mind the profound remark of a Harvard philosopher, who is rated as having had the finest critical mind of his generation. "At a technical school," said William James, "a man may grow into a first-rate instrument for doing a certain job, but he may miss all the graciousness of mind suggested by the term 'liberal culture.' He may remain a cad, and not a gentleman, intellectually pinned down to his one narrow subject, literal, unable to suppose anything different from what he has seen, without imagination, atmosphere, or mental perspective."

Am I going too far if I suggest that we political scientists have indulged in featherbedding? I do not think that my choice of the word is unfair. My inquiries about college curricula have turned up no cases of political science firemen who, "having tenure," ride in departmental cabs and do nothing. Nor have I ever heard of anything in our "racademic" careers that is similar to the setting of bogus type.

---

14. I withhold judgment on "area studies," but surely they should be fruit carefully rationed to undergraduates save in exceptional cases.

(When reading what some of my younger colleagues write, I suspect that the time may not be far distant when automation will do the writing for them.) But I think that the term featherbedding is one explanation of the multiplication of courses: some of us have wished to take advantage of our current academic interests, unmindful that our interests, as Professor Oakeshott has forcibly told us, "may be in an entirely unsuitable condition for undergraduate pursuit." I add that in many cases they will be unsuitable for pursuit by graduate students.

Secondly, the proliferation of specialized courses must, in some cases, have been due to the desire to give a small teaching load to someone engaged mainly in research. Or graduate professors who have had an intelligent and agreeable Ph.D. candidate may have thought it would be pleasant to keep him around for a while. In each case the new course must seem not to duplicate another course. And I imagine that some proposals for instruction in political cytology, for example, have been motivated by a desire to create an attractive berth for a personal friend and to lure him from another institution. I add that when I reflect on how some political science departments have profiteered in personnel, I confess having no sympathy with complaints about the low level of university salaries. Departments should have kept themselves small and divided up the available money.

As I have said above, no course in our field of study can intelligently and honestly be said to be a necessary prerequisite to the profitable taking of another course. Yet, as I inspect college catalogues and see prerequisites listed, I suspect that their *raison d'être* is a desire on the part of certain givers to be absolutely certain that they have some recipients. On occasion there seems to be an insensitivity to colleagues lifting their eyebrows. At a state university that I know of, only one course is required. It is given by the head of the department, and unhappily for the students, it is a course in state government! To inflict a course in "state government" on undergraduates is not merely a misdemeanor but a felony. If there should be students who profess an interest, let them read a textbook and/or the newspapers and draw up a list of questions to which they have not been able to find adequate answers. Then a professor or so in a lecture or two could provide the answers.

By and large I think too many specialized courses are provided for graduate students, all less literate than they should be. Until we have ridded ourselves of featherbedding, courses will probably be too numerous, but I suggest that those required be almost nil. During my time at Columbia we told Ph.D. students that they could take all their courses in Chinese and swimming, and if they could thus prepare to pass their oral examinations, this was all right with us. We did require masters' students to take some work in the department, but this was only to protect ourselves from having to bother with masters' essays by students in other departments. As for the courses (Columbia had a point system), the students needed only to be fiscally, not physically, present. And as for undergraduate majors in political science, I think there should be great liberality. If, say, four courses are required, I would for one of them allow the substitution of any history course, and for another of the four any course in English Literature which dealt with writers who, either personally or by way of their prose or poetry, had some connection with the political life of their generation.

As I have already suggested, half a century ago there were first-rate universities that gave no undergraduate work in political science. Our association dates from 1907 and until World War I had a small membership. At the end of World War II a committee of our association in a pamphlet entitled "Political Science and the World of Tomorrow" reported that, "as compared with over 150,000 physicians and an even larger number of lawyers in the United States, the number of political scientists giving full time to the study and teaching of government in colleges and universities is very small, probably not over 1,500 for a nation of 140,000,000 people." In 1951 a committee reported that there were 5,000 persons "teaching in Political Science in the United States." The secretary of the association informs me that the number is now 8,500.[15] The earlier committee solemnly declared that "a heavy responsibility for the public welfare falls upon the small number of men and women who make a profession rather than a part-time avocation of the study of government." I wonder.

Is there anything in the comparison with the medical profession?[16]

15. In the decade student enrollment has increased by about 50 per cent.
16. "The medicine man of an earlier age," writes Kenneth W. Thompson, "was turned into a physician as philosophical and scientific inquiry gave him new insights

To be sure, like physicians, we have had some individual patients—graduate students working for advanced degrees, politicians who need ghost writers, and government officials not above seeking advice. Some of us have written and published prescriptions for better political behavior by office holders and for improved institutional functioning, but is there any virtue in desiring a large increase in our number *qua* number? When I recall my tyrociny, and when I reflect on those whom we have speeded from the faculty of political science at Columbia—some very good and now on the faculties of major league universities and colleges and in the government service; some good and doing useful work in the minor leagues; and some lost in the sticks—my feelings range from pride to uneasiness. When I think of the figure of 8,500, I am inclined to shudder.

Did not Huxley (the elder) tell us that while in a multitude of counselors there is wisdom, the wisdom is to be found only in a few of them? Mr. Justice Cardozo has warned us that "the output of a multitude of minds must be expected to contain its proportion of vagaries. So vast a brood includes the defective and the helpless." After he had reviewed some new recruits for the British Army, the Duke of Wellington was forced to remark: "I don't know if they will scare the enemy; but by God they scare me."

> 'If seven maids with seven mops
> Swept it for half a year,
> Do you suppose,' the Walrus said,
> 'That they could get it clear?'

and resources. In the same way, the policy-maker of today is handicapped by the fact that his rough generalizations are drawn from a single experience. With better data and more accurate theories he can become more nearly 'a physician of policy.' " Writing of the task of the historian, Sir Lewis Namier says that, as in the case of medical diagnosis, "a great deal of previous experience and knowledge, and the scientific approach of the trained mind, are required, yet the final conclusions (to be re-examined in the light of evidence) are intuitive: an art." The greatest physicians, Sir Lewis suggests, have a flair, as do the greatest historians, of whom he was one.

Two further observations: (1) A physician's patient has nothing to say on whether he shall get a quarter or a half grain of morphia to relieve his pain, on which wonder drug shall be used to treat his pneumonia, or on how large a segment of his intestine shall be removed. The body politic tells its would-be physician what it will and will not stand for. (2) Those who use the medical analogy hopefully have forgotten Moliere's *Le Medicin malgré Lui*. "I find it the best of trades," says Sganarelle, "for whether we are right or wrong we are paid equally well. . . . A shoemaker can't spoil a scrap of leather without paying for it, but we can spoil a man without paying a farthing for the damage done. The blunders are not ours, and the fault is always that of the dead man. He can't protest." The body politic does protest.

'I doubt it,' said the Carpenter,
And shed a bitter tear.

IV

If one throws a net rather widely, one may say that the *New York Times Book Review* annually pays attention to 175 volumes on the "recent history" that Edward A. Freeman termed "past politics" and on the politics that he called recent history. The *American Political Science Review,* the organ of our learned society, each year publishes more or less lengthy discussions of some three hundred volumes within its field of interest and lists six or seven hundred additional titles as "received." Many of these books remind one of Charles Lamb's remark: "They look like books but they are not real books because they cannot be read."

Our *Review* ignores many of the volumes discussed in the *Times Book Review* on the ground (I suppose) that they are meant for popular consumption and thus have no "scholarly interest." I confess that I have always thought that brilliant political journalists—Walter Lippmann, James Reston, and Raymond Aron, for example—merit the attention of scholars and students just as much as do Professor John Doe and Professor Richard Roe who have written textbooks or monographs. We should not forget that Walter Bagehot was a journalist, and I cannot recall any American professors (save Charles Beard and Thomas Reed Powell) who have been as provocative and as illuminating as Walter Bagehot was and still is.

Nearly two hundred periodicals ranging alphabetically from the *Administrative Science Quarterly* to the *Yearbook of World Polity* make current politics one of their major interests.[17] Annually, hundreds of thousands of pages—rarely seen by the non-specialist—deal with the governmental problems of the world in which we live and the ways in which these problems should be investigated and discussed and how the investigation and the discussion can be made more "scientific." All this may not be luminous, but as Sheridan said of Gibbon, it is certainly voluminous.

17. When I was young channels of publication were much more limited, and I do not think that we found this inhibiting. We might have, if "political scientists" had then been as numerous as they now are. Formerly one could read pretty nearly everything that one's colleagues wrote. This (happily?) in now impossible.

For the most part, the writers of these books and articles are the 8,500 men and women who teach political science in American colleges and universities. Some of them feel that they must publish or perish, for in certain misguided academic quarters, a "productive output" is a *sine qua non* for promotions in rank. Many teachers have a real urge to say things in print; some are associated with research institutes, agencies, centers, etc., which use funds granted them to publish pamplets and books in the hope that they thus will obtain additional funds. Inevitably some who inspect the results of this authorship will be reminded of Macaulay's remark: "So great is the taste for oddity that men who have no recommendation but oddity, hold a high place in the vulgar estimation." Should one modify this slightly and say "scholarly estimation"?

On the first page of the *New York Times Book Review* a few months ago, W. M. Frohock of Harvard University referred to academic studies "which, by the close reading of familiar texts, illuminate what is already not badly lighted." Such literary activity, he said, "goes on everywhere—professors writing for other professors in periodicals which other professors edit." This "academic discipline," he added, "has little to do with the literary life of the country as a whole." The academic activity I am discussing has little to do with the political life of the country. Few executives, legislators, columnists, or editorial writers take note of it.

I give an example of a failure to explore our "Waste Land," or more probably there were explorers who found nothing worth while. Since the end of World War II, in books and learned journals tens of thousands of pages have dealt with the workings of our federal system. But in his recent Godkin lectures at Harvard University, *The Future of Federalism,* Governor Nelson A. Rockefeller cited only two political scientists: Lord Bryce and the late Harold J. Laski. I think it is safe to say that only very rarely does any academic product in our field of endeavor find its way into literature written in an endeavor to educate laymen.

You may be saying to yourselves: "What has all this to do with . . . the teaching of political science?" I reply that even if we are not guilty of the crime of inflicting our own academic interests on our students, we may harm them by urging them to read too many of the hundreds of thousands of pages that pour from subsidized presses.

I have always urged my students to read the *New Yorker* before they turned to the *American Political Science Review*. The *New Yorker* has as good political correspondence as any other publication in the world. Those who write regularly from London, Paris, and Washington are first-rate, and roving reporters write frequently from other capitals. The *New Yorker* published the best discussion I have seen of the Berlin Wall and a superb report on the Vatican Council. A few months ago a brilliant young Indian writer analyzed at length the theories, the crochets, and the controversies of a remarkable group of British historians—a group that unfortunately has no counterpart in any other country: A. J. P. Taylor, C. V. Wedgwood, Arnold Toynbee, Sir Lewis Namier, Herbert Butterfield, Isaiah Berlin, E. H. Carr, etc., etc. No one who wishes to be literate in the field of politics can afford to ignore these historians.[18] (I wonder how many political science students have been urged to read these articles.) What comparable discussions appear in our *Review*? I now turn for a moment to what may seem to be an irrelevant digression.

According to Leonardo da Vinci, "small rooms or dwellings set the mind in the right path; large ones cause it to go astray." In a letter to a friend, John Locke warned against general theories. "It is easier," he said, "to build castles of our own in the air than to survey well those that are on the ground."[19] To De Tocqueville an abstract term was "like a box with a false bottom; you may put in it what ideas you please and take them out again without being observed."

"It is the fashion of youth," wrote Hegel, "to dash about in abstractions. But the man who has learnt to know life steers clear of the abstract and adheres to concrete." To my mind, Hegel remained something of a boy because he failed to follow his own advice, and I never have been sure I understood him. Frederick William Maitland (the "royal intellect of the Victorian Age") said that "people can't understand old law unless you give a few concrete illustrations; at least I can't."[20] That felicitous contemporary essayist, F. L. Lucas,

18. Dr. Hannah Arendt's five *New Yorker* articles on the Eichmann case are the most provocative discussion of the trial that has yet appeared.

19. Another quotation from Locke is pertinent. The busy mind of man is unwilling "to stop when it is at the utmost extent of its tether, and to sit down in a quiet ignorance of those things which, upon examination, are found to be beyond the reach of our capacities."

20. The Harvard law professor, John Chipman Gray: "The use of homely ex-

speaks of "the type of a philosopher who sometimes from a sound instinct of self preservation, consistently refuses to illustrate his meaning by *examples.*" Likewise, to Archibald MacLeish, "abstractions have a limited, a dehumanizing, a dehydrating effect on the relation of things to the man who must live with them." One is reminded of Dr. Johnson's complaint of Poll Carmichael: "I never could persuade her to be categorical." I am not saying that academic writers on politics wiggle and waggle, but they are enamored of generalizations that are too broad, abstractions that are too puzzling, and refinements that are too deep.

Some years ago the Yale philosopher, Brand Blanshard, delivered a lecture at the University of Manchester on "Philosophical Style." Since it was published, no student of mine has failed to hear about it and to be asked to read it. Mr. Blanshard sounded off on Macaulay's familiar diary entry anent a translation of Kant's "Critique": "I tried to read it but found it utterly unintelligible, just as if it had been written in Sanskrit." Macaulay said that the only thing he was sure he understood was a Latin quotation. Mr. Blanshard tells us that "most men's minds are so constituted that they have to think by means of examples: if you do not supply these they will supply them for themselves, and if you leave it wholly to them, they will do it badly. On the other hand, if you start from familiar things, they are quick to make the necessary generalizations." In other words, unless you can point to an event or situation and say: "Now you see what I mean," there is no meaning in what you said. Or, as T. H. Huxley once put it: "There is nothing like a brutal fact to kill a fine theory."[21] You are now saying to yourselves: "Why does he not 'think by means of examples' "? I shall endeavor to do so.

Take one of our fraternity, whose many critiques of American

pressions and examples helps one to keep a grasp on the facts of daily life, the loss of which is the chief danger in the moral sciences."

21. Mr. Blanshard pointed out another aspect of the matter. "On the great issues of philosophy," he says [I add politics], "many of men's hopes and fears do hang and plain men feel that their philosopher should be alive to this and show it. It is not that they want him to give up his intellectual rigor and scrupulousness—at least they do not think that it is; it is rather that when men are dealing with themes of human importance, they should not deal with them as if nothing but their heads, and somewhat dessicated heads at that, were involved." Mr. Blanshard adds that "academic tradition does not require clearness," that, on the contrary, "there seems to be a presumption that anyone who writes in such a way as to be understood of the many is debasing the coinage of scholarship. But plain men do not see why this should be true, and being one of them, neither do I." I am a plain man also, and neither do I.

foreign policy during the last decade have been as trenchant and as persuasive as those of any other commentator save perhaps George Kennan and Walter Lippmann. The man I am citing criticizes our "obsession with military alliances." Here he is specific: The Baghdad Pact, the Eisenhower Doctrine and, "more particularly," the Southeast Asia Treaty Organization—each a *brutum fulmen.*[22] But then the critic goes on:

> It is also worthy of note that quite a number of our allies have turned out to be handicaps for the United States in political as well as in financial terms. They have been able to dictate to the United States the policies we are supposed to pursue with regard to them. Where they have not been able to do that, they have, in many instances, been able to impose a veto upon the foreign policies of the United States. What has been generally noted in recent years as the sterility of American foreign policy—the lack of initiative and determination, the immersion in old and safe routines—is in good measure the result of the limitations which the alliances impose upon the United States. Wherever there is need for a new departure, there is also an ally pulling at our coat-tails and saying, "No. If you want to keep me as your ally, you can't do that."

Which allies? When? Why? Which "dictated"? Which pulled at our "coat-tails"? "No" to what?

Or take a recent discussion of the importance of political parties in the study of politics. The writer deals with "the problem of the logical model" in such a study. He discusses "the relationship of parties to public opinion and political representation," deals with "the significance of comparative politics," and then divides party systems into four types: the Representative-Majority Type, the Responsible-Majority Type, the Multi-party Coalition, and the Predominant Single-Party." Finally he goes in for "institutional and behavioral analysis."

The reader of these pages is never able to tell whether the author has in mind British parties, French parties, or American parties; or whether, within a particular political system, he considers that there are different types of parties. All we are certain of is that they are political parties and not tea parties. One assumed that by "Predominant Single-Party" he means the Communist party, but even in this case there are no specifics. Is it unfair to recall Carlyle's wife, who said of Browning's poem "Sordello" that she read it through without being able to make out whether Sordello was a man, a city, or a book.

---

22. Sometimes I thought (before the Supreme Court school prayer decision) that each morning a State Department chaplain prayed: "Give us this day our daily pact."

Or take the floods of words that yearn for the excogitation of "theories" of international relations. Oftentimes in reading them one feels that obscuration is deliberate because clarity would take the cover off and let the reader see that the bucket was empty.[23] When in the floods of words there is a drop of reason it is oftentimes hailed as something new—a "breakthrough"—when it is actually one dropped long ago. Here I must obey Brand Blanshard's injunction and give an illustration of what I have in mind.

Thus, one of our company tells us that his book "is a pioneering [sic] attempt to establish what lately has come to be spoken of as a 'conceptual framework.' " The "conceptual context" to which his discussion is oriented is this: "Is power concentrated in the hands of a single power holder or state organ, or is it mutually shared and reciprocally controlled by several power holders or state organs?" To pose such a question as an original one shows shocking ignorance of the literature of our subject. In 1914, W. Morton Fullerton published a volume which he called "Problems of Power"; there was a revised edition in 1920. An explanation (not an excuse) for this oversight might be that Fullerton was only a brilliant foreign correspondent and not a scholar, but how about the distinguished Italian historian Guglielmo Ferrero? Shortly after the outbreak of World War II he put down "his own intellectual testament and crystallized the tragedy of the Western world" in a trilogy, the third volume of which he called "Principles of Power."[24]

As a reviewer in *The Economist* said of this search for "theory" and the attempts to find new "approaches," they would seem to consist "either of attempts to denature the subject so that it ceases to be an affair of individual men or communities making agonizing choices,[25]

23. Not long ago in *The Times Literary Supplement,* a reviewer said that he did not understand what was meant by this sentence: "The relevant model for world politics was less a two-person zero-sum game than a multi-person non-zero-sum game." I do not understand either.

24. In 1831 there was published in Boston a little volume, *The Political Class Book; Intended to Instruct the Higher Classes in Schools in the Origin, Nature, and Use of Political Power.* Its author was William Sullivan, counselor at law.

25. "In order really to know anything about government, you must see it alive," wrote Woodrow Wilson, "and the object of the writer on politics should be nothing less than this: to paint government to the life, to make it live again upon his pages." Perhaps Wilson was recalling what his "master," Walter Bagehot, had written about Guizot. The Englishman was reading the Frenchman on "principles"—"The principle of Legitimacy, the principle of Feudalism, the principle of Democracy." One principle grew, another declined, and a third crept slowly on. "The mind is immensely edified," said Bagehot, "when perhaps at the 315th page a proper name

but becomes instead a meaningless minuet of abstract concepts; or, on the other hand, particularly in America, a set of mathematical or quasi-mathematical formulae that obliterate the distinctions between one set of concrete circumstances and another." Here it is pertinent to quote Macaulay again, this time on writers who "conceive classes of composition which had never existed, and then investigate their principles." This, he says, is as absurd "as the demand of Nebuchadnezzar, who expected his magicians first to tell him his dream, and then to interpret it." Or, if a more modern authority is desired, I cite Peter de Vries and use one of his atrocious but wonderful puns: It is all a "welter mitty" in their heads.

One final example of the sins that are being committed in the name of political science. Sidney Smith once said of Bentham that he "loved method itself more than its consequences." Of many contemporary Benthams who love method more that its lack of consequences, I choose those who have recently been interested in quantitative rather than qualitative "approaches" to the study of "judicial behavior." They seek to emulate Samuel Butler's "Hudibras" who

> . . . by geometric scale,
> Could take the size of pots of ale;
> Resolve by sines and tangents, straight,
> If bread or butter wanted weight;
> And wisely tell what hour o' th' day
> The clock does strike by algebra.

Macaulay (and I quote him for the penultimate time) put the same thought in prose: "A man would not have been more likely to walk a thousand miles in a thousand hours if he had known the place and name of every muscle in his legs."[26] Macaulay went on to say that "Monsieur Jourdain probably did not pronounce D and F more correctly after he had been apprised that D is pronounced by touching the teeth with the end of the tongue, and F by putting the upper teeth on the lower lip." The comparisons may not be on all fours, but they are worth pondering.

We get the "sines and tangents" and the "D's" and the "F's" in

---

occurs, and you mutter, 'Dear me,—why, if there were not people in the time of Charlemagne! who would have thought that?' "

26. This is from a Chinese philosopher (third century B.C.): "Let me remind you what happened to the child from Shou-ling who was sent to Han-tan to acquire the Han-tan walk. He failed to learn the steps, but spent so long trying, that he ended by forgetting how one usually walks and came home to Shou-ling on all fours."

the quantitative analysis of judicial behavior. We are given statistics
on pressure groups, or, to put it another way, the "trends in *amici*
participation." Here the numerology is only arithmetical. But not so
when we get to the "dissenting blocks" and the "indices of cohesion"
of individual justices: the judicial behavior of those who are senior—
do they dissent more or less?; "scalogram" analysis; the "game
theory" of justices competing for power. "Do the center justices exercise more or less of their proportionate share of power. . . . can a bloc
of two or three justices be equal in power to a bloc of three or four
justices?" Since "game theory assumes that there will be a 'pay-off'
to the players"—theoretical pay-offs—quantitative analysis of judicial
behavior may be able to determine whether there are "side payments
among the justices." One form of side payment may be "the assignment of the writer of Opinions." The premise underlying all this is
that judges are gamesmen, which they are not. "Why isn't it [the
judicial process] in the nature of an art?" Learned Hand once asked
and gave his answer: "It is what a poet does."

You may be saying that I am not discussing the "teaching" of
political science but only writings. This is true. I cannot go into
classrooms and listen to what is taught, but I do look at (and for the
most part refrain from reading) what is being published. Is it not
certain that many of our 8,500 brothers inflict written oddities on
the unfortunates in their classrooms? A former student of mine does
this under instructions from his department head. "Don't you tell
them that it is tripe [a *five*-letter word!] and that they should pay no
attention to it?" I asked. He replied: "No, that would not be cricket."

On much current writing—and I can cite some horrible examples
from the field of public administration—I think we should take to
heart the reply of a keeper in a zoo to the woman who wanted to
know whether a hippopotamus was male or female. The keeper did
not know himself and the woman asked him to find out. "I will not,
Madam," he answered. "That information should be of interest only
to another hippopotamus." Many oddities in present-day political science should be of interest only to those who attempt oddities. We do
not want our students in later years to have the attitude that Hilaire
Belloc had toward some of his Oxford Dons: "I stifle when I think
of you." G. K. Chesterton (Belloc's intimate) described his university

days as "the period during which I was being instructed by somebody I did not know about something I did not want to know."

In his brilliant inaugural lecture as Regius Professor of Modern History in the University of Oxford, "History: Professional and Lay," H. R. Trevor-Roper asserted his belief that history was a humane subject. If this is true, and I believe it is, then the study of politics, which instantaneously becomes history, is the study of a humane subject also. Humane subjects, Mr. Trevor-Roper declares, "have no direct scientific use; they owe their title to existence to the interest and comprehension of the laity; they exist primarily not for the training of professionals but for the education of laymen." Technical specialization in respect of humane subjects

has no value in itself; it owes whatever value it has entirely to that degree to which it makes those subjects clearer, more comprehensible and more interesting to the intelligent laity. I do not dispute that by a completer professionalism we may arrive at a more perfect knowledge of history [politics] and literature: I merely state that that perfect knowledge may be so fine and so uninteresting that nobody, except its discoverers, will wish to possess it. If we believe, as I do, that a knowledge of history and literature is essential to a civilized society, this would be a great loss.

For my part, I agree with Mr. Trevor-Roper.

V

I now turn briefly to another inaugural lecture—perhaps the most discussed one ever delivered; it was argued about in the British newspapers and a second edition was necessary. Unless I am more ignorant than I know myself to be, American political scientists have paid little attention to it. In some remarks that he made before our association, Thomas P. Peardon discussed the lecture along with other views of the newly inaugurated professor. Another of my colleagues, Neal Wood, published an article in the *Journal of Politics* (1959). Have there been any other mentions in the literature of our subject? How many of us have urged that our students read Michael Oakeshott's *Political Education,* which does not lose in interest because Oakeshott had been appointed to the professorship at the London School of Economics that Harold J. Laski had long occupied?

Oakeshott is allusive and elusive; every paragraph contains evi-

dence of a fine intelligence and an exceptional literacy. Epigrams tem-
per the despotism of the judgments,[27] but if he had read Brand Blanshard's lecture on "Philosophical Style" he failed to heed the admoni-
tion which I have already quoted to you; after a generalization he
rarely says, "for example." I give two quotations to indicate the
flavor of the lecture:

> In political activity, then, men sail a boundless and bottomless sea;
> there is neither harbour for shelter nor floor for anchorage, neither starting-
> place nor appointed destination. The enterprise is to keep afloat on an
> even keel; the sea is both friend and enemy; and the seamanship consists in
> using the resources of a traditional manner of behaviour in order to make
> a friend of every inimical occasion.

I interject that the ship of state is one of a few vessels which is
endangered by leaks at the top. The second quotation is the lecture's
concluding paragraph:

> The more profound our understanding of political activity, the less we
> shall be at the mercy of plausible but mistaken analogy, the less we shall
> be tempted by a false or irrelevant model. And the more thoroughly we
> understand our own political tradition, the more readily its whole resources
> are available to us, the less likely we shall be to embrace the illusions
> which wait for the ignorant and the unwary: the illusion that in politics
> we can get on without a tradition of behaviour, the illusion that the abridge-
> ment of a tradition is itself a sufficient guide, and the illusion that in politics
> there is anywhere a safe harbour, a destination to be reached or even a
> detectable stand of progress. The world is the best of all possible worlds,
> and *everything* in it is a necessary evil.

In his book, *Rationalism in Politics and Other Essays* (which
appeared several months ago), Michael Oakeshott reprints his inaugural lecture and concludes with a hitherto unpublished essay under
the title, "The Study of 'Politics' in a University: An Essay in Ap-
propriateness."

"'Politics' found its way into English University education in a
somewhat tortuous manner," Mr. Oakeshott tells us, "quite unlike
the simple and naive manner in which it entered American University
education." There has been an ominous silence (not in the United
States) "about the manner in which this study is to be conducted":
whether it is politics as political behavior, as power in society, or
political institutions and political theory.

27. "What is an epigram? A dwarfish whole, Its body brevity, and wit its soul"
(Coleridge).

Mr. Oakeshott makes much of the distinction between a "language," by which he means a manner of thinking, and a "literature," by which he means what has been said from time to time in a "language." Vocational education is a literature and not a language, and he thinks that it has no proper place in a university, which he defines as "an association of persons, locally situated, engaged in caring for and attending to the whole intellectual capital which composes a civilization." Such an intellectual capital is not "a reliable collection of information, or a current condition of knowledge," but it is "a variety of modes of thinking or directions of intellectual activity, each speaking with a voice, or in a 'language' of its own and related to each other conversationally. . . ."

Thirdly, the university is a place for education, not merely for learning and research. "There appears in a university what cannot (or cannot so easily) appear elsewhere, the image of a civilization as a manifold of different intellectual interests, a conversation between different modes of thinking; and this determines the character of the education it offers." Finally, the university is an association of persons "engaged in formal teaching." Teachers should not teach what they are in the process of learning or what they discovered yesterday. Their job is to impart "familiarity with the modes of thought, the 'languages' which, from one point of view compose the whole intellectual capital of a civilization." They should offer "not information but practice in thinking." In short, "what undergraduates may get at a university and nowhere else in such favourable circumstances is some understanding of what it is to think historically, mathematically, scientifically or philosophically and some understanding of these not as 'subjects' but as living 'languages' and of those who explore and speak them as being engaged in explanatory enterprises of different sorts."

In Mr. Oakeshott's opinion:

Politics offers the most difficult of all "literatures," the most difficult of all collections of "texts," in connection with which to learn to handle and manage the languages of explanation: the idiom of the material to be studied is ever ready to impose itself upon the manner in which it is studied. Nevertheless, if we recognize what we should be doing at a university, the difficulty may itself be an attraction; if we recognize that our proper business is not with politics at all but with teaching, in connection

with politics, how to manage the "language" of history and philosophy
and how to distinguish them and their different sorts of utterance.

Unhappily, as I have said, Harold Laski's successor rarely says "for
example."

The late Alfred North Whitehead expressed his conviction, "based
on no confusing research [sic] that as a training in political imagination the Harvard School of Politics and Government cannot hold a
candle to the old fashioned English classical education of half a century ago." I venture to express a conviction based on no confusing
research and ask you to challenge it!

In Great Britain the intelligence and the literacy of the magazine,
newspaper, and parliamentary discussions of political questions are
no less impressive than they are in the United States. The British
civil service is not demonstrably more incompetent than its American
counterpart. In their universities our cousins have been able to expose
themselves to much less "political education" than is offered in American institutions of higher learning. What conclusions should we draw?

VI

When in 1921 I left Harvard to join Columbia University's Faculty
of Political Science, a principal reason for making the change was
that I would deal only with graduate students and hence have more
time for non-university activities. In the twenties and thirties, the
graduate student crops were uniformly good. Are you doubtful?
During that generation a graduate professor of political science at a
good university could think of the inscription on a door at St. Paul's,
written by Sir Christopher Wren's son: *Si vis monumentum circum-
spice.* Then, also, publication of the dissertation was a requirement
for the award of the degree of doctor of philosophy and one's standards were known to one's colleagues in other graduate schools and to
the prospective employers of dissertation writers.

But not long after the end of World War II, when I returned to
Columbia after five years of part-time duty with the International
Labour Office in Montreal, it seemed to me that graduate students
were less interesting than they had been. The abler undergraduates
who had majored in political science were now apparently plumping

for law rather than for graduate work. More students turned up who were in their thirties or even forties; those who came from foreign countries were not so well prepared as their predecessors had been, and too many (American as well as foreign) could not write English. Each batch of graduate students seemed to be less literate than the previous batch. I remember telling one student that I was sure a student of his might refer to the Sermon on the Mount and find that he had no comprehending hearers. Columbia, one of the few institutions that had retained the publication requirement for dissertations, now decreed that microfilming would suffice. The "sponsoring professor" and the author no longer had to wait nervously to learn whether reviewers in "learned journals" or "literary magazines" praised or blamed or were uninterested. Pride (or shame) could remain undetected.

Hence, I decided that during the last few years before my retirement (slated for 1959), re-exposure to undergraduates might be more exhilarating than dealing only with graduate students. So I offered to give a seminar for a half-dozen college seniors, who were majoring in political science or history and who thought that they might want to do graduate work or go to a law school. What kind of a seminar should it be?

Ruling out a seminar whose members would do research and endeavor to become more "scholarly," I decided to experiment with a reading seminar. At the time I was not conscious of having any educational doctrines more profound than those loosely expressed by Macaulay and Francis Bacon. History, Macaulay said, is frequently best studied in works that are not professedly historical. This, it seemed to me, was true of politics also. "Reading maketh the full man; writing, an exact man, talking, a ready man" was the familiar Baconian maxim. The seminar members could read anything that had some connection with politics (any thing that resembled a textbook was ruled out) and would write 750 words to be read to the seminar. The words would deal not so much with what had been read as with the impact of the writing on the seminar writers, who would be asked to keep in mind the maxim of Boileau as translated by John Dryden: "Polish, repolish, and every color lay; sometimes add, but oftener take away." (I had read John Dryden in high school and Boileau in college, but no seminar member that I encountered had read either.)

The experiment worked.[28] Seminar members thought it was a howling success. After we parted company many wrote to tell me that they had had the richest experience of their college life, and some still keep in touch with me. In saying this I am not boasting. Whether a seminar works depends on the way in which its members make use of their opportunities. When other engagements took me away from the university, the students would foregather by themselves for just as profitable, although probably more relaxed, sessions than when I was in the chair. When I was absent the seminar would appoint a *rapporteur*, who at the next meeting would relish telling us how poorly his brothers had done in choosing what to read and in describing how the reading had affected them.

The range of reading was wide—from *Anthony and Cleopatra* to *Zarathrusta*; from Thucydides to Toynbee. Biography was always a prime favorite. "Read no history; nothing but biography, for that is life without theory," was Disraeli's rather extreme judgment in *Contarini Fleming*. Students took this to heart, although they did read a good deal of history. Political novels—Disraeli, Trollope, Balzac, Macaulay's essays, some of Burke; political satire—*Gulliver's Travels*,[29] and Voltaire's *Candide*; Shakespeare's historical plays.

I recall a report by one student who, with exultant originality, maintained that *Coriolanus* was as illuminating on the nature of dictatorship as any textbook or tract for the times that the deponent had ever come upon. When I told him that William Hazlitt, a great and neglected essayist, had expressed the same idea more felicitously and at greater length, the student had a fine time turning to Hazlitt. Pepys, Samuel Johnson, William Godwin, Maitland, and Keynes, a "royal intellect" of the next generation (*Essays in Persuasion* and

28. I tried it at Johns Hopkins in 1960 and it was a colossal failure. The seminar was too large and its members seemed strangers to each other. They had not joined in taking the core of courses that all Columbia freshmen and sophomores were required to take—Contemporary Civilization, etc. In 1962 I tried the experiment at Occidental College, Los Angeles. My nervousness quickly vanished. All the Occidental students had been in a course on "The History of Civilization." To use Mr. Oakeshott's terms, there was some "literature" with which they were all familiar, and they were eager to try to polish their "language."

29. When Wendell Willkie published his book, *One World,* Sir Winston Churchill told a cabinet meeting that *Gullible's Travels* would have been a more accurate title.

Essays in Biography); Bernard Shaw (prefaces as well as plays)—
but enough of this random sampling.[30]

As I have said, I began the experiment with little pedagogical
theory. But, as so often happens when one begins to think about
something that one is doing, and so to speak, carries a mental basket,
eggs which are old but forgotten and new eggs drop into that basket.
Thus, in one of G. M. Young's essays I came across this definition
of a university:

> I remember one morning, many years ago now, William Temple [a
> future Archbishop of Canterbury] and I were walking back from a lecture
> on the monadology of Leibnitz, and Temple said: "After all, the only
> things we really learn at Oxford are the things we say to one another
> between lectures." That observation, having germinated for sometime in
> my mind, produced at last the definition of a University to which I have
> ever since adhered. "A University is a place where young men and women
> educate one another by conversation, under the guidance of people a little
> older, and, more often than they might imagine, somewhat wiser than
> themselves."

Or take the oft-quoted verdict of an eminent English educator, William Cory, as requoted by Professor Oakeshott in his recent book of
essays:

> You go to a great school [Mr. Cory said] not so much for knowledge
> as for art and habits; for the habit of attention, for the art of expression,
> for the art of assuming at a moment's notice a new intellectual position,
> for the art of entering quickly into another person's thoughts, for the habit
> of submitting to censure and refutation, for the art of indicating assent or
> dissent in graduated terms, for the habit of regarding minute points of
> accuracy, for the art of working out what is possible in a given time, for
> taste, discrimination, for mental courage and mental soberness. And above
> all you go to a great school for self-knowledge.

The late Learned Hand was in agreement:

> I venture to believe that it is as important to a judge called upon to
> pass on a question of constitutional law, to have at least a bowing acquaint-
> ance with Acton and Maitland, with Thucydides, Gibbon and Carlyle, with
> Homer, Dante, Shakespeare and Milton, with Machiavelli, Montaigne and
> Rabelais, with Plato, Bacon, Hume, and Kant, as with the books which
> have been specifically written on the subject. For in such matters every-

30. This kind of seminar should not be given in a bare classroom; there should
be books around: a "Britannica" (the Eleventh Edition!); some book of quotations;
a good dictionary (not the new Webster's!); and (for me at least) Fowler's *Dictionary of Modern English Usage*.

thing turns upon the spirit in which he approaches the questions before him. The words he must construe are empty vessels into which he can pour nearly anything he will.

Montaigne! A man who had read and pondered him, as Goethe said of a man who had been "under the palms," will never be the same again. If such a prescription is good for judges, it is good for those who discuss contemporary politics and institutions and tell their readers how they should choose between alternative public policies or, as is more likely, what compromise is a tolerable substitute for victory by either side: what difficulties lurk in each suggested solution.

Or consider the judgment of a contemporary critic (writing in *Harper's Magazine*): "Too many colleges," David Boroff complains, overload students and leave them "little or no time for the kind of contemplative activity that alone can make an educated man." Students are insufficiently encouraged to learn on their own in ways that will make them keener to learn more. These may be precepts that are frowned upon by (if they are known to) the authorities on education in teachers' colleges, but to a layman like myself they seem to make sense. And they have, I think, made sense to political science students at Morningside Heights and in Los Angeles. As Stalin once said to H. G. Wells: "Education is a weapon whose effect depends on who holds it in his hands, and at whom it is aimed."

VII

Noel Annan, Provost of King's College, Cambridge, has recently told us that "the focus of all education is the personal impact of the teacher upon his students." Crucial questions are two in number: how can pupils be taught "to use their own minds and develop originality" and how can they be "persuaded to renounce cramming and question spotting"? Mr. Annan does not attempt to answer his questions, and I do not think that anyone can. Each teacher is more or less successful than his fellow teachers. All of us feel indebted to some who years ago were our teachers, but I doubt whether we can phrase our indebtedness in concrete terms. Willoughby had so many students who turned out well that he must have been a good teacher. He must have succeeded in getting minds off trivialities and onto important things. He must have been a good critic, but if you challenge me (as Brand Blanshard suggests you should) by saying "for example," I am unable to reply.

When my students of yesteryear come to see me (their desire to do so suggests that they have a slight feeling of indebtedness), I have sometimes asked for specifics: "What is your most vivid recollection of what has been called 'the meeting of the minds of pupil and teacher?'" The answers are almost always trivial and are sometimes ludicrous. For one student, whom I recently questioned, the high spot was a description of India's foreign policy as one of "Nehrutrality." Another, now a dean at a state university (not in the South), thought for some time and came up with a nugget. "You once asked someone in a class the date of the Australian Constitution"—to hear that I had asked such a question made me wince—"and when there was no reply, you said: 'Mr. So and So, would you guess that it was before or after 1900?'" Is it not better that recollections be completely blank? My recollections are blank in respect to the two most memorable experiences of being taught that I have ever had.

Years ago on the Crescent Limited en route to New Orleans one of my fellow passengers was Frank J. Goodnow. Until then I had met him only casually, but I introduced myself and we spent some of the evening and the whole of the next day together. Curiously enough, my second memorable experience was also on a train which, happily, was delayed by a violent snowstorm. My companion then was Charles A. Beard. As I say, I can recall no specifics, but these two men expressly came to mind when I read what Learned Hand had once written of the famous law professor, Samuel Williston, who died a few months ago at the age of 101. "While this Socrates of ours never coerced our assent," wrote Judge Hand, "like his prototype he did not let us alone until we had peered into the corners of our minds, and had in some measure discovered the litter they contained." Judge Hand was not explicit on the locale of the meetings between the modern Socrates and his students. Circumstances under which I encountered Frank Goodnow and Charles Beard were such that, even though we were on trains, we could have recalled Cowper's lines: "There shall he learn, ere sixteen winters old, that authors are most useful pawned or sold; that pedantry is all that schools impart, but taverns teach the knowledge of the heart."

In these remarks I have several times expressed the belief—perhaps you will call it an obsession—that political science should be kept a humane subject and that we should not inflict our specialized interests on our students. "How much *minutiae* can a man take—it would require a Hercules to clean such academic hodge-podge from the stables." This from an anonymous letter that I received a couple of years ago. (The writer had read something that I had written and had concluded that I would sympathize with him). "The thought of one or two more years in this 'discipline,'" the letter went on, "elicits a vision of a man devoid of zest, grinding out insignificant publications in order to obtain a meaningless academic J. Alfred Prufrock status." The letter was signed "A soon to be ex-graduate student of political science."

Someone had said that a teacher can strike a spark and cause a conflagration. As this letter disclosed the spark may cause smoke that stifles those who have to endure it. "A parent gives life, but as parent, gives no more," wrote Henry Adams. "A murderer takes life, but his deed stops there. A teacher affects eternity; he can never tell where his influence stops." It is a somber judgment and I do not challenge it, although, as I have suggested, those influenced are often unconscious of what has happened and are unable to dot any i's or cross any t's. At least Henry Adams' judgment is more flattering to those of us who have endeavored to teach political science than is Bernard Shaw's wisecrack: "He who can, does, he who cannot, teaches."

VIII

STRANGER. Do you think that the multitude in the state can attain political science?

YOUNG SOCRATES. Impossible.

STR. But perhaps in a city of fifty thousand men there could be a hundred or, say, fifty who could?

Y. SOC. In that case political science would be the easiest of all sciences; there could not be found in a city of that number as many really good draught-players, judging by the standard of the rest of Hellas and there would certainly not be as many kings. For kings we may truly call those who possess royal science whether they rule or not as was shown in the previous argument.

(Plato, *Statesman*; Jowett translation.)

AVERY LEISERSON

The behavioral approach

[T]he inspiration of science for four hundred years has created the values of our intellectual life and, with the arts, taught them to our civilization. . . . It is the lesson of science that the concept is more profound than the laws, the act of judging more critical than the judgment. . . . The values by which we are to survive are not rules for just and unjust conduct, but those deeper illuminations in whose light justice and injustice, good and evil, means and ends, are seen in fearful sharpness of outline.[1]

If the philosophy of the sciences of energy and matter can produce such a value-oriented conception of its role and mission, it comes as no surprise to find that "the roots of [the social and behavioral sciences] lie in . . . the needs of modern society for empirical, quantitative, policy-oriented information about itself."[2] The paradox is that it is not the established institutions of society, indeed, but the spirit of scientific intelligence that calls for openness to new ideas and the infusion of as much knowledge (natural, social, artistic, moral) as possible into the processes whereby a vigorous, dynamic society adapts itself to change. We need not worry too much about this contradiction, or opposition, if we consider the historical linkage between the rise of science and technology, the ensuing rate of social change, and the subsequent increase of human problems themselves requiring investigation and understanding. Whether the base-values and institutions of society themselves can survive the process of self-transformation, whether public attitudes, reactions, and policies will turn out to be progressive or retrogressive, are debatable and problematic questions, not pre-judged or pre-determined by scientific knowledge. But the challenge of our times is not whether we like or dislike, choose or reject science. The issue rather is whether the methods of rational

1. Jacob Bronowski, *Science and Human Values* (New York, 1959), pp. 93-94.
2. Daniel Lerner (ed.), *The Human Meaning of the Social Sciences* (Cleveland, 1959), p. 19. Note that this is not a definition of social science.

intelligence will be more effectively mobilized by apocalyptic forces of hate and destruction or by political systems whose leaders and decision-making processes are animated by the sense of human brotherhood, personal responsibility, and "a decent respect for the opinions of mankind."

This paper starts from the assumption that the so-called "behavioral" study of politics is virtually coextensive with the scientific outlook toward man and society. By scientific outlook I mean an identifiable mode of human experience which is not only distinctive, but probably crucial, to the survival of our civilization. The scientific attitude consists of a syndrome of belief, method, and value. The *belief* is that there is an underlying continuity between man's natural and human environments to which he can gradually penetrate through his creative powers of imagination (formulation of symbolic concepts and relations), logical reasoning, and observation (experimental or systematic verification). The *method* requires that ordering concepts and propositions, procedures of selecting and analyzing evidence, and modes of interpretation be public, communicable, and ultimately connectible with the experience of others. The *values* lie in the enjoyment of the common motivation and heritage known to men who seek the truth. The incentive is found partly in the urge to explore, partly in the rewards of insight into the hidden relationships (uniformities) between theoretical units of analysis whose variable interaction constitutes the "truth" of human understanding.

Of course, the scientific outlook has its costs. These include the personal and collective anxieties that follow the displacement of established certainties, the hostility of disturbed, vested interests, the evil as well as the good consequences to which knowledge may be put, but above all the Promethean bonds to one's fellow men in helping them to cope with the changes wrought by advancing knowledge upon their personal and public lives. Now what has all this to do with teaching?

Assuming the desirability of extending the range and capacity for scientific understanding of human behavior and organization, including the *political,* I shall argue that:

    1. It is not sufficient for the political philosopher solely to criticize and evaluate political events, behavior, institutions in terms of the great moral ends and purposes of

man; his function includes the systematic, critical analysis of: (*a*) the role of values in organized political society; (*b*) the effects of politics, viewed as a universal dependent variable, upon the operative values of individuals, groups, and institutions.

2. The teacher of politics requires knowledge of the concepts and methods of scientific inquiry in order to avoid self-deception and misrepresentation to his students of the nature of the political environment, the role and skills of the political calling, and the conditions and consequences of personal involvement (participation) in politics.

3. Regardless of whether the student of politics is oriented merely toward "citizenship," or actively committed to the practice, study, or teaching of government, his progress toward comprehension and competence depends largely upon his ability to separate analytically, while recognizing in action the relations between *knowledge, value,* and *judgment* in public affairs.

4. The quality and contribution, let alone the survival, of political science as a significant discipline in the family of sciences is closely related to the profession's standards in recruiting its replacements.

Political Theory and the Behavioral Outlook

There is a necessary and healthy tension in the relationship between the political philosopher and political scientist. At times, it can take on a futile, nightmarish quality, as when questions are framed in such a way that they cannot be answered meaningfully, communication fails, and discussion degenerates into petty argument over vocabularies. Of course, a mere optimistic enthusiasm for science is no substitute, taken alone, for intuitive speculation, logical brilliance, historical insight, legal reasoning, or trained experience with the "important problems" of politics as conventionally defined. The often-used analogy of medicine may suggest the more interesting and fruitful context of discussion that I have in mind. The climate in which progress in medical knowledge seems to have occurred arose when investigators began to collect information systematically related to hypotheses about disease and pathological malfunctioning, rather than contenting themselves with conventional bromides about the causes and conditions of healthy, normal states of the body. When there is a problem to be solved, or when we are genuinely curious about a question, there is something unsatisfactory about reasoning to a quick answer from a restrictive definition of what science is and what science can or cannot do. When we are in trouble we tend to ask the basic epistemological questions in a more constructively critical frame of mind: (*1*) What do we know that is relevant to the problem? (*2*)Are we sure that what we have accepted as knowledge is the whole truth of the matter? (*3*) Are there other variables (factors, conceptual innovations) which might lead to a different formulation of what we think we know, and thereby enable us to give a more satisfactory interpretation and application of intelligible principles to the observed facts?

The great teachers of politics have been those who asked themselves not only what politics in human associations is for, i.e., ends and purposes, but have provided at least implicitly working hypotheses (viable propositions) which help to explain the power-and-authority structure in political systems generally; the roots of power in the historical, social-psychological, economic, and technological linkages with the society (culture) in which they are imbedded; the institutions and processes whereby political systems adjust cleavages and controversies, resist or adapt pressures for change, or meet or fail to meet the requirements of survival, foreign and internal. Socrates, Aristotle, Machiavelli and Francis Bacon, Hobbes, Locke and Rousseau, Hamilton-Madison, Bentham and the Mills's, Lenin, all are important teachers of politics not only as figures in intellectual history, but because their questions about the structure and functioning of political systems produced meaningful, consequential (if not universally valid) concepts and principles for understanding political organization and behavior. The great teachers assumed the importance of politics; they analyzed the functioning of power-oriented behavior in individuals, groups, public and private organizations; they showed the relationships of these "facts" and ideas to the central, integrative institutions of conflict resolution, of policy formulation and control they called "the state" (polity, commonwealth, system, or "constitution-in-action"). In our century men like Wilson at Princeton, Dunning and Goodnow at Columbia, Lowell and Holcombe at Harvard, Merriam at Chicago, Barker and Lindsay and Laski in England, Weber in Germany live with us today because of their ability to transmit their own fascination and recognition of the requirements of governance, their rejection of formalism and idol worship, their hospitality to new concepts and methods for attacking the timeless problems of "the political." As writers and teachers they imparted the sense of commitment to what G. B. Shaw used to call *political comprehension,* rather than a fixed set of moral absolutes by which political inquiry must be conducted, behavior judged, institutions transformed.

The latter statement fairly screams for clarification. Although these men shared certain common qualities as teachers, they varied widely with respect to political involvement and identification. The point involves not partisan or ideological position, but the connection between philosophy, theory, and action. If these roles are placed diagrammatically on a circle rather than on a straight line, it can readily be visualized that the philosopher in some respects is closer to the political activists than to the contemplative-analytical, theorist-researcher. Plato and Dionysius, Aristotle and Alexander, Machiavelli and Borgia, Bacon and James I, Bossuet and Louis XIV—these thinkers and leaders represent a broad range of role relationships under the old royal regimes. In American history, Adams, Madison, Hamilton, Jefferson constituted a rather rare combination of intellectual power and active political energy. With further democratization the separation seems to have set in again, at least in the United States (witness Henry Adams). But it was no accident that the American Political Science Association was formed in the period of intellectual ferment and political reform that we now call the "progressive era." Woodrow Wilson, a successful teacher but a frustrated college president who went on to a meteoric career, had serious doubts about the possibility of a science of politics, as did the historian Charles Beard. Lowell and Goodnow eschewed politics themselves but contributed to the development of the discipline as scholars and university administrators. Charles Merriam, a born Bull Moose politician, nipped in political infancy by defeat in the 1911 Chicago mayoralty race, helped to organize not only the association but the Social Science Research Council, and went on with unconcealed delight to pool his interests in planning with Louis Brownlow's ebullient efforts to introduce administrative rationality into the New Deal. A. D. Lindsay became a spokesman for the Labour Party in the House of Lords.

The recital could go on, but the point which needs to be made is that while a brilliant and successful career in the study of political values, institutions, and practices may pave the way for an active political or administrative role, such experience and training does not guarantee success in executive, legislative, or electoral application any more than a physicist need be a good engineer, an economist a businessman, or a biologist a doctor. Both *personal* factors of motivation, character, judgment, and will, and *situational* variables of time, events, group affiliations, and interpersonal relations intervene. Nor does the relation necessarily work in reverse. The man of action who knows how to operate in the political process frequently lacks patience with the requirement of analytical precision, the drudgery of research, and he often has difficulty in formulating ideas in explicitly analytical, explanatory terms, in contrast to imperative, normative, or illustrative language.

Accepting a functional division of role between the philosopher and the ruler does not mean that the former must or can isolate himself from the political currents and controversies of his time. Whether or not he wishes it, the philosopher is "involved"; he either does or does not make a contribution. The point at which he renders disservice, and fails as a teacher and colleague, is when he assumes that the *only* function and mode of discourse is that of moral critic and preacher, or when he insists that his concepts and analytical procedures are the *only* respectable tools for dealing with political reality. Indeed, he intensifies his students' sense of the gulf between theory and practice, and widens the breach between himself and the world of action with his rigid, compulsive, exclusive methodology. It is not the scientific or behavioral outlook, but philosophical narrowness that inhibits the dialectical process of conceptual inventiveness, critical interchange, and symbolic transformation out of which man gains in theoretical understanding. Who is qualified to help in the intellectual, educational process of anticipating change and adapting innovations in the environment at "least cost in terms of all values" that are desired to be preserved?[3] The contribution that the philosopher and

3. H. D. Lasswell, "The Political Science of Science," *American Political Science Review*, L (1956), 961-979.

theorist-researcher alike have to make to the political actor, operator, or executive is "to broaden and deepen their capacity for judgment, not to provide answers. . . . to help in the reformulation of the problem, not to fill gaps of factual knowledge."[4] This is the criterion of utility which the practical man under the impact of science and technology is beginning to understand as the contribution of basic (theoretical *and* useful) research, rather than the acquisition of facts or application of knowledge already acquired.[5]

Turning now to the differentiation between the philosopher and the scientist in politics, I hope with Truman, Dahl, and Snyder that the discipline has matured beyond the point of ill-tempered, ill-informed, irrelevant disputation as to whether scientific procedures have been and are being incorporated into the study of government and politics. At the same time, Eulau and Sibley probably are right in insisting that the traditional methods of philosophy, law, and history are likely to persist for longer than the short run.[6] Here the critical question really goes to the *willingness* of the philosopher to engage in the rigorous analysis of concepts and hypotheses relative to an accessible body of empirical data. Here one meets the preference for speculative insight freed from the difficulties of "hard" facts, the contempt for the trivial or obvious or unsavory world of experience, the familiar desire to find sureness and certainty in defining the issues. There is a continuing cleavage, or tension, in the discipline between those empirical theorists who seek more satisfying models for explaining behavior, and worry about the "payoffs" of alternative strategies of inquiry, and those normative philosophers and practical empiricists who believe the important political problems already are known, and therefore worry primarily about the moral regeneration of the human data, or else how we might somehow transform the "institutional facts" which would somehow enable us to find the saving answers. In short, the gap that needs to be bridged in political science lies not

4. Max F. Millikan, "Inquiry and Policy: The Relation of Knowledge to Action," in Lerner, *op. cit.,* pp. 167-169.
5. H. D. Smyth, "Role of the University in Basic Research," in National Science Foundation, *Proceedings of a Conference on Academic and Industrial Basic Research* (NSF 61-39, 1960), pp. 17-20; see also American Association for the Advancement of Science, *Symposium on Basic Research* (Washington, 1959), pp. 1-72, 249-258.
6. R. A. Dahl, "The Behavioral Approach in Political Science: Epitaph for a Monument to a Successful Protest," *American Political Science Review,* LV (1961), 763-772; American Academy of Political and Social Science, *The Limits of Behavioralism in Political Science* (Philadelphia, 1962), pp. 31 ff., 91 ff.

so much between philosophy and action, as between philosophy and theory.[7] It is the great teacher indeed who, given the state of the discipline in his time, can formulate in his mind, exhibit in his life, and transmit through his students a sense of the vital balance between political philosophy, a scientific theory of politics, and personal participation.

Emergent Concepts in Political Science

It is not necessary for the teacher to share the commitment to the goal of a science of politics to realize the importance of those conceptual shifts and transformations that come about in a period of vigorous intellectual ferment and empirical inquiry, such as occurred in American political science before 1915 and after 1945. He knows only too well the attraction for young, eager, able minds of developing fields of knowledge, which seem to offer powerful and exciting tools with which they can come to grips with problems to which they have just been awakened. Fifty years ago it was the recognition of such disrespectable phenomena as political parties, interest groups, and administrative bureaucracies, so essential to understanding the formation of public opinion, policy, and law-in-action, that brought many of our best teachers and scholars into the discipline during the twenties and thirties. Before 1900 the discipline had centered upon the history of political thought, comparative government, and constitutional law. The post-World War II reinvigoration had its roots in the seminal work of such men as Lasswell and Herring, who pressed forward empirical inquiries illuminating the concept of politics as interpersonal and intergroup power relations in society, in contrast to conventional, descriptive, legal, political, administrative case studies. Once the dynamic potential of the analytic concept of power was grasped, the way was open to perceiving the relevance of work in anthropology, psychology, and sociology for political scientists eager to understand the significance for politics of the personal and social meanings of the vote and other forms of political participation; the motivation and skills of leadership; the effects of personality, role, and informal group affiliations upon the formal authority structure

7. Arnold Brecht, *Political Theory* (Princeton, N. J., 1959) has helped as much as any to make this point clear.

of organizations; the functions of symbolism in civic education, propaganda, and mass communication.[8] Awareness of economics as providing a theory of rational choice was less immediate and largely restricted until Dahl and Lindblom in 1953 elaborated its utility for comparative analyses of planning and decision-making processes (maximization of values and resources).[9] It scarcely needs to be emphasized that these strange curiosities and terms were not only not "new" to political science, but indeed simply reformulation of problems as old as Plato and Aristotle from which nineteenth-century legalistic, historical, and ethical preoccupations with "the state" had cut themselves off.

The conceptual ferment of the forties and fifties produced several movements, some of which seemed to converge, while others literally exhibited a centripetal tendency to fly off into space. Searchers for more fundamental, dynamic units with which to explain political activity (behavior) tended to probe more deeply into the dynamics of human motivation and adjustment, employing on the one hand Freudian (and other psychological schools) subunits (drives and mechanisms) within the personality, and on the other the cultural imperatives and restraints identified by social psychologists and anthropologists.[10] These and the sample survey researches into the dimensions of opinion and attitude may be described as forays into "micropolitics." Emphasis upon explicitly political functions and processes, useful for comparing behavior in societies in different stages of "modernization" or development, led to Almond's concept of *political culture,* while Easton, Deutsch, Kaplan, and Liska elaborated in different ways the notion of the *political system.*[11] Whether by way of adaptation or reaction, these explorations in "macropolitics" were strongly affected by the sociologists, Parsons and Shils, whose formulation of the pattern variables for analyzing the value components of different cultures led naturally to the effort to identify the functional components of social systems in general.

Thus, in one direction the behavioral scientists sliced deeper within the human personality to find the origins and parameters of political

8. Charles Edward Merriam's *New Aspects of Politics* (Chicago, Ill., 1925), *The Making of Citizens* (Chicago, Ill., 1931) and *Political Power* (New York, 1934) explicitly foreshadowed each of these lines of development.
9. R. A. Dahl and C. E. Lindblom, *Politics, Economics and Welfare* (New York, 1953).
10. R. E. Lane, *Political Life* (Glencoe, Ill., 1959).

behavior, while in the other they expanded the boundaries of the formal, legal organization of government to include a general theory of political action, systems, and cultures. A somewhat less cosmic, middle-ground position was taken by students of formal and informal organizations who saw in "the group" the empirical, connecting link between the individual and the political system, and who sought in the interaction of group politics, class politics, party politics, and bureaucratic politics the key to unravelling the complex relationships between individual perception, group organization, and political rule.[12] On this middle level, also, the work of Herbert Simon and Richard Snyder should be mentioned, the former for his unremitting attention to the formal analysis of conditions for rational action in administrative organizations,[13] the latter for systematic development of the concept of "decision-making" as an instrument of empirical analysis.[14]

No sketch, however brief, of the behavioral impact upon political science would be complete if it did not mention the revival of interest in the method of comparative politics. The term itself reflects the shift from descriptive specialization upon government in particular areas to search for more reliable, "functional" indexes and bases for cross-cultural classification of fundamental socio-political processes common to all political systems, preparatory to generalizing from a large number of cases and reducing the number of cultural variables to be controlled.[15] The degree of process here should not be overstated. Difficulties in "tooling-up," the temptation to indulge in extravagant conceptualism, problems of access to field data and reliable methods of observation pose truly formidable obstacles to realizing the promises of enhanced theoretical sophistication. The gains from

11. David Easton, *The Political System* (New York, 1951); Karl W. Deutsch, *Nationalism and Social Communication* (New York, 1953); Morton A. Kaplan, *System and Process in International Relations* (New York, 1957); George Liska, *International Equilibrium* (Cambridge, 1957).

12. Robert K. Merton, *Social Theory and Social Structure* (Glencoe, Ill., 1949); D. B. Truman, *The Governmental Process* (New York, 1951); O. Garceau, "Research in the Political Process," *American Political Science Review*, XLV (1951), 69-85; G. C. Homans, *The Human Group* (New York, 1950); S. M. Lipset, *Political Man* (New York, 1960).

13. *Administrative Behavior* (New York, 1947); with Smithburg and Thompson, *Public Administration* (New York, 1950); with March and Guetzkow, *Organizations* (New York, 1958).

14. Ronald Young (ed.), *Approaches to the Study of Politics* (Evanston, Ill., 1958); Snyder, *et al.*, *Foreign Policy Decision-Making; An Approach to the Study of International Politics* (New York, 1962).

15. Sigmund Neumann, *Modern Political Parties* (Chicago, 1956); Daniel Lerner, *The Passing of Traditional Society* (Glenco, Ill., 1958); G. A. Almond and J. S. Coleman, *The Politics of the Developing Areas* (Princeton, N. J., 1960).

clarification of assumptions underlying comparative work, however, as well as the improved statement of methodological problems, pitfalls, and opportunities, can scarcely be denied.[16]

The "behavioral shift" in the study of international politics had one contextual advantage lacking in the domestic or comparative fields, namely, the recognition of the unsatisfactory gap between normative philosophy and the variety of competing analytical models for investigating politics among nations.[17] Here, however, there was a more fruitful interaction between academic centers and present and former public servants in the field of foreign policy, with the result that a considerably more continuous, mutually reinforcing exploration of the respective roles of scientific theorizers and policy planners took place at Yale, Princeton, Columbia, M. I. T., and Johns Hopkins.[18] In the hands of a theorist like Arnold Wolfers, for example, the analysis of foreign policy-making in terms of "actors-as-decision-makers" constituted, if not a transposition of the old "states-as-sole-actors" concept, an extension and refinement of it.[19]

In summary, then, earmarks of the behavioral-scientific approach to politics are:

1. An explicit conceptual focus upon power- and policy-oriented activity (attitudes, resources, strategies of actors seeking to influence outcomes);

2. openness and receptivity to ideas and communication with other scientific disciplines, centering upon the interaction of personalistic, cultural, resource, and structural "variables" that may be visualized as a "system";

3. emphasis upon theoretical analysis and formulation of hypotheses capable of empirical test and, so far as possible, quantitative evaluation of limits of sampling generalizability and probable error;

16. D. B. Truman, "Trends in Political Science," *Liberal Education,* XLVII (1961), 280-303.

17. Quincy Wright, *The Study of International Relations* (New York, 1955); Ernst Haas and Allen Whiting, *The Dynamics of International Relations* (New York, 1956); Klaus Knorr and Sidney Verba (eds.), *The International System* (Princeton, N. J., 1961).

18. W. T. R. Fox, "Frederick Sherwood Dunn and the American Study of International Relations," *World Politics,* XV (1962), 1-19.

19. "The Actors in International Politics," in W. T. R. Fox (ed.), *Theoretical Aspects of International Relations* (Notre Dame, Ind., 1959), pp. 83-106.

4. insistence upon the importance of explicitly differentia-
ting the structural and contextual relations between social (informal and non-governmental) and political
(overt and institutionalized) forms of power, and upon
comparative investigation of the conditions under which
the behavior of the influential actors seeking to satisfy
the demands of their internal and external constituents
tend to conserve, expand, or transform the capacity of
the authority system to meet the requirements of survival.

To the teacher of government and politics, the significance of the
developments on the cutting edge of the research "advance-guard"
may be stated provocatively in some such terms as the following. He
is obliged to recognize that it is no longer intellectually respectable
for him, either in locating his own position or in introducing the students to politics and politicians, to content himself with making explicit his own value position (the uneasy compromise reached between
the value-oriented philosophers and the empirically oriented institutionalists, or positivists). Even if he doubts or depreciates the ability
of the discipline to become a science, he must recognize the role and
competence of limited, theoretical generalizations about the organization and distribution of political power, or how political action is
generated and decisions reached, which have important consequences
upon the validity and tenability of a priori, preconceived prejudices,
preferences, and premises. Achievement of this kind of competence
comes hard, but recognition of it is growing, and with that comes
relinquishment of such self-deceiving canards as: "Political science
demonstrates that Ideology A is correct and B bad," or, "Political
science teaches what politicians and policy-makers ought to do," or,
"Political knowledge depends on one's point of view," meaning thereby it is either a matter of opinion, a derivative of a philosophical
value position, a predetermined product of bio-physical or social-class
factors, or a special kind of knowledge restricted to a self-selected or
"culturally chosen" elite which is entitled to manipulate the ignorance
of others in the light of their own estimates of the requirements of
the system in which they rule. To end on a positive note, although
much scientific effort terminates negatively in clearing away mythical
notions, one can hardly point to a better statement than that of James

B. Conant in describing the nature of the scientific calling. We paraphrase it here as "a policy for guiding research into the unknown, in the form of wagers [hypotheses] about the structure of reality, the proof to be submitted to the test of his colleagues' judgment, in advance of which the bettor is prepared to commit his energies, his resources, and his reputation."[20]

Education for Politics

Perhaps the salient observation about civic or political education is that although children ordinarily get no systematic, critical instruction in political analysis worthy of the name until their first or second year of college, they absorb implicit political ideas about authority, prevailing values about how power ought to be exercised (credenda), and myths about how it is organized (miranda), from the earliest days in the family, play groups, school, church, newspapers and other mass media, parents (even if by way of reaction) and friends with whom they most naturally and frequently associate, and the situations in which they earn their own living. So far as formal education below the college level goes, explanations usually take one or more of the following forms: (*1*) politics is controversial and contains no really objective information or tools that can be taught reliably; (*2*) society needs to protect itself and transmit its political heritage by indoctrination of preferred values, symbols, rites, and institutions until children reach some age of presumed discretion when they can be exposed to the dangers of alternative theories and methods of organizing the public business; (*3*) the curriculum is already crowded, and civic education can be adequately intrusted to teachers of history, language and culture, or *physical* education!; (*4*) politics on the level of method or technique is bad and should not be taught, whereas on the level of value and critical analysis it is a form of "the higher learning" which ought to be postponed until the child has acquired the classic, humane, and literary tools of history, grammar, logic, and rhetoric; (*5*) outside the humanities, creative thought is not recognized beyond mathematics and the "hard" sciences. These are weighty considerations; all of them contain considerable elements of truth; and little

20. *Modern Science and Modern Man* (New York, 1952). See also Vernon Van Dyke, *Political Science: A Philosophical Inquiry* (Stanford, Calif., 1960), chap. xv.

is to be gained by indulging in the parlor game of castigating elementary and secondary school teachers for failing in what they are neither trained nor allowed to do.

On the college level, political science faces two sets of problems, namely, those that it shares with the other sciences of man and those of organizing and presenting its own subject matter. With respect to its interdisciplinary relations, political science shares a common interest in the following areas of knowledge, which provide the general grounds of mutual recognition and communication essential both to the liberally educated man and the professional specialist. These are (1) social and psychological factors in motivation, learning, and adjustment: (2) the basic elements of logical and material reasoning, including the requirements for analyzing and making valid inferences (generalizations) from empirical (both qualitative and quantitative) data; (3) the theory of rational choice under conditions of maximizing value satisfactions from limited resources; (4) the history of political thought, interpreted in terms of the effects of alternative arrangements and restraints upon authoritative decision-making in situations of interpersonal and intergroup conflicts of interest and power. To this list may be added, or perhaps incorporated in (2), the history and philosophy of science.

Now, it can be argued that these are precisely the analytical concerns of the several social (behavioral) sciences, and that the student can acquire these by taking the appropriate basic courses in each field. In my judgment, this is a possible and partial answer but neither wholly sufficient nor germane to the problems that gave rise to this paper. As an approximation of the present university organization and curricula, it has failed to contribute to the resolution of "the value problem" dealt with in departmental scope-and-methods courses, the sociology of knowledge, and the notorious philosophical disputes in the history of ideas. It confirms and prolongs the separation among and between the natural and social sciences. Proliferation of statistics courses adapted to the "data" of each field is an example of the same type of thinking. It heightens the difficulties of students who transfer from one field to another in the transition to graduate training, where they have to undergo elementary methodological retooling. It maintains the misleading illusion that the social sciences are radically different disciplines, although they are all dealing with the human behavior of people. But most of all, it focuses attention on the differences rather than what the sciences share in common, the "understanding and welfare of Man."

Both from an administrative and an educational viewpoint, therefore, the interdisciplinary interests of political science suggest constant reconsideration either at the college or divisional level of appropriate courses, aimed at all college undergraduates, focused upon the common problems (not the technical specialties) of logic and scientific method, statistics, social psychology, and the politico-economic determinants of public policy and decision-making.

With respect to its internal problems of organizing and presenting its educational offerings, political science still is facing the problem of the introductory course and the appropriate classification of its sub-field. The first problem is perhaps less urgent for a "final" answer, partly because there is a legitimate difference in the demand of the general college student, who may properly approach the subject of politics either from the desire to understand the political institutions of a particular country, or the relatively rare and mature desire to acquire the rudiments of political analysis (both psychology and sociology straightforwardly have adopted the latter course, while economics has come back from an early emphasis upon "principles" to a combination with "institutions" and "processes"). There are also the perennial differences between those who would offer the introductory student the approach to politics in terms of the dramatic conflicts of opposing values and ideologies, or alternatively, those who would present the pros and cons of contemporary issues and problems, along with the "inside dope" on the strategies and tactics of winning and losing political battles. The field has been so pre-empted by advocates of one or another form of appealing to students' competitive, emotional involvements over values that "the behavioral persuasion" is a tiny and lonely voice indeed in advocating return to *comparative analysis of political cultures, systems, and processes, utilizing elementary analytical concepts as tools for empirical observations.* However, given the state of most students' preparation and commitment, the overwhelming weight of contemporary opinion favors the approach of proceeding *from* value involvement *to* case study description, *to* analysis and observation. This relegates independent empirical investigation and theoretical inquiry in all but a few institutions to the final year of undergraduate concentration or the first year of graduate training—if then—where it almost invariably starts *de novo*.

The question of how political science should be organized and classified for purposes of instruction is properly a matter for decision at the graduate level, and it is squarely raised again by recognition of the differences between the scientifically oriented behaviorists, the empirically oriented institutionalists, and the value-oriented philosophers. (If anybody thinks that the natural sciences do not face intra- and interdisciplinary classification problems, look at the relation between physics and chemistry since the rise of sub-atomic nuclear science, the development of bio-physics, bio-chemistry, geophysics, or the relations between "classical" and "molecular" schools in biology.) Unfortunately, knowledge seems to resist fixed, eternally valid subdivisions, and modern political science is in distinguished company in having strong external linkages and internal divisions. Internally, we have philosophers, administrators, lawyers, and social psychologists, among others. Proposals for sub-classifying the discipline range from unity to eight or more. Perhaps only the neo-Thomists advocate restoration of the medieval unity by presupposing the primacy of natural law over positive laws in worldly affairs, but since natural law is subordinated to eternal reason and divine revelation, the trinity is re-established as levels of being above and beyond "positivistic, man-made science."[21] George Catlin has recently suggested that "systematic politics" consists of philosophy and theory, both empirically based. The *trivium* has had its advocates, ranging from the three I's (ideas, institutions, and interests) to Finer's philosophy, institutions, and systematic (positive) politics. In the United States, perhaps the most orthodox classification rests upon the *quadrivium*: theory, American government, foreign and comparative government, and international relations. The University of Chicago introduced a *five*-fold, "process" classification, consisting of politics (voting, electorate and parties), administration, theory, public law, and international law and diplomacy. The American Political Science Association's Committee on the Teaching of Politics came forward in 1951 with an *eight*-fold division, which amounted in essence to a further breakdown of Chicago's "politics" and "international" categories.[22] Some be-

21. Eric Voegelin, *The New Science of Politics* (Chicago, Ill., 1953).
22. *Goals for Political Science* (New York, 1951).

haviorists have argued for a separate field of methodology, but this indicates either an emphasis upon intra-university bureaucratic considerations or a tendency to divorce methodology from the analytical-empirical investigation of politics. Thus, the prevailing opinion among behaviorists is to incorporate methodology partly through special courses on scope and methods with empirical-analytical theory and the history of political thought, partly in the combined work with the other social sciences (see p. 64, above), and partly in the subdivisions of subject matter. The behavioral approach no more than any other leads to a final or necessary classification. The same body of analytic-empirical theory underlies and should permeate each of the sub-fields, but as long as the different schools and methods have to be differentiated, we shall have to have a field of (*1*) theory. The divisions of subject matter probably would be (*2*) comparative political systems (structures), (*3*) policy and decision-making processes (strategies), (*4*) international politics.[23] It is not too difficult to arrange comprehensive, senior undergraduate and graduate, preliminary doctoral examinations on this basis at the present time.

It is to be hoped that the foregoing paragraphs will not be interpreted as advocating that political science as a discipline should cut itself off from the critical and historical aspects of the humanistic tradition. On the contrary, it is upon the foundations of an appreciation of the evolution of political ideas and instituitons, and the roots of science in history and philosophy, that hopes for progress in human development through free inquiry are built. The behavioral political scientist does argue, however, that the "valuational" and "judgmental" schools in the discipline have been vastly overweighted in the undergraduate presentation of the subject, and that a more soundly based conception of "political knowledge" is essential both for the education of citizens and the preparation of professionally competent analysts and teachers. Whether one starts from what some have called the decline of political theory, or from the separation of theory from fact, and whether one does or does not accept the dictum that judgment cannot be taught and that values have to be learned by faith or indoctrination, none of these current maxims reflect a satisfactory theoretical situation from the standpoint of the political behaviorist.

23. A more conventional breakdown might be (*1*) theory, (*2*) comparative politics, (*3*) public law and administration, (*4*) international politics. The international field potentially could be subsumed under the other heads.

His diagnosis would be that in our undergraduate program there has
been a failure to discriminate and to maintain a proper balance between the intellectual operations of (*1*) critical inquiry and determination of tested knowledge, (*2*) the detection and ranking of priorities
between values at stake, (*3*) the skills of practical judgment in public
affairs.

The Recruitment and Training of Political Scientists

The editor of this volume was "not sure that the behavioral approach
has much to do with teaching" political science at the undergraduate
level.* He seemed to think it was more relevant to the training of
graduate students in research methods. Even the most extreme behaviorist would agree that at the undergraduate level political science
should have in mind more than "catching" and training its own professional recruits. If the discipline is more than a branch of philosophy
in the college curriculum, however, it is also more than a special way
of looking at history, a training ground for the professions of law,
business, journalism, and government service, or a set of entertaining
courses for teen-agers and adults in "how to think about" politics and
citizenship. Political science does all of these things. As a body of
knowledge developed from systematic concentration upon government, the public life of the commonwealth, it ought to exhibit in some
more explicit, systematic way than it now does the problems, difficulties, and methods of arriving at empirically based principles of political
knowledge. With some notable exceptions, what we do now for undergraduates is to show them how to look at politics through different
sets of ideological spectacles and to develop either a contemptuous or
an admiring attitude toward politicians and their "manifest" techniques.
The behaviorist wants the undergraduate's education to include the
technical rudiments of inquiry, analysis, and generalization about
politics in the observable world, which amounts to an introduction
to the requirements of competent research into the behavior of people
acting in political situations. This is an expensive, time-consuming,
and exhausting teaching operation, but if it is approached in the spirit
of redressing the balance rather than a wholesale substitution for

* Editor's note: Evidently this provocative challenge did achieve its purpose. It
induced the author in the midst of a very busy spring to sit down and write this paper.

existing methods in departmental administration, a growing number of qualified, young political scientists are available and willing to help.

Put in such reasonable terms, it is easy to say: "What's new about that? Aren't we doing it already?" The answer is "yes" and "no"; "yes" in the sense that we emphasize the importance of descriptive "facts" about how courts decide cases, congressmen get elected, presidents nominated, and government workers employed; "no" in the sense of elementary training in how to isolate a problem, identify in exploratory terms a few critical, explanatory variables, formulate two or more of them in a researchable proposition or hypothesis, and go about getting and analyzing the relevant data by which the original guess or hunch could be checked. Only in a few departments is this kind of instruction given, but where they are is very quickly evident to one who reads statements of interest on graduate school and fellowship applications. I refrain from mentioning what proportion of postdoctoral, research-grant applications exhibit this primitive level of competence.

The justification for training in empirical theorizing extends far beyond the "practical" means of getting money for research later on. Incapsulated, this kind of thinking is the earmark of the *trained* mind: the ability to conceptualize in precise rather than pretentious and fuzzy language, to make discriminations in terms of variables and attributes rather than uncircumscribed or undifferentiated wholes, to identify problems in terms of operational concepts and accessible data rather than conflicts between definitions, schools, or approaches. It also is the foundation for learning how to communicate in "variable" language with the other social and natural sciences.

There is still another pragmatic justification for empirical political theory. This has to do with the importance of imparting to the able student "the sense of the political," the assumption that political theory constitutes an objective skill and competence in its own right. A great many students come into political science under the impression that it is a recognized profession of secular preaching, in which the holder of an advanced degree obtains the license to expound "correct" views and "approved" schemes of politico-governmental reform. The discipline would do a much better vocational counseling job, as well as public relations, if its undergraduate curriculum contained more of the kind of training that made students appreciate the work of arriving at principles, getting at facts, discriminating between opinion and evidence, distinguishing between theory and policy. Many fine, highly motivated men and women would save precious years they now waste before discovering that a political scientist is not a lecturer-provocateur or a journalist-advocate.

The behavioral viewpoint is more than a revival of interest in *methods* of teaching and research.[24] Let me illustrate the kind of theoretical training behaviorists see, hopefully, along with philosophers and empiricists. It could take the form of a series of short-answer propositions to which the reader would be invited to agree or disagree, but we will play the game in the form of questions:

1. Does our theoretical training produce: (*a*) explicit criteria for discriminating between propositions that are politically significant, irrelevant, or unimportant? (*b*) models (theories) of the world that clarify rather than obfuscate when the student tries to relate the imagined (conceptualized) world to the observed one? (*c*) students who within their own limitations are able to formulate and carry out autonomously their own research priorities and strategy?

2. Do our students believe that the purpose of political analysis is: (*a*) to prescribe for political society as if it were a clean slate on which the appropriate ends of man should be written? (*b*) to produce tautological, internally consistent positions based upon premises that cannot be proven or disproven? (*c*) to discover uniformities and differences in political behavior and institutions, expressible in generalizations and hypotheses of explanatory and predictive value?

3. Do our students view and enjoy political theory as exercises in formulating fresh statements supposedly: (*a*) contributory to the understanding of a problem? (*b*) self-consciously relevant to the question being asked?

4. Are our students prepared: (*a*) to distinguish, on the discriptive level, statements of observable and preferred

24. D. Easton, "The Current Meaning of Behavioralism in Political Science," in J. C. Charlesworth, *The Limits of Behavioralism in Political Science* (Philadelphia: The American Academy of Political and Social Science, 1962), pp. 7-25.

facts? (*b*) to accept the requirement of not presenting, on the analytical-explanatory level, statements as universals which contain concealed assumptions of time, place, class, or ethnic identification? (*c*) to recognize and apply the distinction between basic and applied research to the resolution of policy problems?

5. Do our students habitually: (*a*) employ ordering concepts which have referents capable of reasonable precise verification or diversification and whose range of variation can be specified? (*b*) assume the likelihood of multi-variate explanations rather than positing singular causation in terms of topical or *post factum* statements of personal experience? (*c*) seek to reduce the number of explanatory variables to the minimum number essential to give an equally adequate answer? (*d*) self-critically emphasize problems of accessibility and reliability of data, and validity of methods of analysis and interpretation?

If these illustrative questions are interpreted to mean that undergraduates should get the same kind of concentrated training as graduate students, I would be disappointed. Political Science 1 has to precede Political Science 2, 3, 4, . . . *n,* but there is some theory even at the lowest level and continuity from the lowest to the most high. Deepening specialization and widening horizons challenge the thoughtful mind with new relations and interdependencies. The rational and the empirical, the idealistic and the pragmatic, the literary and the scientific, the deductive and the inductive, all are parts of the humanistic tradition, interests, and heritage of mankind. As the student grows from social unconsciousness through class consciousness to self-consciousness, the teacher hopes he will acquire an appreciation of those intellectual values that sustain him and are shared in common by all the disciplines and sciences of man, society, and nature: respect for truth, freedom of thought and expression, justice and dignity in human affairs, the welfare of the polity which makes these possible. May we hope to instil in our students more of the skills, commitment, and insight that we strive to find in ourselves, and in so doing endeavor "to transmit our commonwealth greater, better and more beautiful than it was transmitted to us."

EDGAR H. BROOKES

Through British eyes

We have rather lost our way as university teachers. All of us do some good work, but the burden of our duties is heavy upon us, and we have little time to stop and reflect. An opportunity such as the present when we can take stock of our situation is to be welcomed.

Any one charged with my task is handicapped from the outset, not only by his own faults, but from the patronizing and superior attitudes in past years of so many English speakers and writers about America. I approach my subject, therefore, with some trepidation, and I hope with due modesty and humility, realizing how much I myself am learning in an American university. Nevertheless, if I do not articulate clearly what I feel, I shall have failed in my duty, and it is in this spirit that I have agreed to participate in this project.

In some countries, and particularly in England, we have assumed that university education is for an elite. That view, even in England, is beginning to break down. In this country it is accepted that university education is for the many. This not only means that there must be very many universities but universities with large student bodies. The effect of this is to create vast and rather amorphous universities, in which the student has little chance of making contact with any one directing or guiding spirit, knowledgeably interested in him as a person and in his studies as a whole.

On the Preparation of College Teachers

We must add to this the phenomenon which I venture to call Phiddity—the tyranny of the Ph.D. My own country and many others suffer from it, but it is found in full flower in America. I was told in Oxford that the doctorate in philosophy was introduced there because American students would be satisfied with nothing else. I have known cases of graduate students going from South Africa and merely taking a further bachelor's degree at Oxford or Cambridge, so that their qualifications would read "B.A. (Capetown et Oxon)" or "B.A. (Natal et Cantab)," but this practice is less common today. The danger is, then, that of the many thousands of political science graduate students in the United States, every ambitious one will aim at the Ph.D. The instructor, if he does not already possess it, will be using all his extra time to acquire one himself. Since a Ph.D. must involve original research and since good subjects are being taken one by one, the process of producing a Ph.D. thesis in spite of the argument that every year produces new subjects, is coming to be more and more, in Sir Eric Ashby's phrase, "crawling along the frontiers of knowledge with a hand-lens." Since an appreciable proportion of those who take the Ph.D. in political science do so in order to qualify for academic posts, it would not be altogether unfair to say that we have Ph.D.'s in order to teach others to take Ph.D.'s in order that they in turn may teach a still further generation to take Ph.D.'s—much of this genuine and praiseworthy work having little relation to personal experience, the world of politics outside the universities, or that student life which is the real aim of a university to produce. This is Phiddity *in excelsis.*

Now some of this cannot be altered. It is unlikely that in our day, if ever, universities will go back to ministering to an elite. Nor is it likely that America will give up the Ph.D. habit. It is far more likely that it will extend elsewhere, as it is doing in pretty well every other Commonwealth country and up to a point even in Britain itself. We shall therefore have to consider how to introduce personal intimacy into the vast modern university and how to improve the Ph.D. degree rather than how to abolish it.

And here let us consider the limitations of the Ph.D. degree. If our system had existed in Elizabethan England, Shakespeare might have got a Ph.D. by submitting some critical notes on Marlowe, but never by offering *King Lear* or *Cymbeline* to the Examiners. Plato would have had a rough passage with *The Republic.* The university would have refused to accept a thesis "On Justice," and if they had approved the title they would never have approved the treatment, which involved little research but just came out of Plato's head. It would have been considered non-factual, over-imaginative, too literary in form, too non-technical in diction. We are rather suspicious of Ph.D. theses which do not have a quality of polysyllabic dullness in them. No one could have rejected Aristotle's *Politics* for lack of original research, but he would certainly have been told that his subject was far too wide. Hobbes might have crept through, but Milton's *Areopagitica* would have been rejected out of hand, and Mill would have had *On Liberty* referred back to him for further consideration and the provision of footnotes and bibliography. In short, most of the great political texts which we use in our courses would be considered incompatible with the Phiddity of our day. So we go on turning out Ph.D.'s in order that they may turn out more Ph.D.'s. "Playing golf?" asked one man of another. "Yes" was the reply. "One must keep fit, you know." "Why?" "Well—to play more golf."

Now, I do not want to be unfair in this paper. I admit at once that not all Ph.D. theses "crawl along the frontiers of knowledge," and I am very sure that hundreds of teachers of political science are, like myself, trying to do their job well with some touch of inspiration and freedom. Nevertheless, the picture which I have drawn has enough truth in it to make us think seriously about our methods.

There are countries, like my own Republic of South Africa, where research still has many important fields to conquer and where at the same time the issues of life and death before the people are so vividly urgent and apparent as to fight against that scholastic "crawling along the frontiers of knowledge." Circumstances such as these may produce theses more vital and powerful than some political science theses in more stable and certain societies. Perhaps, indeed, similar spheres of what we might call passionate knowledge exist even in countries less frighteningly aware than mine of that need. A book like James Baldwin's *The Fire Next Time* might be ranked for its literary beauty, its spiritual passion and fervor, and even its conclusions (with not all of which I agree), with the best of more orthodox Ph.D. dissertations. But whether, in an advanced country like the United States or in a more divided and uncertain one like the Republic of South Africa, we ought to encourage that true passion and passionate truth which spell creative activity and not merely cold-blooded and not very useful "research" is an open question.

Such encouragement would have its own dangers, for once we get away from the strait path of depersonalized research there is the danger of propaganda, the danger of cheap feelings glibly expressed, and these are from no point of view worthy of academic encouragement or recognition. But surely as at present we see through and reject shoddy research, we ought to be able to see through and reject shoddy analysis, simulated passion, or unreal vision.

What I am leading up to is a revolution about Phiddity—the acceptance of the principle that analysis, thought, and vision ought to be more readily accepted than they are for a Ph.D. degree. If we were lucky enough to have a twentieth-century Plato's *Republic* presented to us, it should earn its doctorate. If it were only a Cicero's *De Republica,* we could insist on the presentation of a shorter thesis of the more orthodox type as an additional requisite. If it were a mere presentation of potted passion and popular prejudice prepared by a popularity-hunting popinjay we should, even without "alliteration's artful aid," reject it outright.

Lest it should be thought that these views are merely the one-sided ideas of a foreign visitor, I would draw your attention to a purely American document which possesses considerable authority and must have great weight given to it. I refer to the recent "Report of the Committee on Policies in Graduate Education" of the Association of Graduate Schools. I shall allow myself to quote at some length from this report.

We see many a man *less* mature, *less* self-poised and *less* confident after two years in a graduate school than he was as an inspirited college senior.

The emerging Ph.D. is not what we mean by an *educated* man, a man who combines wide-ranging learning with an attitude of simplicity and vividness, and who commingles good taste with an excited curiosity. Rather he likely has become a sort of expert plumber in the card catalogues, or other areas and neither as teacher or scholar will he throw off this inhibiting heritage.

We reaffirm what we take to have been the original idea and intent of the Ph.D.; namely, to train men to do advanced work of an original nature, without either maiming them spiritually or assuming that they are Methuselahs.

Few theses conform to these prescriptions. Generally their fantastic bulk not only prolongs graduate years, but too often inculcates bad lessons. The idea of discrimination in citing references or the thought that there is something good about a vivid and graceful English style too frequently go down to defeat before mere undigested mass. It is not by such ways that a man will learn to write either a book or an article of merit and interest. And as for the subjects themselves, one pauses to decide what to complain of first.[1]

My remarks, which might otherwise be dismissed as the somewhat brash views of one not well acquainted with the American scene, must surely challenge consideration when they coincide so nearly with the considered opinions of so distinguished a group of American scholars. What is it that they and I object to in the Ph.D. degree? Neither they nor I propose its abolition. Neither they nor I suggest that it should not involve original thinking. But both they and I feel that it is beginning to harden into an uncreative system of pedantry, of research for research's sake, not only kindling the creative intelligence and emotions of students but even quenching the divine fire that is already there. If, as we are told, the time will come when we need to turn out 20,000 Ph.D.'s a year, the prospect of 20,000 such Ph.D.'s fills one with foreboding, almost with horror. The fact that America may need 20,000 more university teachers is something to be welcomed, but may we have grace to turn out inspired and creative teachers, not mere plumbers of card indexes. My own feeling is that the Ph.D. should sometimes be awarded on outstanding original and creative work, even if it is not research in the narrowest sense of that term.

On Excessive Specialization

But if this new spirit of life and freedom of which the Committee on Graduate Education speaks is really to prevail in our universities, we must set the spirits of our faculties themselves free from the burdens of overwork and overspecialization in depersonalized institutions. For while an outstanding noble personality can succeed as professor or student in any environment, none the less the vastness of many modern universities makes it harder to be personal, harder to think, harder even to find time. Theoretically, when there are many specialists each ought to find more time, but it does not seem

1. Association of Graduate Schools in the Association of American Universities, "Report of the Committee on Policies in Graduate Education," *Journal of Proceedings and Addresses* (1957), pp. 35-41.

to work that way. There are, it would appear, Parkinson's Laws of intellectual activity as well as of administration.

We must therefore approach the question of the size of universities, not taking for granted that present developments are either inevitable or right or both. But before we do so we ought to examine the advantages and disadvantages of the extreme specialization which now prevails. In the very early days of my own University in South Africa there was a professor of English and philosophy—*all* philosophy—and a professor of history *and* modern languages—*all* modern languages. And though in conditions of specialization not much better than these a great humanist like Alan Paton received his university education, we should all agree that they are undesirable and indeed ludicrous. The other extreme is illustrated by a talk which I had when four years ago I was dining in one of the Oxford colleges. The man who sat at my right hand had not indeed been introduced to me, but I felt that, even in England, this did not preclude dinner-table conversation. Ignoring the obvious topic of the weather, I asked him, "What is your special field of study?" He answered promptly, "Henry I." Here was an able man apparently devoting his whole life to the study of England from 1100 to 1135. Perhaps when he wanted a sort of intellectual "binge" he ran over into Stephen (1135-1154), but he would soon return to the paths of intellectual sobriety and Henry I. And he complained that there was too much competition in his subject.

It reminds me of the story of the old-fashioned general practitioner who had agreed not without some reluctance to his son's becoming an ear, nose, and throat specialist. One day the son came home and said that he felt his chosen field was too wide and that he wished to specialize only on the nose. "Which nostril?" growled the old man.

No argument on my part is needed to prove the value of intensive work in limited fields of research. The labors of my friend at Oxford will undoubtedly prove beneficial to anyone who has to handle medieval history as a whole. Someone must do this kind of work. But if a faculty is composed mainly of men thus specializing, and if there is no one to give the student more general direction, he will have to work hard against the atmosphere of his university to see life as a whole, even to see his subject as a whole. And this is surely as true of the United States as it is of Britain.

T. F. Henn, in the *Harvard Educational Review*, says:

The individual must publish. In order to publish he must specialize
on a comparatively narrow field. Once his reputation is really established
he will teach in that field and in little else. Because he has written well
in it there is an inevitable assumption that he will teach it well. (But the
fallacy in this was exposed more than once in conversation: "If a man's
got a big name, we don't give a damn whether he can teach or not.") . . .
The American Professor is considerably more learned, in a limited field,
than his British counterpart. His output in published matter is almost
certainly greater; his training in dealing with subjects which have very
broad or complicated aspects is perhaps less.[2]

I should like to advocate that as many university teachers as possible should be encouraged to combine a course of intense specialization with similar responsibility for a much more general one. Even
where this is already being done, as of course it is in many cases,
the spirit of departments, in particular of political science departments, should be oriented in this direction—this combination of
genuine and specialized knowledge with a broad view of the subject,
and even of life as a whole. We surely must not exclude Socrates
from the university!

All this being granted we must return to the question of the size
of the modern university, for almost every part of our task would
be rendered easier if we had fewer students to handle. In England
the two old universities, Oxford and Cambridge, have met this difficulty in the course of centuries of history by the collegiate and tutorial system. Divided up into historic colleges of manageable size,
Oxford and Cambridge are able to give their students personal attention and a sense of "belonging" which is partly met in American
universities, but only partly, by the institution of fraternities. In
Britain an adequate provision of tutors means that the student is
assured of some guidance while being left almost completely free of
the obligation to attend university lectures. I am aware that attempts
have been made in America, notably by Harvard and Yale, to trans-
plant this system with suitable modifications to American soil. But
the system can no more be imitated in detail than can the House of
Lords. It has not even been copied fully in the newer English universities. Scotland has never had it. In that country in earlier days

2. T. R. Henn, "Some American Universities as Seen Through British Eyes,"
Harvard Educational Review, XXIV (1954), 207.

the professor's duties were confined to his lecture room, and the student was left to sink or swim for himself in such lodgings as he could find. It was a system grim and intellectually spartan. Rarely are men quite so good or quite so bad as their theories, and in any case Scottish university education has improved a great deal since those austere days.

In my own country, South Africa, the Afrikaans-speaking universities have modeled themselves on the Scottish and Continental universities, and of the strange new tribal or "ethnic" university colleges set up by the government for men of color it is too early to speak, though not too early for signs of foreboding. The four English-medium universities have had many Oxford and Cambridge men on their faculties, but, much as they would like to introduce a tutorial system, their financial state is not such as to make it possible on any extensive scale. Apart from Oxford and Cambridge, then, the differences between British and American universities are to be found rather in spirit and outlook than in formal organization. There is, perhaps, more stress on a broad outlook as against over-specialization, though as my story of Henry I shows this is by no means universal. There is certainly less insistence on assiduous attention at lectures and a great freedom in organizing one's own studies. Even in South Africa our universities are in general content if our students attend three-quarters of the lectures given, and this requirement is not harshly applied.

In Oxford and Cambridge this non-insistence on lectures is carried very far. Once at Oxford I asked an undergraduate at St. John's College how many lectures per week he was going to attend, and he answered, cheerfully enough: "None at all. You see I'm preparing for an examination." In the Joseph Payne Memorial Lecture, delivered at the London College of Preceptors in 1954, Sir Charles Morris summed up this system as follows:

It has sometimes been thought that it is not necessary to teach young people of this sort, in any positive sense of the word, at all. All they should need is access to libraries and laboratories with occasional advice, as sought on occasion by themselves, from senior and more established scholars. Like everyone of course who devotes himself to an arduous and exacting pursuit, these young men will need social comfort and encouragement to sustain them in their disappointments and to fortify them in their devotion to study. But this they will gain in good measure from living with one another, and with their elders of like purpose with themselves, in the way of life of a university. But understanding and true knowledge come only to him who teaches himself; and libraries, laboratories and occasional self-sought advice and encouragement should be enough. For such people, it might be thought, the educational duty of a university is confined to welcoming them to its common life and giving them their opportunity.[3]

A little later in the same lecture Sir Charles sums up this point of view by describing the university as a "home of learning" and contrasting this conception with that of the university as a place for educating the young. I refuse to accept this as a legitimate antithesis. A modern university is and must be both. And here a comparison might be drawn with two other great institutions, the Navy and the Church. In the Navy and in the naval schools a young officer must be educated, not only in technical details. But the spirit of the Navy surrounds him, he learns its prides and its traditions, he is part of something which is much more than a teaching agency. A Church may and indeed must have its confirmation or other membership classes, but its atmosphere from early childhood, its hymns, its sacraments, its ways of living, its example, must matter more than its formal teaching. Both are needed. It would be a sad day when our universities became merely educational institutions, but it would be an equally sad day when they ceased to be such. Probably the third and fourth undergraduate years should approximate more closely than they do now, and the postgraduate years almost wholly, Sir Charles Morris' ideal, but the first two years should contain a good deal of genuine teaching, which should be professionally good teaching as far as this is possible.

My first impressions of American university life have been very happy. My students have won my heart from the first day and revealed qualities of maturity, sanity, and good will which are encouraging indeed. They work hard. They know they have to read, and they do read. But they give me the impression of being too much coerced to attend lectures, and too dependent on their teachers for assignments of work. I get the impression also that they know a lot of things in detail—sometimes adequately related to one another and sometimes not—but that they cannot always see the wood for the trees; a general philosophy of life comes rather in spite of than be-

3. Sir Charles Morris, "The Idea of University Education," *Universities Quarterly,* VIII (1953/54), 327.

cause of the teaching system. What they know they know well, often better than my own students in South Africa, but it often consists of unrelated pieces of possibly premature specialization. Is the process of Phiddity—I promise not to use this word again—seeping back into the training of our undergraduate students?

There is much talk today of "disciplines." I am not sure that "disciplines" differ as much as we say they do. We all tend to suffer from over-departmentalization. What is this political science which we teach? I should like to offer the thought that a university teacher's job is not so much to teach political science or economics or history as to teach the ultimate wisdom of life, the accumulated treasures of the ages, through the medium of political science or economics or history. "The proper study of mankind is man," and man is not merely political man or economic man, man the lover, man the worshiper, but quite simply man, and this we must remember in all our teaching. But let me repeat and try to answer from a somewhat different point of view the question, "What is this political science which we teach?" The British universities have been slow in recognizing it as a separate discipline. In my own country while some universities so recognize it, others hook it up with history or philosophy or economics or local government. But whatever differences we may find in organization, it is almost universal that the syllabus includes some sort of political philosophy and some careful factual and analytical study of governmental institutions. As we would not lightly eliminate either Plato or Aristotle from the accumulated treasure of human learning, so we would not lightly give up either element of political science. The careful study of institutions is valuable in itself and is a very necessary element of the subject, giving it "body" as it were. The treatment of political philosophy should not be an unrelated, "airy-fairy" body of speculation. It should not be a mere study of the *history* of political thought but should constantly be related, by teacher and student alike, to those passing problems of present-day concrete political life which form the subject of the other half of the syllabus. But to see politics as what it is, an intimate part of life, it must be related to life as a whole. The very difficulty of classifying it in so many universities shows how it is in fact closely related to other fields of thought. To deprive it of the standards and values of either is to improverish it beyond words. Even religious faith cannot be excluded from a subject which includes St. Augustine and St. Thomas Aquinas, Bertrand de Jouvenel and Jacques Maritain, among its doctors. It is surely society as a whole which must be the living background of our study of the state as a part. G. D. H. Cole writes of the value of what he calls "link" courses of lectures, designed to bring out the interconnection between philosophy, politics, and economics. In short, it must be our ambition both for ourselves and for our students.

"To see life steadily and see it whole."

I yield to no one in my admiration for the able and knowledgeable American professors whom I have been meeting day after day. In the political science department of a great American university there is little that you cannot find out from one or another of them. The student who has access to them as a whole is fortunate indeed, and I say this with deepest sincerity. But does he have access to all of them? Does not the system of selecting a number of semester courses mean more-than-average knowledge and efficiency in patches, often without the wisdom or inspiration to see the whole picture and relate it to life as a whole? And there is another point to remember. Does the student in fact have access to his professor except in the lecture room? The more studious the professor, the more conscientious a research worker, the more he will be tempted to be bogged down in his study—shall we say of Henry I, or some other specialized subject of research. The more able and energetic he is, the more he is likely to be on numbers of committees, and to end up in university administration, according to the peculiar university system of promoting any first-rate teacher by taking him away from teaching.

I want to put to you the view that some close personal contact between professor and student is greatly to be desired in university teaching. It need not be so, probably it cannot be so, between every professor and every student. But if it is generally absent, the university has failed. And I suggest, with becoming humility, that every department of political science in a great American university should ask itself very seriously whether in the accumulated work of all its members there is a general vision of life, or even of political science, presented to all its students and how many of them have become in any real sense friends of their professors? Even as I pose the question I think of cases within my own knowledge where it would be an impertinence to ask it; but as a general question it still needs to be asked.

More time could be made for personal contacts between teacher and student by reducing the teaching load after the first two years of university life, by reducing (if one may be permitted to give expression to so blasphemous a thought) the number of committees, and by mitigating somewhat the demands of research.

It is the last of these three suggestions which seems most in need of defense. Every good university teacher will want to do some research. A political science teacher, in particular, is compelled to do so merely to keep up to date with the facts. But it is the undue stress laid by university authorities on research and publication which is the trouble. It is as though at some period in the past they had realized that a few university teachers would not do research work without pressure from above. Every university system in the world must, I suppose, contain a few people who look upon their jobs as opportunities of abundant and uncreative leisure. I think that your university authorities might well have trusted American integrity. Even if they could not bring themselves to do that, they ought to have realized the existence of American virility and American ambition. There is no real danger that American professors as a whole will not do research work. But the feeling that research must constantly be done and that publications are one of the most vital factors in promotion means that almost all spare time is given to these things. No similar inquiries are set apart to insure that men give time to their students as individuals. This does not count for promotion. Will anyone seriously maintain that the American university system would be sensibly weakened if one-third of time now given to research were devoted to individual students? Will any one seriously maintain that the reduction of the number of lectures by one-third and the devotion of the time thus served to work with individuals would reduce the standard of university education? These are practical reforms which do not destroy the whole background and tradition of American university life and are not a slavish imitation of a foreign system. Why should the number of lectures given be so sacrosanct?

Some years ago in the University of Pretoria a number of the professors were asked to answer the question, "What is education?" One defined it as "the ability to use an index intelligently" and another as "humility and a sense of humor," but no one defined it as the "ability to take good lecture notes in a receptive spirit and learn them off by heart." In the deepest sense I should think that education might be defined in one of the great phrases of the Anglican Prayer Book as "the increase of faith, hope and charity," but never as the increase of wise passivity and a good memory.

On Political Activity and Teaching

It is time now to speak of a question which affects us deeply as political scientists, namely, whether we should remain in our ivory towers of academic impartiality or descend into the arena of practical politics. If I may be excused for being personal, I have always been glad that I did my laboratory work. I was Professor of Political Science and Public Administration at the University of Pretoria from 1923 to 1933, a member of the Senate of the Union of South Africa elected by the Africans of Natal and Zululand from 1937 to 1952, and I then taught political science at the University of Natal from 1953 to 1962. My years in Parliament did not involve me in violent party controversy until toward the end, and I found them most enriching when I began to teach political science to university students again. In the last few years real problems have presented themselves. The party struggle in South Africa, real and bitter enough, was preoccupied with the relations between the two white groups—English-speaking and Afrikaans-speaking. In recent years it has been swept into the vortex of African nationalism, the Russo-American struggle for Africa, and the active, and as many think reactionary, apartheid policies of the Afrikaner Nationalists. In these circumstances it has been difficult to remain silent.

When a university finds itself set in the midst of an area and a period of violent change in which high moral issues are involved, is it desirable that either professors or students should remain silent or detached in spirit from it all? Every man must follow the star of his own conscience; no man can lay down an unvarying role for his associates. But there have been moments when I myself have felt with Martin Luther: "Here I stand: I can no other." I have remembered the words of a great American poem: "Then to side with truth is noble, when we share her bitter crust." The words of Milton have come back to me about the arena "where that immortal Garland is to be won, not without dust and heat." I may have said more than I should at such moments.

In 1960, after the massacre at Sharpeville, our government proclaimed a "state of emergency" and there were a large number of arrests. Our senior lecturers (or as you would say associate professors) in English and botany, who had been active members of our non-racial Liberal party, were sent to jail where they remained without trial for ten weeks. Feeling ran high among the students, who were anxious to parade through the city in protest. In the then frame of mind of the government and police, this might have led to a baton charge and the injury or arrest of students. My colleagues paid me the compliment of thinking that I was the one member of staff to whom the students would listen most readily on this subject, and asked me to address a mass meeting in which we recorded our sympathy with the families of the arrested men and persuaded the students not to stage a provocative demonstration.

I succeeded in my task and at the time was inclined to feel pleased with myself, but when a year or two later I realized that there had been a recession in student feeling, I found myself wishing that there was something that needed to be restrained. When still more recently a student demonstration was planned and I was asked to quiet the students, I said I would rather head their procession. Armed police were placed at the university gates, and while I was busy elsewhere students surged down there and were persuaded to turn back. I was troubled because the great fault of English-speaking students in South Africa is apathy, political timidity, and absorption in sport and careers. Yet I must say that the very impassioned political activities of Afrikaans-speaking students in defense of Nationalist policies have seemed to me harmful, and the intimidation of Afrikaans-speaking professors who would not toe the Nationalist line an infringement of academic freedom.

About ten years ago the council of Fort Hare University College, at that time a "free" institution for Africans, now one of the government's ethnic seminaries, asked me to serve on a private commission on inquiry about certain difficulties at the college. We found the dominant—I will not say the majority—student opinion to be a kind of mixture of African nationalism and Trotskyite communism. We found evidence of extensive intimidation of students who did not respond to this view. African members of the faculty, including some who were outstanding in their public work, were currently described as "sell-outs." It was impossible to be happy about this state of affairs, grievous though the disabilities of Africans were.

It must seem to those who are following this paper as if I am against political activities at universities which are contrary to my own sentiments and in favor of those with which I agree. I have to face this all too human charge with modesty and honesty, and to realize that there may be something in it. Yet I do not think that this is all there is to it. Let me therefore try to sum up some general impressions arising from my own experiences.

1. Political apathy is not a good quality, nor is it a help to impartial thinking. If we must exercise restraint let us have some emotions to exercise it on. In the words of our South African poet, Roy Campbell,

> You have the snaffle and the curb all right,
> But where's the bloody horse?

I have seen many inspiring examples of national patriotism and civic duty among American students, but there is still too much apathy among too many.

2. Intimidation of any kind, open or subtle, whether of students or of faculty, should be resisted as the enemy of academic freedom which it is.

3. Faculty members should not exploit their students for political ends or "work up" feelings which have not arisen spontaneously among the students.

4. Political excitement must not take the place of serious and —as far as is humanly possible—impartial study.

The ivory tower issue has to be faced, however, not only in crisis countries like my own but also in countries like the United States with a stable atmosphere and democratic institutions such as to make revolution unnecessary. Here the question that may arise is whether a faculty member should seek political office or take a prominent part in party politics while still retaining his teaching position.

No general rule can ever be laid down about this, but a few comments may help to lead us each to formulate for himself the principles which must guide him personally. One point which might certainly be borne in mind is that the balanced, sane outlook on political philosophy which is characteristic of the Anglo-American tradition at its best is to be found most markedly in men who have taken part in practical politics. Both Locke and Burke held public office. Burke was twenty-nine years in Parliament and John Stuart Mill four. The too much neglected Halifax was in the heart of public affairs during three reigns and was in effect prime minister of England in the first year of the reign of William III.

Other great names in political philosophy evoke different reflections. To me Hobbes, Rousseau, and Marx, however great and influential in the history of thought, are men who have given unbalanced views of life because they never knew true life. Hobbes's long walks for meditation in the countryside (not to speak of his clinical drunkennesses three times a year) would have yielded better fruit in political thinking if he had borne some part, however small, in the government of his country. Had he done so he would soon have discovered what practical limitations exist on the theoretical sovereignty which he preached. Rousseau, in the intervals of fathering five illegitimate children and writing on the beauty and purity of family life, might have found even in the homogeneous and minute cantons of central Switzerland, if he had truly been a citizen of one, some cases where the General Will did not quite work. And if Karl Marx had spent some of those long hours devoted to study and writing under the gaslight of the British Museum in really getting to know the workingmen in the country of his refuge, their hopes, their aspirations, and their political feelings, he would have learned that humanity is not so easily bisected as he taught, and some salutary reservations and exceptions would have made more real and more wise the terrible successes and the dialectical infallibilities of Communist orthodoxy, for no orthodoxy is more pitiless than the orthodoxy of the heterodox.

By this time I shall have made enemies of half the teachers of political science in the United States, and doubtless these obiter dicta have said more than they should. However, the main point, I suggest, is well taken: an experience of practical citizenship is no unworthy equipment for a political philosopher or a teacher of political science. This work, provided that it brings one into the stream of life, need not necessarily be of a party nature. Experience in local government or in national work not of a party character may be as useful and less dangerous. Perhaps, after all, if it does not sound too old-fashioned to say so, the real tests of political involvement are moral. Is the political scientist moved by ambition? Is his academic work a mere step toward a career elsewhere? The real danger lies in his giving his students a bad example of selfishness masquerading as honest civic interest. The clear eyes of youth may see through him; the shrewd eyes of age and experience certainly will.

Are there not in this matter apt comparisons to be made with other fields, such as law and science, where the same considerations apply?

No study of university life can be complete without some study of the work, often most valuable work, of university presidents. It is easy to see that genuine participation in national activities may be a strength to such leaders, while absorption in party politics must be a weakness; but this is not decisive in our own case, since some things may be improper in a commanding officer which are permitted to his subordinates. I would rather take a different point of view, namely, whether a president has the time to give real intellectual and spiritual leadership to his university, for the answer to this may help us to evaluate our own duties as professors more clearly.

In my own country, where few universities possess any considerable endowments and where the government's contribution to higher education is clearly inadequate, the main task of the president of a university is often the collection of funds. In short, he has to "sell" the university to the wealthy. To do this he may well feel that he has to give much time to adapt himself to their way of life and very specially not to say anything that could dry up contributions.

From our point of view it is incredible that the well-endowed universities of America, equipped with fabulous buildings and libraries that have to be seen to be believed, should expect their presidents to submit themselves to the same ordeal. Yet they often do. "Much would have more," and in my own limited experience I have never yet discovered a university which was satisfied with what it had. This would not matter so greatly if it did not make such inroads on the time and the inner life of those distinguished scholars who are chosen to be heads of universities.

And yet an even deeper inroad into the life of the university president is made by the hundred and one questions of administration. A man who should be, and often is, chosen because he is a great scholar or a great teacher or both, is directed into office work and finance. There is nothing wrong with these things, but in the end, what with money-raising, administration, and the cultivation of potential donors, a university president is left with neither the time nor the spiritual resources to give leadership to his colleagues and students in the things that matter. I hunger to see more university presidents who really inspire their students and staff. What could be more important than that? And if this is so even for the president, how much more so for us. We should of course do research; we should publish. These things give our students more confidence in us. But our students should get the best of our time, not just the few scraps that can be saved from other things.

And if the president is a great scholar, so much the better for his relationship with his students. Only with respect and almost with reverence would I discuss the danger of over-administration, since our universities owe so much to good administrators. Yet it is here that the president—and we—get caught out. Returns and the completion of forms become ends in themselves, and by some refinement of torture they are so often in triplicate. In the end one has the fear that in our obsession with statistics we may be led to the conclusions of the girl who was writing a Ph.D. thesis on marriage in Missouri. "Careful examination shows," she concluded, "that more men than women were married in Missouri in 1959." We need to ask ourselves and one another, sometimes ruthlessly, what exact purpose is served by some of these laborious researches which deprive us of the chance to entertain our students in our homes, to talk to them unhurriedly in our studies, to know them and care for them.

A famous definition of "genius" speaks of it as "1 per cent inspiration and 99 per cent perspiration." While these percentages are utterly wrong, the fact remains that the work of university presidents and university professors needs inspiration and perspiration both. Neither can be dispensed with. And, indeed, a readjustment of the sadly misleading percentages may give us a much-needed clue to what our universities lack. Whatever the right figures, they are certainly nearer 50:50 than 1:99, and indeed the ultimate condemnation of a university system would be to say the opposite. None of this comprises a picture of an ideal president; it is rather a grim analysis of what over-administration can do to the fine scholastic material of which a president is often made. It is using a razor to cut blocks; and it is, do you not see it, a picture of our system at its worst.

I should think that a less grim and perhaps more accurate analysis of a president would often be: inspiration, 5 per cent, grinning sociabilities, 35 per cent, perspiration, 60 per cent.

Throughout this study we have been driven on strongly to insist on certain fundamentals. Let us try to gather these together before closing.

We may begin by saying that every system has much to learn from every other system, and therefore that it is reasonable that the English system may give some pointers to the American. As it is not now my task to say what the American system has to teach, I will not elaborate on this except to say that no man worth his salt can come away from the American universities other than moved by the honesty, scholarly integrity, and almost incredible hard work of the American university world as a whole. There is little that is shoddy or pretentious or superficial about it. What is there is good.

You could not, however, import the American system as it stands into the English universities, nor could you to anyone's advantage make an exact copy of the Oxford and Cambridge collegiate and tutorial system in an American university. We must keep the traditional and accepted framework, if for no other reason than the immense opposition which would be caused by any proposals for substantial change. We should find ourselves fighting years hence for organizational changes, which do not greatly matter, instead of concentrating on the changes of spirit and content which matter a great deal. I would sum up our real conflict as follows: (*1*) fighting against the narrowness of subject specialization, including the exaggeration of the idea of different "disciplines"; (*2*) fighting for more time, so that we may give to our students not so much a tutorial "system" but more of ourselves; (*3*) making it possible for the Ph.D. degree to be awarded wholly or partly on original or creative work, not only on research work in the narrower sense; (*4*) refusing to be so dominated by the requirements of research publicity and committees as to have no time for our students; (*5*) saving some time now devoted to lectures for personal contacts and tutorials, in particular, giving fewer lectures than at present, once the first two undergraduate teaching years are over, and cutting down requirements for compulsory attendance at those lectures.

No one can deny that this modicum of reform is possible. Few can deny that some reform is necessary. I would feel that those of us who think this way should go out in a bold and well-sustained effort to carry some such program through.

WILLIAM ANDERSON

In ancient Greece

Since my retirement in 1957 from the teaching of political
science at the University of Minnesota, many of the questions that
are involved in the scientific development, study, and teaching of
political science have been much in my mind. Indeed, I have been
trying to write a *History of the Study and Teaching of Politics* in the
Western world.[1] What I have to offer in this article is primarily a
condensed version of one of the topics dealt with in the first volume
of this work, namely, the study and teaching of politics in ancient
Greece, with special reference to Plato and Aristotle. In this paper
I have tried to limit the introduction and the conclusion to only what
seems necessary to provide a setting for the central theme.

In the first volume of my work I have tried to survey, as fully
as time and the available information would permit, the writings of
the ancient Mesopotamians, Egyptians, Hebrews, Greeks, and Romans, in order to ascertain in what ways and to what extent they
reveal any serious study and teaching of politics among these outstanding peoples. I have sought to find the leading early students
and teachers of politics, the proto-political-scientists, and their principal successors. Who were they? Under what conditions did they
work? What and how did they teach, if they did teach? These were
my leading questions.

In order to carry out this plan, and to make my findings of some
pertinence and value to present-day political scientists, I had to set
certain standards and guidelines, and not wander too far afield. To
me, politics and government are human activities which, potentially,
at least, affect everybody in any organized society. When I use the
word "politics" alone, I intend, as a rule, to include both politics

1. The first volume of this work has been published. See William Anderson,
*Man's Quest for Political Knowledge: The Study and Teaching of Politics in Ancient
Times* (Minneapolis, 1964). The second volume, now in preparation, will bear a
similar title and will deal with the medieval and modern period.

and government. All persons who become aware of the important and pervasive effects of political events upon themselves and others are likely to have thoughts about them and about the men and women who acquire leadership and exercise power in the field. In the long course of history, many persons, including leading philosophers and other scholars, have written down thoughts or speculations about politics, ranging from single sentences and brief comments to long and systematic works. Some of these writings reveal a strong aversion to politics, and by no means all of them give evidence of any careful study at first hand of political personalities and affairs. The histories of political theories and the histories of utopias mention many of these writers, and it is not my intention to compete with any such works. They have their own values and usefulness, but I am not engaged in writing another history of political theories or digest of utopias.

Instead, with the modern development of political studies in mind, especially in Europe and the United States, I am seeking the origins and the development of scholarly attempts to make relatively un-biased and scientific studies of politics as a group of human activities. Many political theorists and utopianizers have operated under condi-tions and preconceptions that made them either fear or disdain to study and write about politicians and rulers, or about systems of politics and government, as they really are or were. On the other hand, modern political scientists, along with many historians, sociol-ogists, and publicists, who to some extent share the field with political scientists, take the direct social-science approach to the study of politics. They endeavor to ascertain the facts concerning political lead-ers, institutions, activities, organizations, and problems, as other sci-entists study animals, plants, the elements, and the forces of nature. In their writings they present their evidence as to the facts of politics, as they see them, and they draw therefrom such conclusions as seem to be warranted. As a rule these students of politics are teachers and researchers in universities, colleges, and other institutions. In the course of their activities most of them write up and publish what they think they have discovered, and they also teach what they believe they know to their students. As a rule they do not speculate at large and without regard to the facts.

In the sense that I have described, the study and teaching of politics always have been especially dangerous to tyrants, whether individual tyrants or collective ones. Furthermore, because really free and popularly controlled governments have been the exception rather than the rule in the past, there have been but few times and places in man's existence on earth when such free study of politics as we enjoy today has been possible. There was a brief period in ancient Greece when a freedom not unlike ours prevailed. The beginnings made by the Greeks at that time were clearly limited, but it would be difficult to overstate their importance. After that brief and localized episode, many centuries passed without any real political studies anywhere in the world, at least in the sense in which I use that term.

When the serious study of actual politics was picked up again after many centuries, it was in Europe and primarily from northern Italy through Switzerland, Germany, Holland, France, and England that it reappeared. From there it leaped across the Atlantic to the American colonies which became the United States, and it is here that the study has had its freest and fullest development to the present time.

Near the beginning of his great work *Politics,* Aristotle says that "In this subject as in others the best method of investigation is to study things in the process of development from the beginning."[2] This is the principle that he followed not only in the study of biological species and other physically existent things but also in the consideration of men's studies of various things and subjects. In his school at Athens, the Lyceum, he required each of his assistants to study historically the methods and findings of their predecessors before they began seriously to carry further their own studies. He himself undertook, among other things, to report on the history of the study of politics. He found very little Greek historical material to report, and he mentions nothing coming from peoples other than the Greeks. His main finding on previous studies of politics related to one Hippodamus, a Greek architect and city planner,[3] "the same who invented the art of planning cities." Aristotle said of him that he was "the first person not a statesman who made inquiries about the best form of government." In other words it was Aristotle's judgment

2. *Politics,* 1252a, Book 1, 3-4 (H. Rackham translation). The Jowett translation is substantially the same.
3. *Ibid.,* 1267b, Book 1, chap viii.

that certain statesmen, but only statesmen, had studied what was the best form of government before Hippodamus did—and Hippodamus was only about a century earlier than Aristotle himself.

I confess to having been persuaded by Aristotle, among others, that to know his subject thoroughly any student and teacher needs to know who were his predecessors in the field, what conditions and problems they faced, what attitudes they held toward their subject, and how these and other factors affected and might help to explain the work they did and the findings and ideas they put forth. With some such evidence concerning his predecessors in mind, and with some knowledge of the conditions under which he himself labors and of his own presuppositions and possible biases, a modern student can be more aware and more critical of his own methods and results. Aristotle's insistence upon the historical approach has been widely influential down through the centuries.

With respect to the study of politics, however, Aristotle seems to have failed to look into the writings and the studies of contemporary and earlier non-Greek populations. Considering how widely through-out the Mediterranean basin and the Near East the Greeks themselves were settled, it is clearly conceivable that the Greeks might have picked up from others some of their ideas about the nature of politics and of political studies. To make up for this omission by Aristotle and later writers on politics, I have spent considerable time and effort in examining the standard histories of the ancient Mesopotamians, Egyptians, and Hebrews, as well as the more readily available writings of these peoples. The Mesopotamians and the Egyptians developed advanced systems of public administration and foreign relations, as the Mesopotamians did also in the field of law, and so these peoples evidently made important studies of political problems as they arose. These studies were carried on within the government or by the personal servants of the ruling monarch. Beyond the training of a sufficient number of civil servants to carry on the work of the governmental departments and the courts, there seems to have been no real interest in teaching the facts about government to the people. Also, although the laws were put forth in writing to some extent for the information of the people, there seems to have been little or no practice of the publication of government reports.

As to the Hebrews, their long history in ancient times is unique. Much of the time they were not self-governing in any true sense. Their earthly rulers were usually aliens to them. Fairly helpless for long periods in the face of these alien rulers, the Hebrews, following the advice of their priests and prophets, turned to God. He was their refuge and their strength. The priests and prophets were their principal teachers, and these men tried to keep the people thinking about God and relying on Him, no matter who their earthly rulers might be or what those rulers did. Thus, religion prevailed over politics, and the general secular study of politics did not develop.

How little Moses, for example, thought or knew about government as a human activity is well illustrated by the story of Jethro, the priest of Midian, who was the father-in-law of Moses. In Exodus 18:13-27, Moses, having brought his people out of the Egyptian bondage into the desert near Mt. Sinai, seemed to have no idea of the need to organize a government for them, or of how to do it if he ever thought of it. Instead, he sat all day, from morning till night, playing the roles of sole priest of God, judge, and secular ruler, all rolled into one, for the entire unorganized multitude. The people stood about or came and went, presenting their numerous problems to him, and he sat there trying to do everything expected of him. Observing that Moses was wearing himself out with this self-assumed burden of caring for all the problems of the people, Jethro gave Moses a terse lesson on how to organize a government by dividing the people up into thousands, hundreds, fifties, and tens; setting men over each of these divisions to settle respectively the smallest, the medium-sized, and the larger cases at the corresponding levels; leaving only the most important problems for Moses himself to handle. Moses evidently was relieved and happy to put this system of decentralization into effect, and there is no report of any grumbling about it from the people.

Whether this little episode actually took place, or took place as described, I do not know. In any case it makes a good story. On the whole the Old Testament books say much that is interesting about rulers and governments with whom the Hebrews had contacts, but they reveal no general concept or practice of the study and teaching of politics.

The Greeks

Coming then to the Greeks in the time of Plato and Aristotle, in the fourth century B.C., let me try to summarize in a preliminary way the conditions under which they lived and worked, for while these conditions will not explain the work of Plato and Aristotle in the field of politics, or show how the two men living in the same environment could have practically opposite views on major philosophical and political questions, they at least may portray conditions under which political studies by important men are possible. A pattern of conditions under which political studies are produced in one time and place is likely to be very similar to the pattern of conditions when and where such studies arise again.

The ancient Greeks were one people with a common language, traditions, and interests, occupying a rather small land area, divided into many self-governing city-states, all small and within easy reach of each other. Cultural and economic exchanges were well developed among them, and government was deemed by the people to be very important to them, because each *polis* or city-state was sovereign, each with a full array of governmental powers. All were engaged in making and remaking their constitutions or forms of government from time to time, so that at any one time there was a considerable amount of political activity and a variety of political forms and practices in operation. Moreover, there were many educated, intelligent, and inquisitive leaders among the Greeks, men who had considerable time for making studies and comparing experiences. They enjoyed considerable freedom of speech and writing and had had, at least since Solon's time, a generally secular attitude toward human affairs. In short, they looked to themselves and not to the gods to improve their conditions on earth.

As far as I know, an exact duplication of these conditions has not taken place at any time in the West, in Europe or America. But conditions sufficiently similar have arisen, and when they have, the study of politics has also shown a tendency to spring up and flourish.

It is interesting to notice, however, that Aristotle, the man among the ancient peoples who most fully took advantage of the opportunity for the comparative study of the actual governments of the Greek city-states, was one who, though of Ionian Greek descent, had been born outside of Greece proper. He had associated with various monarchs including the great Macedonian conqueror, Philip, and his even greater son, Alexander. He had no fixed abode in Athens where he studied, taught, and wrote, and needed special protection from Alexander and his vice-regent Antipater, while there. To be sure, he had traveled widely, not only in Greece but in other countries, so that he had gained an overview of politics such as had few if any other Greeks of that time. The many constitutional histories of Greek city-states that he collected and used for his studies had been written by local historians for their own cities. Probably very few if any of these local historians had the background for comparative studies that Aristotle had developed in his travels and in his work in comparative biology.

The study of politics among the Greeks flourished from the seventh century,—and perhaps earlier—to near the end of the fourth century B.C. This span of time takes in Solon near its beginning and Aristotle at its close. Following Aristotle there was a precipitous decline and practical disappearance of the study among both the Greeks and the Romans, although later writers such as Polybius and Cicero are worthy of mention. Little that was really new developed in the study of our subject for many centuries after Aristotle either in the West or in the East, as the empires that followed Alexander succumbed to the Roman Empire, and that seemingly world-dominating entity succumbed to internal decay, religious revolution, and the repeated mass intrusions of the numerous barbarian peoples in the West and to the Persians, Arabs, and Turks in the East.

Although I have already summarized some of the conditions in ancient Greece that permitted the rise of political studies, I think it desirable to examine the ancient Greek situation in a little more detail. By twentieth-century standards the ancient Greeks comprised a relatively small nation, occupying a very small part of the world's land area. The Greeks were probably fewer in number in Aristotle's day than they are today, when their population is reported to be about eight million, and not much more populous then than the average present-day American state, say about four million. By the time of Aristotle and Alexander at the end of the fourth century B.C., Greeks were scattered in many colonies that they had founded from

the western end of the Mediterranean to its eastern end and well in-
land beyond the sea, and also around the Aegean and Black seas
and on various islands. Most of the Greek population probably was
concentrated, however, on the Greek mainland, the nearby islands,
and the cities along the Ionian shore.

The present-day area of Greece is about 51,000 square miles,
less than the area of Illinois, Iowa, or Wisconsin, each of which is
smaller in area than the average size of our fifty states. It was mainly
within the area that constitutes the Greek national homeland today
that the ancient Greeks developed their remarkable civilization and
culture, had their most decisive political experiences, and undertook
their studies of science, history, philosophy, mathematics, and politics.

Until they were unified under Macedonian rule by Philip and
Alexander in the time of Plato and Aristotle, the Greeks were not
united in a single state or political organization. Instead, they were
divided among many small sovereign political units, each one a *polis*
with a full range of powers to manage its own foreign affairs, provide
for its defense, and carry on all the other functions of government.

How many of these places there were, and of what sizes, is not
known with census bureau precision as of any particular date, but
a reasonably close estimate can be made for Aristotle's time. As I
discuss this problem, try to keep in mind the state of Illinois with its
102 counties and about the same total area as ancient mainland
Greece. There is no complete list of the city-states available, but
Aristotle is known to have made a collection of Greek and other
"constitutions," and he refers to many places by name in the *Politics*.
Some five hundred years later Diogenes Laertius reported that there
were 158 "constitutions" in Aristotle's collection, but whether this
means 158 separate city-states is doubtful. The Greek city-states did
not have formal written charters or constitutions in the sense that the
fifty American states do. What Aristotle collected and used were
apparently brief constitutional histories such as Aristotle himself
wrote for Athens, and such as many local historians wrote for their
respective city-states during the fifth and fourth centuries B.C. From
this and other evidence compiled for me by several research assistants,
I have concluded that the actual number of Greek city-states in
Aristotle's time was about a hundred, but it may well have been more.

In other words, the Greek city-states on which Aristotle largely based his comparative studies in the *Politics* were about the same in number and in area as the counties of Illinois in recent years, but, even if Cook County which includes Chicago is excluded from the Illinois population figures, the Greek city-states were of considerably smaller population than the counties of Illinois. No doubt Athens, Corinth, Sparta, and a few other city-states had populations of more than a hundred thousand each, counting not only the male citizens but also the women, children, slaves, and non-citizen males, such as Aristotle himself was. Some evidence as to the population of the Greek city-states may be inferred from Hippodamus' argument that the ideal size for a city would be one that had ten thousand citizens and no more.

In short, then, the cities whose "constitutions" Aristotle mentions and comments upon were very small places by modern standards for national states, and his study of politics was based upon about a hundred or more (compare the present membership of the United Nations!) city-states of fairly simple structure and diminutive size. His was a study of government in miniature. He did almost nothing to describe the confederations of city-states that began to arise to make up for the deficiencies of these small places, and it was premature for him to write about the empire that Alexander was putting together in his time. But at least Aristotle collected a considerable number of accounts of the governments of the city-states, and from these and other materials he made a somewhat comparative study of their governments. It is unfortunate that they were already on the way out as independent units of government when he wrote about them, but fortunate for later students of politics that he actually completed his account of them before it was too late. If he had not written the account, who would there have been to record the picture of them?

If we take a comprehensive view of the political situation as it existed among the Greeks in the time of Plato and Aristotle, I think we must concede that the essential conditions existed for a fairly scientific study of politics. On the other hand, these conditions had not been present in such large monolithic states under one-man rule as Mesopotamia or Babylonia and Egypt, or among the Hebrews during most of their history.

The Greek city-states, were numerous, close together, and small enough to be studied by one man without spending a lifetime of labor on each one. They were politically active, and they exercised an extensive range of political powers and functions. They had problems of interstate relations, military defense, legislation for all domestic needs, adjudication of disputes, law enforcement, public works, public finance, and others, including relations with and some support of religion. Furthermore, the governments of these city-states, ranging from monarchies and oligarchies to advanced democracies, underwent frequent changes, so that the processes of constitutional modification were widely observable.

Thus, the materials for a comparative study of governments were close at hand and in considerable variety. Moreover, the Greeks with their considerable leisure class, high level of education and culture, inquisitiveness in many directions, and their direct dependence upon their local governments for the safety and welfare of all that they possessed and loved, proved to be just the sort of people to take a keen interest in their local politics. How else can one explain numerous essays about the governments of the different cities that Aristotle was able to collect and the many other things that are known to have been written about public affairs? The advantages the Greeks had in being one people, with a single language, and no doubt brothers, cousins, and other relatives and friends widely distributed among the various cities, a fairly high level of education and culture, and considerable freedom of speech and writing—though not without danger, as Socrates, Plato, and Aristotle all came to realize—all suggest conditions not wholly unlike those in the United States today. Not to make this catalogue of conditions unduly long, let me mention in closing the generally secular attitude of the Greeks toward public affairs and the belief in human responsibility for human well being, the widespread availability of the writings of leading statesmen and learned men generally, and the existence in some of the leading city-states of rival political parties to present the issues of the day.

It is against this background of political conditions and interests that we need to consider the leading teachers and writers on politics whose names and works have come down to us. Although there were others who wrote in the field—Solon, Isocrates, and Thucydides, for example—the historians of political thought have justly given most attention to two men, Plato, and his most famous pupil, Aristotle. Let us look at these two in particular.

Plato was born in Athens about 427 B.C., and he passed away there about eighty years later in 347 B.C. He came of a family of considerable means and conservative connections. At about the age of twenty he struck up an acquaintance with Socrates, the famous streetcorner philosopher, and he remained one of his most devoted followers until and after Socrates' death in 399 B.C. It was after that event that Plato wrote the famous Socratic *Dialogues* and the *Letters*. Attracted as a young man to a life of public service, Plato began to work with the aristocratic party in Athens, only to quit in disgust and shock when he saw the methods pursued by that party. Then the democratic party came into power, and Plato decided that it was even worse than the aristocrats. As if uttering "a plague on both your houses," he gradually turned against all politics and politicians, and developed the idea that only philosophers were qualified to rule over men and cities. He also had a strong feeling of revulsion against the rhetoricians and their schools for young men; he decided that although they pretended to prepare men for political careers, they in fact merely were teaching them tricks of speech and political dodges that could in no way improve the governments of the city-states.

When the democrats came to power in Athens, Plato, because of his former association with the aristocratic party, decided it would be better for him to absent himself from the city until perhaps his early connections with that party had been forgotten. He traveled for some years, therefore, and in the course of this time visited Syracuse, in Sicily, where he became acquainted with the new young tyrant of that place, Dionysius II, and with the latter's scheming uncle, Dion, who had plans to get rid of his nephew so as to be able to rule Syracuse himself. This connection led to a sad chapter in Plato's career as will be related below.

Permitted to return to Athens in 378 B.C. when he was forty years old to set up a school for young men, he apparently decided, and may even have agreed with the democratic rulers of the city, not to engage in Athenian politics or even to teach politics at his school. The Academy, as it came to be called, was established in the outskirts of Athens, and there it apparently stayed for over nine centuries, until abolished in 529 A.D. In that long period the school went through many changes in personnel, curriculum, and fortunes, and never in all those exciting and fateful centuries, as far as I have been able to ascertain, did it openly offer a single course in politics. In Plato's time it offered instruction in mathematics (arithmetic, plane and solid geometry), astronomy, music or harmonics, dialectic, and philosophy, the latter including logic and ethics.

The assistants that Plato recruited for his staff were evidently permitted some freedom to pursue their own researches in these fields and even in others outside the curriculum. Thus, young Aristotle apparently began his natural history studies there and possibly may have begun to collect city-state "constitutions" there as well. Plato was inclined to poke fun at Aristotle's collection and classification of biological specimens, but I have found no mention of Plato's reaction to Aristotle's library-collecting interests.

Thus, Plato's program of instruction was openly non-political, but it seems to have been tacitly more or less anti-political. His purpose was to train philosophers or masters of wisdom of such superior preparation and capacity that cities would voluntarily choose them rather than politicians as rulers. The complete program of instruction and contemplation designed to this end is said to have extended over a thirty-year period, or from about age twenty to age fifty for the average man enrolled. By that time a man was supposed to have become so wise in philosophy and so free of personal ambition that he could be trusted to decide wisely and fairly any and all questions concerning a city's governmental problems and its policies in a perfectly selfless spirit, without having had any technical instruction for the task. The first students, enrolled at the opening of the school in 387 B.C., if any stayed for the full course, would have been ready to be philosopher-kings in 357 B.C., ten years before Plato's death. That the Greek cities did not rush in to recruit any of these Academy-trained philosophers to be their rulers should not be a cause for great surprise to any one who has studied practical politics.

One episode that throws some light upon Plato's innocence in matters political needs to be reported and pondered. Perhaps foreseeing that none of his personally trained philosophers was ever likely to become a king, Plato allowed himself to get sucked into the political power struggle in Syracuse. He attempted in vain to turn the young ruler of that city, Dionysius II, who was already enjoying the exercise of power and the adulation and pleasures that went with power, into a philosopher by tutoring him first in mathematics and then in the rest of the Academy's curriculum. The idea seems to have been that if philosophers cannot be turned into kings, perhaps one king can be turned into a philosopher. Dion, the young king's uncle, who desired the kingship for himself, was apparently a leading promoter of this absurd venture, which Plato apparently entered upon in all innocence. Perhaps having a famous philosopher like Plato come to Syracuse as his personal tutor appealed to his vanity, and Dionysius agreed to the plan.

This preposterous enterprise turned into a complete fiasco. The tongues of the young king's associates around the court began to wag. Plato was merely the tool of the young king's uncle. Dionysius soon began to believe this himself. Dion was exiled; Plato was placed under house arrest, escaping from Syracuse only with the aid of a friend at court. Apparently other members of the Academy also had become involved in Dion's scheme and in Plato's effort. When it failed so miserably they all apparently stopped meddling even in non-Athenian politics. Thereafter the instruction at the school turned even more decisively against politics. The idea of training philosopher-kings seems to have been dropped. The Academy became a sort of cultural finishing school to which not only Greeks but also Romans and others came to acquire the proper polish for their stations in life. And so the school lived a long and innocuous life, until it was abolished centuries later by the Emperor Justinian because leaders of the Byzantine or Orthodox Christian church thought that it was a dangerous pagan institution and a competitor to their own schools—and perhaps because Justinian needed money as always, and wanted to seize the school's assets for his own use, which he did.

If Plato's Academy avoided direct instruction in politics and government, Aristotle's Lyceum certainly did not. Aristotle was born in 384 B.C., the son of a Greek physician at the court of Philip in Macedonia, three years after Plato had set up his school at Athens. At the age of seventeen Aristotle enrolled at the Academy and for twenty years he was successively a student, assistant, and part-time teacher in the school. Plato admired Aristotle as "the Brain," but later when Aristotle came to reject much of what Plato had tried to teach him,

Plato is said to have remarked that Aristotle spurned him as a colt kicks its mother. Aristotle tried hard to accept Plato's theory and philosophy of universal ideas and even undertook to write out his thoughts in dialogue form in imitation of Plato. He even may have tried to accept Plato's anti-political views, but that would have been hard to do in view of his early life with his father in close touch with the court of Philip. In addition he carried on some independent investigations of a scientific nature while at the Academy.

Basically an empiricist and a scientist, Aristotle found himself turning more and more against Plato's position on every major point. The intellectual break between the two came some years before Plato's death. When that event brought another Platonist into the headship of the Academy, Aristotle gathered up his books, notes, and other effects, and left Athens with one or more like-minded friends.

During the following twelve or thirteen years Aristotle engaged in marine biological research in the Aegean Sea, hobnobbed with a liberal-minded ruler and his court circle in Asia Minor, tutored young Alexander in a broad program of studies at the request of Philip, and no doubt did much reading and writing. In the meantime Philip and Alexander had gained control over Greece and had demoted the Greek city-states to a subordinate status. When Alexander, though still young, succeeded his father as ruler of Macedonia and Greece, and set out in about 335 B.C. upon his conquest of the Near East, Aristotle returned to Athens with a large endowment and a guaranty of protection from Alexander. That protection was needed because Aristotle was a non-Athenian and a friend of Alexander's, and Athens was a hotbed of actual potential anti-Macedonian agitation. There in the vicinity of Athens, not far from the Academy, Aristotle set up his school, the so-called Lyceum, recruited a small staff of assistants, and proceeded to make it a rival of the Academy as a place for young men to acquire learning and to prepare themselves for life. For the next twelve to thirteen years Aristotle lectured in his school, carried on research, assisted in and helped to direct the research of his staff, and wrote most of the great works in various branches of learning and science for which he has become famous. He is credited by various writers with having been the founder of scientific philosophy and of the history of philosophy and of science, the father of logic, the originator of the study of psychology, the creator of philol-

ogy, and the principal beginner or at least an important early contributor to other branches of learning. He was truly a polymath.
We who work at political science are not able, therefore, to claim
him as entirely our own, and yet most of us recognize him as the
writer of the first real treatise on politics in the West if not in the
entire world, and as the founder of the study of comparative government or of comparative constitutions.

As a student and as a teacher Aristotle in his mature years took
positions almost diametrically opposed to those of Plato. I will not
take the time to try to analyze in detail the respective views of these
two men in all their ramifications. Only those points that concern
their views with regard to politics will be considered.

Plato developed and defended the philosophical doctrine of real-
ism, which is in brief the notion that universal ideas or concepts have
a real existence, while the concrete examples we see and know on
earth do not. Aristotle in effect took the opposite or nominalist view,
namely, that the general or universal mental concepts that one develops and under which one subsumes the many individuals according
to their different characteristics are not existing entities. Thus, dogs
exist severally and separately as individuals, but the general concept
"dog" is only a mental construct of the distinctive qualities that dogs
have and that distinguish them from human beings, and from cats
and trees and countless other kinds of things. The same principle
applies to non-physical things; thus, "law" is a general or universal
concept, but "law" does not exist. Instead, there are the countless
laws of nature, laws ordained by men, and, some believe, laws made
by God, and so on. The specific laws of nature exist and can be
discovered by scientific research; the laws made by men can be found
by research in legislative records, court decisions, administrative proceedings, and other places.

As a consequence of this initial and basic difference in views,
Plato felt no need to study in detail the government of any actual
city-state, although in practice he departed from this position to some
extent, while Aristotle found it necessary to examine many separate
existing states in order to ascertain not only their specific identifying
characteristics as states, but also to learn their many variations and
mutations.

The two men also differed fundamentally in their attitudes toward politics, government, and the rulers of men. Plato's disillusioning and devastating experiences with politics and politicians in Athens and Syracuse had badly deflated his ego and turned him completely sour on politics as it was carried on in his time by politicians and rulers. For them he wanted to substitute philosophers trained by himself. Aristotle, on the other hand, had been brought up by a father who was friend and physician to the Macedonian ruler, Philip. Aristotle himself had later associated on intimate terms with other rulers, had tutored young Alexander at Philip's request, and had received from them remuneration for his tutoring services, endowments for his future teaching and research, and protection for his school at Athens. While Plato seems to have longed secretly to exercise political influence if not actual power, practical circumstances disqualified Aristotle from participating in politics or trying to become a ruler in Macedonia, Athens, or anywhere else; and he seems to have had no ambitions in that direction. It is in his Seventh Letter or Epistle that Plato shows why he renounced the study of constitutions, namely, because all governments in his time were bad. His own "correct philosophy" was the only possible solution for the political problems of the race. Philosophers educated by him were to rule without constitutions to hamper them.

On the other hand, neither did Aristotle condemn all politics or all politicians. Instead, he treated men in politics and political units such as the city-states of Greece very much as he did the biological specimens that he collected, examined, and classified for his studies in natural history. They were things to be studied and understood for what they were. Thus, while Plato was trying to get at the realities of life by postulating the universal ideas, by training the soul, by long contemplation, and by studying subjects such as mathematics that were far removed from people's lives, Aristotle was collecting, examining, and classifying in his laboratory actual specimens of biological species, and the written evidences of the political life and governments of the city-states—written evidences, because one cannot bring into one's library the real or "living" constitution of any state.

These two men differed quite fundamentally, not only in their methods of searching for truth but also in their ways of teaching. Plato employed primarily the dialectical method of group discussion

of an abstract idea, concept, or problem, and used analogies extensively to bring out his points. Socrates was his chief spokesman in
the dialogues, of course, and some of the analogies that he reported
Socrates to have used are exceedingly farfetched and unconvincing.
They were, however, such as Socrates could employ to drive his
opponent into a corner where he finally had to let Socrates have his
own way, even though obviously not convinced. Read the *Protagoras*
again, for example, and see how Socrates sets the trap for the older
man, Protagoras, just returning from a wearisome journey, with the
question whether virtue is one or whether it is not like a face composed of many features. How can one really compare an intangible
thing like moral or political excellence with a many-featured physical
thing like a human face? Protagoras does not clearly see the trap
that has been set for him, and he finally quits the argument, apparently from sheer exhaustion. What light the discussion throws upon the
issue of whether virtue can be taught is questionable to this day.
The argument seems to be that because a subject is complex, or composed of many features, it cannot be taught, a line of argument that
would throw out the teaching of almost every subject one could name:
mathematics, language, biology, medicine, government, *good* government, child rearing, and so forth.

Returning for a moment to the *Protagoras,* it is clear that in this
dialogue, speaking through the words of Socrates, Plato denies that
the art of politics and the practice of good citizenship can be taught.[4]

SOCRATES. Do I follow you? . . . I take you to be describing the art
of politics, and promising to make men good citizens.
PROTAGORAS. That . . . is exactly what I profess to do.
SOC. Then it is a truly splendid accomplishment that you have mastered, . . . if indeed you have mastered it. I warn you that you will hear
nothing from me but my real mind. The fact is, I did not think this was
something that could be taught, though when you say otherwise I cannot
doubt your word. But it is up to me to say why I believe it cannot be
taught nor furnished by one man to another.

So direct a denial of the possibility of teaching the art of politics and
the practice of good citizenship I have not found anywhere else in
ancient literature.

Perhaps what Plato reveals in the *Dialogues* can itself be called

4. Plato's *Dialogues,* edited by Edith Hamilton and Huntington Cairns, 319 a, b.

teaching. Surely he must have been trying to teach something that was related to politics, but it was not the structure and techniques of politics that interested him. What he tried to do was more in the nature of "forming the soul" or of getting his students and readers into an accepting (and anti-political) state of mind, and thus to get them ready to philosophize with him about abstract and universal ideas. However, because he used Socrates as his principal interlocutor it would have been difficult, on the basis of what he wrote, for any public prosecutor to have impeached Plato for impiety or for speaking or acting against the state. Indeed, in this very dialogue, he avoids trouble by praising the Athenian people for the sensible way in which they conduct public affairs without having had any special training. Socrates himself was, of course, impeached and tried for impiety and other alleged offenses, and he suffered the ultimate penalty. Plato, on the other hand, appeared to be a mere reporter of what Socrates said, and that only after some years had elapsed since Socrates had passed away and his life had been largely forgotten.

It seems to be accepted that Plato as a teacher did not lecture to his students or come out flatly for his own views. Like others of his writings, *The Republic* and *The Laws* are presented as dialogues in which Plato has no part.

It appears also that Plato rejected the idea of study for the discovery or creation of new knowledge. The fundamental and universal ideas in which he apparently believed, having existed from time immemorial or from the very beginning of things, could have been known in any past generation as well as in Plato's time, and thus there was nothing new to discover, much less to create. Instead, learning was essentially a process of soul-searching, contemplation, and discussion, aimed at the recovery within oneself of the perfect knowledge that had always been in existence. In one of the dialogues Socrates professed to demonstrate that even the untutored slave boy whom he used as an interlocutor could, if properly questioned and encouraged by another, "recover" knowledge. That is, he could bring to the surface of his otherwise dormant mind, knowledge that presumably always had been there, but that in his untutored state he had not known that he possessed. On this theory there could be no increase or development or history of science or of other knowledge, but only repeated recoveries of the same knowledge that had been there from the beginning, now by one man, now by another, without change in the knowledge, and so on and on forevermore.

With these ideas dominant in his mind, Plato did not set his students and assistants to doing research with a view to increasing the store of knowledge. The most that he did, as I have already indicated, was to permit them to use space in the Academy for their own researches, a privilege of which Aristotle and several others at that time took some advantage.

On all these points Aristotle in his maturity stood opposed to Plato's thinking. He made his own studies in search of new knowledge; he wrote up his findings in straight expository style; he read the results of his studies to his students and associates without any concealment of his authorship. He had nothing to cover up, and he kept his discussions on a factual and scientific level. There is good reason to believe that chapters of his works on *Politics, Ethics,* and other subjects were delivered by him as lectures at the Lyceum. Of course we must remember that he was under Alexander's protection, but I doubt that there was anything in these lectures that would have incited the Athenians to attack him. Athens and the other city-states that he dealt with in the *Politics* were, in any case, already practically defunct as independent political units.

Aristotle also believed that there were new things to be learned about the world and in the various fields of knowledge that he cultivated. Likewise he believed that scholars had a duty to try to advance knowledge. His researches in zoology have been mentioned. His studies in the field of the governments of the city-states by means of interviews with rulers, and by the collection and examination of the constitutional histories written by local historians, give further evidence of his methods and aims.

Indicative of his belief in the development of knowledge through the years is his emphasis upon the importance of discovering the historical backgrounds and beginnings of knowledge in every field. As already mentioned, he instructed his research assistants and associates first to study and record the history of each subject assigned to them. Only when this had been done was the man responsible for a field of study ready and qualified to make further advances in the field. To Theophrastus he assigned the history of studies in physics and in metaphysical systems; to Eudemus the histories of mathematics, geometry, and astronomy; and to Menon the history of medicine. He took upon himself an imposing array of subjects, including zoology, economics, politics, ethics, logic, general philosophy, psychology, and others—in each case planning to write the early history of the study as a part of his task. This part of his plan was only partly accomplished.

His large and varied library must have been a great boon to his assistants, especially for the historical phases of their assignments. To what extent he asked his students, as distinct from his assistants and associates, to make their own investigations in the field or in his library in order to give them a feeling for research, I do not know, but it certainly would have been in accord with his educational theory to have tried some such experiment.

Aristotle was interested in actual things, especially living things, and most of all in human beings, their ways and their institutions, here on earth. Plato seemed to be more interested in his universal ideas than in people, and more interested in God and heaven than Aristotle was. Both had some prejudices against non-Greeks—the barbarians—but Plato showed both in *The Republic* and in *The Laws* that without qualms he could subject even a majority of the Greeks to the absolute rule of the select few, headed by his philosophers.

Aristotle's approach to politics was, then, more secular than Plato's. He stood in the line of those Greeks, stretching as far back as Solon or even farther, who believe that men had to construct and operate their own governments. The gods had other things to do, and they did not interfere in human affairs either to make men better, or to punish them for bad deeds. Plato, on the other hand, made frequent references to God and the gods in spelling out his ideal republic for men. God was in a sense his greatest idea. He was perfect righteousness, the measure of all things, and an intervener in human affairs. Alongside of God, or under him, men were insignificant things—they were expendable—and Plato was not opposed to expending men, if only his philosopher-kings might be permitted to rule.

I do not mean to leave the impression that I consider Aristotle to have been a paragon of all the academic virtues as we see them today. He discussed the city-states in his book on politics as if they were still sovereign units, when in fact they had lost their independence. He does not discuss the Alexandrian empire that was taking shape right before his eyes, or even adequately consider the confederations of the Greek cities that to some extent made up for the deficiencies of the city-states. Along with other Greeks he refused to consider the non-Greeks as worthy of inclusion on an equal footing with the Greeks in the empire that Alexander was planning to establish, thus abandoning some of the scientific impartiality that he had shown in his biological studies. Moreover, his ideas in economics and in other social fields were rather naïvely elementary.

Despite his blind spots and other shortcomings, of which the foregoing are some examples, Aristotle was a scholar and a teacher of politics whom modern political scientists can look back upon with pride as the one really great contributor in ancient times to the scientific study and teaching of politics. In quality of insight he was certainly no better than Thucydides, but the latter was a man of less far-reaching views and one who concentrated his attention primarily upon Athens in one of its periods of great travail. In short, Thucydides did not have the broad views of politics, of science, or of philosophy that Aristotle had. Aristotle clearly did more to inaugurate the scientific study of politics than any other ancient writer. He examined the history of the subject, cited and quoted from earlier authors, gathered political data on a large scale, interviewed a number of people, and in writing up his results referred to specific places and their distinctive constitutional characteristics. He left a trail that others might follow to verify his results. I find no one but a few Greek historians near his time to compare with him. In the histories of nearby peoples for several thousand years before him and for some fifteen centuries after him, I find no political scientists who did anything like the sort of fact-gathering, scientific writing, and teaching in the field of politics that he did.

After Aristotle's departure from Athens under threat of prosecution for impiety in 323 and his death in 322 B.C., the political situation changed rapidly. Absolute monarchs ruled in the three successor kingdoms that followed the dissolution of Alexander's empire and there could be no free and unbiased study of these monarchies. The Greek city-states declined steadily in power and importance, until they were hardly worth studying. When the Romans in the next few

centuries made one empire of all the lands adjacent to the Mediterranean, the emperors saw to it that there should be no dangerous
subversives studying and criticizing their system of government. Aristotle was the last of the ancient scholars who had any opportunity to
make a truly comparative study of independent states and their governments. Under the Roman emperors, except as one or another
decided to be liberal toward critics, politics was the monopoly of the
ruling emperor and a subject taboo to scholars and ordinary citizens
alike. Under some of the worst of the emperors, Romans suffered
death on the mere suspicion that they were critical of the imperial
government.

I will not attempt here to trace the occasional glimmerings of
the study of politics in the centuries that followed. The rise and fall
of the Roman Empire, the expansion of the Christian church, the
conflicts between the two, the barbarian invasions, the division of the
Empire chiefly for purposes of defense, the crumbling of the western
half followed by several attempts to restore it, the perdurance of the
Byzantine, or eastern half until the mid-fifteenth century, the so-
called Dark Ages in Europe, the several successive resurgences of
culture and education called the renaissances of this and that century
would be fruitless to attempt to describe here in detail.

In the Psalm 90 the Psalmist, whoever he was, puts into the mouth
of Moses the following words addressed to the Lord:

> Thou turnest men back to the dust,
>   and sayest, "Turn back, O children of men!"
>
> For a thousand years in thy sight
>   are but as yesterday when it is past,
>   or as a watch in the night.

The period of more than a thousand years from the birth of
Christ, during which any serious study of politics was impeded begins
to end, perhaps, with John of Salisbury in the twelfth century, the
translation of Aristotle's *Politics* from Greek into Latin in the thirteenth century (about 1250 or 1273), and the writings of St. Thomas
Aquinas, also in the thirteenth century. Some would be inclined to
date the revival of political studies even later, say with Machiavelli's
works, *The Prince* and *The Discourses,* in the early sixteenth century.

Europe in Medieval and Modern Times

If we count the Greek experiment in the study and teaching of politics from the sixth to the fourth century B.C., culminating in the work of Aristotle between 335 and 323 B.C., the first truly significant episode in the history of our study, the second one must be the late medieval and modern European episode, from northern Italy and the Iberian peninsula north and westward to the Scandinavian peninsula and the British Isles. By the eleventh century Lombardy and adjacent areas of central and northern Italy had a number of city-states or entities of that nature that exercised considerable powers of sovereignty, formed leagues, carried on foreign relations, defense, and other functions in a realistic and secular manner. These city-states were not unlike those of ancient Greece. It was in them that Machiavelli acquired his political experience and wrote his works in the fifteenth and sixteenth centuries.

Just to the north of Italy, in the thirteenth century, a number of Swiss communities not unlike city-states began their politically independent careers and began to have the materials for comparative political studies. North of the Alps in eastern and central Germany a number of feudal duchies and principalities arose during these centuries. Larger states were appearing at the same time out of the remnants of the old Roman Empire and out of regions farther north and east that Rome had never claimed. In short, the modern European state system was taking form, meaning that once more the materials for comparative political studies existed. This is one of the basic requirements, I believe, for the stimulation of curiosity about forms and functions of government, and about the actions and behavior of kings, parliaments, and other ruling bodies and personalities. There was not complete freedom everywhere for men to study and to write about their own governments, but the study of the governments of other nations and states generally was not prohibited. Statesmen on their occasional travels, ambassadors, traveling businessmen, students and teachers going to other countries for study, and other travelers would observe unusual features of the governments in the states in which they sojourned and in many cases write home about them. When printing became widely available the amount of political information that crept into the weekly journals and news-papers became considerable.

In the meantime—indeed from the twelfth century—universities had begun to dot the maps of the European states. They were in part church-controlled and in part chartered by monarchs and under their supervision. They varied in organization and in curricula, but they tended to have faculties divided into three or four fields of study. A complete system would include faculties of theology, medicine, law, and arts. There naturally came to be some pressure on these institu-tions to prepare men for state service, as the faculties of theology would prepare them for the church. Public finance and the foreign service were likely fields for university training for state employment. Clearly the faculty of medicine would have little to offer in the way of training for public administration, the courts, or the foreign service. The faculty of law seemed to be the most suitable for training men for any public service, and it came to be used for that purpose. Roman law, although it was mainly private law, was one of the subjects widely emphasized, even in the countries which did not have Roman law. For the study of politics, of course, Roman law had relatively little value.

The study of politics naturally would have fallen to the arts facul-ty, but for centuries there was little encouragement of it. While the faculties of theology, law, and medicine prepared men for specific vocations or professions, the arts faculty, although it did prepare men for teaching, was in respect to subject matter a sort of "omnium gatherum" of classic and modern languages, rhetoric and dialectic, philosophy, mathematics, history, geography, natural science, music, and other presumably cultural subjects. Economics, politics, sociol-ogy, psychology, anthropology, and a number of other subjects known to modern universities were not to be found in the curricula of the medieval and early modern universities of Europe. Each of these subjects had to make its way, sometimes against strong opposition, and in universities under monarchical regimes it is understandable that anything like a free study of politics would not be encouraged. The subject came to be approached, therefore, not directly, but through the study of the Greek and Latin classics—Plato, Aristotle, Cicero—and through philosophy, rhetoric, and history.

Nevertheless, many individual professors, here and there, in their

own studies of the classics, philosophy, and history, did make and
publish studies in the politics of earlier times. Furthermore, some
professors of law undertook to study international law and various
other branches of public law, so that a literature of politics began to
be built up. From about the fifteenth and sixteenth centuries one finds
beginnings in this area of study, and by the eighteenth, nineteenth,
and early twentieth centuries the numbers of such studies are very
considerable. Despite language barriers, lack of encouragement from
university and state authorities, absence of endowments, and other
discouraging factors, the study of politics in modern Europe, both in
and out of universities, has grown to large proportions, and many
excellent books and periodicals have been and are being produced.
In addition, there have come to be some departments and institutes
for the study of politics, as well as many individual university chairs
for the teaching of the subject. All these developments constitute
what I call the second great episode in the history of the study and
teaching of politics in the West. Beyond this little summary I do not
wish to go until my research into this episode has been more nearly
completed.

The United States

For the third and in some ways the greatest episode in the history I
think we are fully justified in taking the United States by itself, and
that from the founding of the several English-speaking colonies to
the present time, a period of just over three hundred years. The conditions for the development of our study in this country have, I think,
been more favorable than they ever have been in any other part of
the world.

It should not take long to run over the main points. The United
States began as thirteen colonies of the British homeland in the seven-
teenth and eighteenth centuries, all properly chartered for limited self-
government, all English-speaking, all intercommunicating and facing
common political problems, and far enough removed from the mother
country to have considerable freedom of self-government from the
start. The Church of England, strong at home, had no power or tradition of dominating thought in the distant colonies—and soon there

were numerous dissenting local churches as well. A general secular attitude toward the problems of government was in evidence almost from the start. The people accepted and indeed asserted their own responsibility for government within their several colonies, and early began to practice politics. This attitude of freedom and responsibility in the area of politics led to conflicts with the home government across the Atlantic, and brought on a Declaration of Independence and a successful War for Independence. Thus thirteen self-governing states came into existence, none with monarchical institutions, all with elective legislatures and ultimately with elective executives called governors. By that time the feeling for, and the responsible practice of, self-government through elective officers, working under written charters and constitutions that defined the rights of the people and limited the powers of their elective officers, had become well ingrained in the traditions and the spirit of the people.

These thirteen colonies that became independent states by a confidence-establishing successful War for Independence thus achieved self-government at an early date. While still only thirteen in number, these states formed a confederation, and later a strong federation, so that now for nearly 175 years the people have had institutions of self-government under written constitutions or charters at three levels, national, state, and local, and—more recently—with opportunities for widespread popular participation through elections at all three levels. Never in history has there been a place in the Western world with so much opportunity for people to take active part in the processes of government. Nowhere else have so many actually taken part or shown so much interest in politics.

The access to political information is almost if not quite unlimited. Throughout the entire nation and in all fifty states there is one official language, English. The nation was born in the age of the printing press. From colonial days to the present, books, periodicals, newspapers, and privately written letters have circulated throughout the entire country. The mail rates for printed matter have been low. The importance of this fact for the spread of political information and propaganda can hardly be overemphasized. Now there are telegraph, telephone, radio, and television facilities also available for the information of the entire people, either at reasonable rates or practically free.

The general attitude toward education also has been important. Elementary and secondary education have become tax-supported and practically free to the individual in every state, while private schools at these levels, many supported by religious denominations at their own expense, also are widely available. Education at these levels for a long time has included practical courses, including instruction in the elements of citizenship and government. Provisions for education at the college and university levels also have increased greatly, and enrollments continue to increase faster than institutions can accommodate the applicants.

College and university education began in colonial times at Harvard, William and Mary, Yale, and other private institutions, partly church-supported and controlled, but by the late eighteenth century (University of North Carolina, 1789, 1795) publicly supported state universities and colleges also began to appear, and soon municipal ones, too, so that today publicly supported institutions of higher education have far the greatest numbers of students and faculty. And the flood of students continues to rise.

The early colleges and universities patterned their curricula after those of similar institutions in England, which meant that there was much emphasis on the classics and on general cultural courses, without specific vocational or professional utility. During the past century or more there has been a great change in college curricula in these respects. The natural sciences have made great advances; so have a number of practical subjects in agriculture, home economics, economics and business, social welfare, and so on, including political science, public administration, and international relations. Intellectual snobbery may not have been entirely eliminated from college and university curricula, but it has been considerably reduced. Students and teachers in the more practical subjects of study long have been showing that by assiduous labors and the use of scientific methods they can make great contributions to the people's welfare and the nation's strength and security.

And so in the colleges and universities of the United States, the study of politics not only has an assured status, but it also can boast of having more teachers of the subject and more students than will be found in the field anywhere else in the world, possibly more than in all the countries of Western Europe combined, which is the next ranking area in the growth of this subject. In 1961 the American Political Science Association, which is the oldest and largest of such organizations in the world, published a directory of its members. In the 283 pages of this book I estimate that some 2,300 or more of the names and biographies printed are those of political science teachers in the colleges and universities of the United States.

Contrast this if you will with Greece in the time of Aristotle, when he stood out as practically the only empirical and philosophical student and teacher of politics. And what a student and teacher he was! With all our numbers and our resources, we face a challenge to try to advance the knowledge and the science of politics in our day and to make the people of the United States the best-informed citizenry in the world in the field of politics.

WILLIAM S. LIVINGSTON

The challenge of numbers

There is little need here to recite the obvious statistics about the impending boom in college enrollments; they are frightening enough without morbid reiteration. As the number of students increase, enrollment in departments of political science will presumably increase at roughly the same rate. But the problems of teaching political science are far from unique; they partake of the same exigencies and urgencies that are to be found throughout the social sciences, and in large part throughout the university. Thus, an attempt to speculate on the teaching of political science in the coming decade(s) is not significantly different from general speculation on the problems of the university as a whole. While political scientists are not directly responsible for solving the larger problem, they obviously will be affected by it and inevitably will have to face up to its consequences in meeting their own instructional task.

"The choice between quality and quantity is not mandatory," says the President's Committee on Education Beyond the High School, but it can be avoided only "if the American people [are] willing to devote a significantly greater proportion of the Nation's rising income to higher education."[1] To which one may answer that the choice may not be mandatory, but it is still pretty troublesome, and money alone will not solve the problem. That is merely the first and minimum essential. Beyond money we shall also need vision, hard work, open minds, a willingness to experiment with new teaching methods, new standards of expectation in regard to the performance of both students and faculty, a different scheme of relations between teacher and student, and perhaps a different sort of organization for the university as a whole.

1. The President's Committee on Education Beyond the High School, *Second Report to the President, Summary Report,* July, 1957, p. 4.

Enrollments and How to Deal with Them

As I see it, the problem of numbers can be met in several different ways. One is to thwart it by cutting down on admissions. Another is to enlarge faculties and facilities. Another is to develop and use improved and more effective teaching techniques. Still another is to make much better use of faculty time and faculty skills. But merely to state these as ways of meeting the problem is to suggest how limited are the means available to us. Each of these will doubtless play a part in our effort to perform the task, but no one of them is easy, and for some colleges some of them are virtually impossible.

Curbing admissions, or refusing to increase them, no doubt will be attempted, but this is not a solution; it is merely a refusal to meet the problem. What confronts us is a general national problem of rising birth rates and a rapidly growing college-age population, compounded by a growth in the percentage of the college-age group that actually goes to college.[2] The traditional American proposition is that education should not be for the select few but for all those who can benefit from it. It directly rejects the traditional European principle of university education for the elite, illustrated by the jingle attributed, of course, to Oxford:

> We are the chosen few—
> All others will be damned.
> There is no room in Heaven for you;
> We can't have Heaven crammed.

Only if we abandon our fundamental principle do we dare talk about solving the problem by more selective admissions. We have the word of the president of one large institution that we are already turning away many students who could profit from a university education,[3] and in any event, for fairly obvious political reasons, a more restrictive admission policy is not a solution readily available to state university systems.

2. The College Entrance Examination Board reckoned that in 1900 4 per cent of the college-age group actually attended college; in 1960 the figure was 33 per cent, and in 1963 it was 36 per cent of a college-age group of 2.8 million. By the year 1965-1966 it was estimated that there would be 3.6 million in the age group, of which 41 per cent would be in college. Growth will slow down somewhat after that, but by 1969 the number of college entrants—1.8 million—will be double the number of 1959.

3. John A. Hannah, President of Michigan State University, in an interview in the *U.S. News & World Report*, (Jan. 21, 1963), p. 59.

The enlargement of faculties and facilities will surely come, and will doubtless help solve the problem, but this, too, has its serious limitations. There simply are not enough trained and able teachers to go around; we are not now training enough college teachers, or political scientists, to maintain even the present student-faculty ratios, to say nothing of improving them—either in political science or in the university faculties at large. The plain fact is that we cannot meet the needs of the future (or even of the present) by getting more teachers. The big universities and the prestige schools may possibly do so, but only at the expense of the smaller and less prestigious institutions. This does not solve the national problem; it only worsens it.

While we should make every effort to increase the number of competently trained teachers, the only real solution I can see is to find ways of making more effective use of the teachers we have. This means two rather different sorts of things: first, improving our methods of teaching, and second, freeing the faculty from functions and responsibilities that impair their ability to teach. It is to these objectives that this paper is primarily addressed.

My own experience and my own concern have been principally, though not exclusively, with the large university rather than the small, and with the state-supported institution rather than the private. I should like to begin, therefore, with a word or two in behalf of the large state university. In the first place, state schools already enroll more than 60 per cent of all college students,[4] and that figure will inevitably increase in the years to come. It is the state universities that will bear the chief burden of the expanded enrollments, and it is the state universities that have to face most directly the question of how to handle them.[5] In the second place, at their best, the state universities are superb and offer an education that is superior, if anything, to that afforded in the smaller private school. There is a widespread and quite false assumption abroad in the land that excellence is the province of the small private college and mediocrity the destiny

4. *Ibid.,* p. 60.
5. The evidence suggests that the pressure of increased enrollments will not be evenly distributed. It is greater (*1*) on the larger schools than on the smaller; (*2*) on the public institutions than on the private; and (*3*) on the technical schools than on the liberal arts schools. Martin Quonbeck, "Implications of Increasing Enrollments for Academic Standards and Methods," *The Educational Record,* XXXVIII (1957), 127-128.

of the state university. This assumption is belied by the most superficial inquiry. The big schools have larger and more specialized faculties, a greater proportion of Ph.D.s, larger and better libraries, laboratories, and facilities; and the education they offer is equal to (I do not say "better than," though in some instances that would be true also) that afforded by the small private school. Where they differ is in the number and quality of their students.

It is not true to say merely that their students are more numerous and less competent. More numerous, certainly, but the matter of quality is more difficult to judge. In comparing the large state university with which I am most familiar with the two medium-size private universities where I have served temporarily, I have found the best students to be of about the same caliber, but the average student, or the student body as a whole, to be of a higher quality in the smaller schools. I believe this same generalization would apply to both undergraduates and graduate students, but the difference is less between the two groups of graduate students than between the two groups of undergraduates. Admittedly, these are highly personal observations, based on my own impressions and not on any sort of scientific measurement.

The difference that is most significant, I suggest, is really not between the public and the private school, but between the large and the small. I contend that the large schools are better prepared to handle the rising enrollments than are the smaller ones. Their faculties are larger, collectively stronger, and more accustomed to dealing with numbers of students; libraries and other facilities are more nearly adequate; they can better afford experimentation with teaching techniques (though, admittedly, they may not be experiment-minded); they are already accustomed to think in large numbers; and they are better organized to deal with those numbers in terms of teaching habits, schedules, administrative facilities, counseling practices, and so on.

The Quality of Teaching

The problem, as it is usually described, is to maintain the quality of teaching in the face of increasing numbers of students. I am not at all sure this is the best way to express it, for it assumes that the quality of instruction at present is all that it should be, which it is not. The 1962 report of the Committee on Standards of Instruction of the American Political Science Association supplies some data that are far from reassuring. Of the 786 institutions offering courses in political science, only 466 had separate departments of political science; in the rest, political science was joined with or dangled from some other department. In 72 per cent of the institutions, political science was being taught by three or fewer persons, but this did not much reduce the number of courses offered. One-, two-, and three-man departments were offering eleven, thirteen, and fifteen courses, on the average. Teaching loads were heavy, eighteen hours being common; in individual cases, they ran to twenty-one and even twenty-five hours per week. In the 297 separate departments of political science having three or fewer instructors, the total number of instructors was 412, or which 236 held the Ph.D. and 138 held the master's degree. "Quite a large number" of instructors have had their training in fields other than political science.[6] These figures all refer to accredited four-year degree-granting institutions. Basically they refer to small colleges, and they do not inspire confidence in the quality of the teaching in political science. This sort of problem, of course, is far less common in the larger schools, but I am by no means confident that instruction there is all it should be. Even in the largest and/or the best, the teaching function is impaired, interrupted, and thwarted by outworn instructional habits, the press of other duties, the frustrations of administrative complexity, and occasionally by sheer incompetence.

The usual statements about growing numbers, large and small schools, large and small classes, and so on, seem to rest on some assumptions whose validity is at least open to question. One is that different teaching techniques must be used in small and large classes, and another is that the teaching techniques appropriate *only* to small classes are inherently better. Thus, we talk as though there were no problem of quality teaching in small classes, and we usually insist that there is such a problem in large classes. This assumption needs to be more carefully examined.

In the first place, the difference that is important is not really

6. "Political Science as a Discipline," *American Political Science Review,* LVI (1962), 417-421; the figures cited are found on p. 418.

the size of the class but the method of teaching. In a small class there is an opportunity for question and answer, for discussion among the students and between students and professor, for oral reports and other exercises—in short, for a more extensive student participation. In the large class there is clearly less opportunity for such things, and the task falls more directly and exclusively on the professor. We usually speak of the former as a "class-discussion" technique and of the latter as a "lecture" technique. But what is important is the technique rather than the class size itself.

Secondly, there is no sharply defined, easily identified line of distinction between the "large" class and the "small." I have seen the "large" class defined as one in excess of a figure that varies from twenty to ninety. At the same time, there is no sharp distinction between lecturing and class discussion as methods of teaching. Each very well may partake of some elements of the other, and one must examine the extremes to see the difference. I do not say there is no difference, but only that the difference is mainly one of degree. In fact, it seems to me that one can more meaningfully distinguish among three types of instruction as they are related to class size, three types which, again, are not sharply differentiated. The first is the real class-discussion method, as described above, involving extensive student participation in the form of discussion, argument, oral reports, individual essays, and so on. But when the class gets larger than, say, twenty or thirty, this extensive student participation begins to give way to another form of instruction. The instructor resorts to a more formalized lecture. The students still play a modest role but are less active than in the smaller class. The basic method of instruction has become the lecture, supplemented, when possible, by question and answer and occasional discussions. The larger the class, the more the instructor turns to the lecture, and at some point the technique becomes exclusively lecture, uninterrupted by any sort of student participation. The point at which student participation disappears entirely varies considerably; it is not determined solely by the size of the class, though that is probably the chief factor. It is also influenced by the skill and inclination of the instructor and by the physical structure of the classroom. In my own experience, I find it possible to ask questions of the class at large, or of individual students, to invite questions from the class, or to develop a brief discussion in classes as large as 150-175, so long as the class-room facilities do not forbid it. At that size, however, these techniques can be used only when a familiarity and personal rapport can be established between teacher and student. Admittedly, it is not easy, and it is virtually impossible in an auditorium or lecture hall, where the teacher is on a high dais or stage. With classes larger than that, I do not believe it is either desirable or worthwhile to invite student participation. The technique must be the lecture. Thus, I conceive three ranges of class size, each with an appropriate teaching technique: (1) up to about thirty; (2) from thirty to about 175; and (3) above 175.

Third, I dispute the contention that there is an inevitable superiority in the small class and the class-discussion technique. If we are to draw our basic distinction between the class discussion and the lecture, it is essential to recognize that either can be well done or poorly done. Each method requires its own distinctive skill, and a teacher may be very good at one and very poor at the other. Or he may, of course, be poor at both, in which case he never should have become a teacher. We sometimes forget that there is no single skill known as "good teaching"; there is, instead, a great variety of methods of accomplishing that result. Different teachers have different skills, and some have skills that are effective with some students but quite ineffective with others. The late Cecil Driver of Yale was one of the very few I have ever encountered who was equally and supremely good in either a graduate seminar or a lecture to five hundred undergraduates.

The best-balanced undergraduate curriculum would include both large and small classes, and both good class-discussion teaching and good lecturing. But inevitably, as enrollments increase, the former will give way more and more to the latter. Increasingly, and especially in such subjects as political science, we will have to resort to the lecture as the technique of instruction. I do not say this, in itself, is a happy or untroublesome prospect. I do say its perils have been exaggerated. Somewhat later in these articles Professor Connery comments that much of the debate over class size may be outdated and that the important factor for good teaching is relating the ability of the instructor to the capacity of the student in a meaningful way. With this position I would heartily agree.

The problem is not really to avoid big classes but to avoid poor lectures. The solution cannot be to insist on small classes and the class-discussion technique—in the first place, because it is impossible, and in the second, because, to do so, we should have to employ poor teachers and poor teaching. A good big-class lecture is far superior to a poor small-class discussion. The only advantage of the latter is that it confuses and benumbs the minds of fewer students. In the words of President Johnson of Fisk University, "Keeping classes small by hiring poor teachers simply enables the teacher to communicate his mediocrity in an intimate environment."[7]

Before undertaking this inquiry into the "challenge of numbers," I was blessedly ignorant of pedagogy. But any examination of this problem has to concern itself with the effect upon teaching of increasing the size of the class. Accordingly, I have tried to find out what experiments have been conducted and what they disclose. There has, in fact, been a great deal of research on the problem, the results of which, I was pleased to find, are not quite so alarming as I had supposed. I shall not try to report upon all of it but will content myself with a few illustrations and a very tentative effort to generalize about the results.

It is worth remarking at the outset that not much has been done in political science; our concern for class size has been very recent. The Committee for the Advancement of Teaching of the American Political Science Association reported a decade ago on some experimental innovations, but these had to do almost wholly with methods of instruction rather than with class size. Indeed, the committee at that time concluded that "because of the large numbers of students who need to be met in many institutions, few of the . . . experiments are of much practical value."[8] The experiments had to do with field trips, internships, case studies, and the like. The few experiments in teaching method that were still taking place were found "in institutions with smaller enrollments."[9]

There have been other experiments in the social sciences, however (notably in geography and economics), and there seems no

---

7. Quoted by Alvin C. Eurich, "Better Instruction with Fewer Teachers," *Current Issues in Higher Education 1956,* Proceedings of the Eleventh Annual National Conference on Higher Education (Washington, D.C., 1956) p. 11.
8. Committee for the Advancement of Teaching, American Political Science Association, *Goals for Political Science* (New York, 1951), p. 289.
9. *Ibid.,* p. 278.

reason why hypotheses derived from general class-size experiments would not apply to political science teaching.

The pioneer research on class size was done by Hudelson at Minnesota in the twenties.[10] From a monumental series of fifty-nine carefully controlled experiments in a wide variety of subject-matter fields, he concluded that the weight of evidence favored the *large* class. Though many of the differences were not statistically significant, the majority of differences that were significant also favored the large class. More recent evidence is less favorable to the large class, but that is only to say that the more recent experiments show no significant difference between the large and the small class.

An Oklahoma experiment in American government involved six classes and three instructors. Two of the instructors had both a small and a large class, while the third had two small classes, teaching one by lecture and one by a class-discussion method. "The amount of achievement, as measured by standardized tests, and the attitudes of students toward American Government, varied as a function of the course instructor and did not vary as a function of size of class . . . the differential skills and abilities of the instructors to present materials to large and small classes is [*sic*] the critical variable."[11]

An experiment at Iowa, also in American government, was rather more complex. It involved an evaluation of television teaching, along with large lecture sections and small-group discussion sections, but the results were not dissimilar. "Students of high and low ability were not differentially affected by the method of instruction. . . . If the method of instruction made the slightest difference, this difference was dwarfed by the general academic-ability factor."[12] The Iowa report also suggests that "it is feasible to conduct a class by the discussion method with seventy-five to eighty students."[13]

Similar evidence suggesting that there is no loss in teaching effectiveness when classes are increased to 150 or even 250 is found in the reports of class-size experiments in geography and economics.[14]

10. E. Hudelson, *Class Size at the College Level* (Minneapolis, 1928).
11. John H. Rohrer, "Large and Small Sections in College Classes," *Journal of Higher Education*, XXVIII (1957), 279.
12. Clearinghouse of Studies on Higher Education, *Special Reports*, U.S. Office of Education, (March, 1959), p. 51.
13. *Ibid.*, p. 52.
14. Wallace B. Nelson, "An Experiment with Class Size in the Teaching of Elementary Economics," *Educational Record*, XL (1959), 330-341. Robert F. Perry, "A Teaching Experiment in Geography," *Journal of Geography*, LVI (March, 1957), 133-135.

Wallace Nelson concluded from his experiments in economics that "the overwhelming weight of the findings is to the effect that large classes of from 40 to 250 are as effective as small classes of less than 40, where effectiveness is defined as student achievement on objective-type examinations."[15] This last point has some importance, however. In most of these experiments, the achievement of students in the different sections is measured by short-answer examinations, and some have challenged the validity and meaning of the experiments on the ground that such examinations do not actually test certain qualities and achievements that are more likely to be found in the small-group, class-discussion teaching situation. The difficulty, of course, is that these other qualities are hard to define and measure. Furthermore, there is no evidence that large classes impair learning of the other things that may not be measured by such examinations.[16] This is not to say they do not, but only that there is no experimental evidence that they do. What can be said is that, despite this experimental evidence, both students and faculty still think that small classes are better. In Wilkinson's phrase, this is only an assertion "on faith."

Several efforts have been made to survey the entire literature on this research, and in general those who have made such efforts reach substantially the same conclusions. The Wilkinson article, cited above, is one such effort. Another is that of Martin Quonbeck, who suggests that the results, particularly with respect to higher education, are inconclusive. "It is possible to argue from this limited evidence that the large classes are at least as effective as the smaller ones. At least we must admit that with respect to many educational outcomes the burden of proof rests with those who contend that smaller classes are better."[17] W. J. McKeachie reached much the same conclusion: "To sum up; lectures of large size are not generally inferior to smaller lecture classes if one uses traditional achievement tests as a criterion. When other objectives are measured, large lectures are on somewhat shakier ground but are not consistently inferior."[18]

One should not, by any means, conclude from these experiments

15. *Op. cit.,* p. 333.
16. Frank Ray Wilkinson, "Class Size in Higher Education," *Journal of Higher Education,* XXIX (1958), 153.
17. Quonbeck, *op. cit.,* p. 130.
18. W. J. McKeachie, "Procedures and Techniques of Teaching: A Survey of Experimental Studies," in Nevitt Sanford (ed.), *The American College* (New York, 1962), pp. 312-364, at p. 326.

or from this literature that large classes are better than small ones. But it is encouraging to find that the experimental evidence does not show that small classes are vastly superior to large classes. Quite frankly, I am rather dubious about the results of some of these experiments. One reason is the fact, already mentioned, that the conclusions rest on the use of short-answer (I forbear to say "objective") tests in the measurement of student achievement. Such tests often measure the wrong things, and they often do not measure the right things.[19] But such objections come with poor grace from those who do in fact use such tests in regular courses for determining the students' grades. Alvin Eurich observes quite rightly that there is nothing wrong in using that sort of test in the experiments if that is the sort of test we use for grading the student anyhow.[20]

A second reservation about these experiments has to do with the difficulty of maintaining control. Class size is far from being the only variable that affects student achievement or teaching effectiveness, and the other factors may not be constant. Teaching method, student attitude and expectation, the character of the subject matter, the instructor's skills and preferences, the instructor's attitudes and personality—all these things can only be presumed to be constant, and they are not. Experimental work of this kind always has to assume at some point that "other things are equal," which is seldom so. Third, most such experiments extend over only one semester and over one, or a few, sections. This is basically a matter of control also, but it reduces, as well, the chance of producing a statistically valid result. Finally, the very fact that it is an experiment may well distort both the students' and the instructor's conduct, interests, and attitudes. Frequent testing, visitors in the room, the use of unusual devices like television—all of these may themselves alter the attitudes of both students and faculty, producing a response to the teaching situation that is not reflected in the measured results.

Even with these caveats and qualifications, however, the evidence is still strong that the resort to larger classes need not be so frightening a prospect as many of us have thought. And even if we retain our faith in the small class and the class discussion, the situation we face will drive us increasingly to larger classes and to the lecture as

19. See Banesh Hoffmann, "The Tyranny of Multiple-Choice Tests," *Harper's Magazine*, CCXXII (March, 1961), 37-44.
20. Eurich, *op. cit.*, pp. 12-13.

the method of teaching. It behooves us, therefore, to see to it that lectures are done well and properly.

The Lecture and the Lecturer

Just as there are many kinds of teaching, so are there many kinds of lectures and lecturers. One dares greatly to generalize about them, or about how to produce good lectures. At this point, my remarks are really addressed not to established teachers of political science but to the oncoming generation of young teachers. To them I would say that there are many ways of teaching and the method must be adapted to the class, the topic, and one's own skills and interests. But all young teachers in one form or another will be expected to lecture, for that is the way American education has developed. And that is the way it will increasingly develop as new numbers of students come into our colleges. There is a great deal of writing on how to teach and how to lecture. A very useful and charming introduction to the topic and to the literature can be found in Gilbert Highet's *The Art of Teaching* and in Jacques Barzun's *Teacher in America*,[21] both of which will repay the aspiring teacher's careful attention. (These are now available in paperback editions.) Both deal with university teaching, but their concerns are different. Highet explores ways of teaching, tells how some of the great teachers have gone about their jobs, and provides some exceedingly sound advice about methods and pitfalls. Barzun is more wide-ranging and deals with teaching as a profession rather than merely as an art. He, too, talks of the great teachers, but he imparts a feeling about the world of the university, its challenge, its excitements, its absurdities.

Since teaching means a lot of lecturing, how does one go about lecturing? The first thing a teacher must do is convince himself that a good lecture is a sound and effective method of teaching. As I have already indicated, there is a widespread impression abroad in the land and in the literature that a lecture is less effective than other methods, that it is merely an exposition of "facts" and therefore bad.

21. Gilbert Highet, *The Art of Teaching* (New York, 1950), and Jacques Barzun, *Teacher in America* (Garden City, N. Y., 1955). The aspiring research scholar, in political science as in other fields of the humanities and social sciences, will find much the same sort of guidance and enjoyment in another book by one of these authors: Jacques Barzun and Henry F. Graff, *The Modern Researcher* (New York, 1957).

I have never understood the curious objection some people have to facts, which always seems, somehow, to imply a preference for "non-facts." Surely what is being complained of is not facts, but trivia. There is nothing wrong with facts, but a lecturer who confines himself to trivia is simply an ignorant man as well as a poor lecturer. Education, they say, is what is left over after one has forgotten all the facts, for which one must read not "facts" but "details." The lecturer must not merely read statistics, chronicle events, or describe structures; he must not merely do what a textbook can do better. He must supply interpretations, show interrelations, assess causes and consequences, portray developments, explain methods, and seek to inspire in his students both appreciation and understanding. He must give them not merely a description of political events but a feeling for political phenomena. This is a difficult task and one not easy to define exactly, let alone perform competently. So much of the character and personality of the individual lecturer must go into the lecture that it is almost impossible to generalize about how to do it well. And yet there are some useful guidelines that may be worth suggesting.

The first key to success is careful preparation. I do not mean merely that the lecturer must know his subject—that goes without saying. I mean that he must give careful thought in advance to the organization of his material, the way in which he will present it, the sequence of his topics, the selection of his illustrations, and so on. He must know what he is going to say before going in to say it. The lecture that is poorly organized is no lecture at all and results in no education for his hearers.

This leads to the second point, namely, that one must come to lecture with careful *notes,* which will be used but not read. One should never, never read a manuscript; it only puts listeners to sleep —intellectually if not literally. On the other hand, the man who lectures without notes is either a genius or a fool, and the odds are that in either case he is a poor lecturer. They are even greater that the student goes away without much to base his further study on. He may be amazed, awed, bemused, or confused, but what does he do next? While it is being given, the lecture should kindle the student's interest and understanding, but it should also provide the means of further study, which means in turn that he must be able to take notes on what has been said. The lecturer who prides himself on "knowing" the stuff so well he does not need notes, or who tries to memorize a lecture, or who does not care whether his lecture is well organized, is not only failing to do his best, he is deluding himself and swindling his students.

A third tip is that the successful lecturer involves himself deeply in his task and in his presentation. He must feel the need and the problem of establishing a rapport and understanding between himself and his students. Too many professors simply go into the classroom and read off their notes, expecting students to take down their words and regurgitate them on call. The process, so someone has said, is to transfer the material from the teacher's notebook to the student's notebook, without its going through the mind of either. If he can communicate his own interest and concern for his subject, he is likely to produce that same interest and concern in the class. Thus, the lecturer is a sentient human being and a perceptive human mind seeking communication with others. Osgood Perkins used to say that he never gave a good performance without having stage fright before going on. Something of the same thing can be said of the lecturer. There has to be a little ham in him, for every good lecture is something of a dramatic presentation. If one plays it too cool, one is likely to cool off rather than warm up the student's perception and understanding.

One objection often made to the lecture as a teaching method is that there is no "feedback," that is to say that the lecturer has no way of knowing how his students are receiving what he offers, or whether they are following him. This is not a problem to be ignored, but its difficulty is often overstated. No doubt there is a more continuous communication in a small-group discussion than in a large lecture hall, but the sensitive (i.e., the competent) lecturer has many ways of measuring student reaction. Inattention, open-mouthed stares, an appreciative chuckle, a defiant glare, a derisive chortle, a sleepy nod, vigorous note-taking at the proper time, paper-rattling, eagerness to ask questions—all these things, as well as their absence, can inform the lecturer of the receptivity and reaction of his students. But he must be on the look-out for these indicators, interpret them meaningfully, and react accordingly.

A final bit of advice is to push the student somewhat harder than he likes or can take. In a large class, the level of student preparation and ability varies greatly and one cannot aim at all students simultaneously. But one should not aim too low; one should try instead to aim just a little too high. This can be done without talking down to the students in exasperating arrogance. George Lyman Kittredge was said to scorn his students and their inadequacies, and consistently talked above their heads. Once, while walking about during a lecture, he fell off the dais and in the startled silence that followed, he picked himself up and growled at the class, "This is the first time I have ever descended to the level of my students." In a way, I think Kittredge was right. It is far better to shoot a little above the students' heads, to disclose but not describe new worlds open to them, to expect more of them than it is likely they can produce, to assume they are rather more knowledgeable than they are —than to do the reverse. It must be done judiciously and with careful skill, but it pays off in horizons widened and interests kindled.

All of this may sound impossible. But what is impossible is not doing it but generalizing about it. Cecil Driver of Yale used to consider the lecture an art form, and in the hands of a master artist like himself, that, no doubt, is what it was. Few of us can hope to make of each lecture a work of art, and not even the master can do it consistently. Yet the challenge of good lecturing is fascinating and the results most gratifying. On too many days one emerges from the classroom saying to oneself, "It just didn't go well somehow." But on those days when one emerges with a feeling of accomplishment and the glow of a job well done, the lecture and the teaching habit seem eminently fine.

The Organization of Large Classes and Courses

It is surely true that we shall have to turn away from the small-group discussion and increasingly to the large-group lecture as our principal means of instruction. But the lecture is not the whole solution, and to some aspects of the problem it is almost irrelevant. Last semester at my own university there were registered in the two halves of our introductory courses in American government a total of 2,729 students. Similar figures, or larger, can doubtless be reported from other institutions. Needless to say, we do not try to put them all in one gigantic lecture section. They are lectured to, all right, but the problem is how to organize such numbers, divide them into sections, provide the necessary teaching staff, decide what they are going to study, and determine how much of what they do shall be done in common.

The introductory course in American government for many years has been required of all students. Hence, we have been faced with a "challenge of numbers" for a long time. Our method is to divide the students into a number of quite separate sections, each one being the full responsibility of the assigned teacher. There is no large central lecture and no breakdown into smaller discussion sections. The sections are manned by staff members ranging from teaching assistant to full professor. Last semester there were forty-eight such sections in the two halves of the course, about half of which were taught by teaching assistants. Our rule is that every member of the staff, from full professor on down, who is teaching full time, must teach at least one section of the introductory course, but the regular staff member usually has only one, or at most two, sections, since he also is teaching advanced or graduate courses. The average section had 57 students, varying from a low of 45 to a high of 94. We make a point of giving the smaller sections (as well as the least popular hours) to the teaching assistants and the larger ones to the regular staff.

The basic difficulty of this method is that of maintaining the quality of instruction in view of the heavy use that must be made of teaching assistants. This raises the very serious question of the use and abuse of these in-betweens, who are both graduate students and apprentice teachers. I am not one of those who believe that the regular faculty member is inevitably a better teacher than the teaching assistant. Indeed, I can remember the day when I thought that very nearly the reverse was true. The Committee on Standards of Instruction of the American Political Science Association reported in 1962 that in "some" of the larger universities "it is said, that lower-division classes fell entirely in the hands of graduate assistants," but they did not "see this practice as necessarily unfortunate. The assistant nearing completion of his doctorate will often bring a freshness of point of view and an enthusiasm to his instructional duties which others may lack."[22] No doubt this is often true, and, in any event, since

22. "Political Science As a Discipline," *American Political Science Review,* LVI (1962), 420.

these assistants are the future teachers of political science in our colleges, they must at some time begin on their teaching duties. Far better for them to start as graduate students, while they have some supervision and assistance, than later on, when they are entirely on their own. The difficulty is that they lack not interest and enthusiasm, but skill and experience.

Whether he has full responsibility for a section or is merely the discussion leader in a small group, the teaching assistant needs and deserves supervision and guidance—a great deal more than merely a general orientation at the beginning of the semester. All sorts of devices are available and will help do the job; the trouble with all of them is that they take faculty time. Ideally, he should be assigned to a senior faculty member who assists him in any way that is useful and desired. They can visit each other's classes, trade off now and then, discuss in advance what they are planning to do, exchange notes (both figuratively and perhaps literally), and develop in each other a feeling of joint pursuit of a common goal. Or, depending on the situation and the numbers involved, perhaps one faculty member or a few can serve in this way with several teaching assistants. Weekly conferences of assistants with a senior man, or among all staff members teaching in the course, are obvious suggestions and valuable practices. What is hard to defend is the too common practice of giving the new graduate student a section of his own and telling him to go to it, ignoring him thereafter until word comes through the (student) grapevine that he seems not to know what he is doing. Small wonder. And small doubt where the fault lies.

Research on the use and effectiveness of closed-circuit or broadcast television as a means of teaching large numbers of college students is still in its infancy. What research has been done can here be reported,[23] but it is very far from being conclusive with respect to either its effectiveness or its economy. It is a natural step, in thinking about increased enrollments, to move from the large-group lecture to the televised lecture, and television has an obvious appeal to the layman whose taxes support the burgeoning state university, for he sees it as a means of handling large numbers of students without hiring ever-growing numbers of professors. But whether television is so obvious a solution to these problems is not yet clear.

23. The research has been surveyed and reported by McKeachie, *op. cit.*, esp. pp. 342-351. This section relies heavily on McKeachie's survey.

The Ford Foundation and its subsidiaries have provided something over $75 million in the last few years for experimentation on college teaching by television, largely for technical facilities and for released time for faculty members to prepare television courses. These funds have supported widely scattered and highly diversified experiments, and the program is still going on. Many schools also have undertaken such research on their own. The bulk of the experiments on which reports are available involve closed-circuit television on the college campus with live teachers rather than film or tape. Not many experiments have involved courses in political science, but enough of them deal in similar courses to make the results of interest.

The elaborate experiments at Pennsylvania State indicate that there is little loss in student learning in courses taught by television, but that students prefer conventional classes. The Penn State researchers investigated a number of factors that one might expect to condition the effectiveness of television teaching, but none of them seem to have had any real significance. These factors included two-way microphone communication, holding a 15-minute discussion immediately after a 35-minute television lecture, holding two television lectures followed by a third hour for discussion later in the week, the use of elaborate "visual aids" in the television presentation, the presence of proctors in the viewing room, large and small viewing groups, and so on. None of these factors seriously affected the results of the television courses or significantly improved their effectiveness.[24]

Television teaching seems to have measurable superiority over the large lecture section, in situations where it is important for the student to see details. There is evidence of both superior effectiveness and more favorable student reaction in courses in medicine, science, and engineering, but not in the humanities or social sciences, except among students who were given seats in the back of a large lecture hall. One of the elaborate experiments at Miami University in Ohio involved a course in "government" in which it was shown that low-ability students achieved more in conventional classes than in television classes; interestingly, the reverse was true in physiology and

24. C. R. Carpenter and L. P. Greenhill, "An Investigation of Closed-Circuit Television for Teaching University Courses," *Instructional Television Res.*, Project No. 1 (University Park: Pennsylvania State University, 1955). Also Project No. 2, 1958. Cited in McKeachie, *op. cit.*, pp. 342-343.

zoology.[25] Students' attitudes toward television classes do not seem to affect their achievement in such classes.

On the basis of his survey of the growing research literature, W. J. McKeachie concludes "that television instruction is inferior to classroom lectures in communicating information, developing critical thinking, changing attitudes, and arousing interest in a subject but that this inferiority is probably not great." Even so, "the consistency of results favoring conventional instruction over television is unusual."[26] The basic difficulty, however, is that we are not going to be able to continue our "conventional instruction," and some means will have to be found to take care of greater numbers of students. With that prospect before him, McKeachie concludes that "when one weighs heavily the necessity for accommodation of higher education to large numbers of students, the differences between television and conventional instruction seem small."[27]

Another major summary of television experimentation is a report by John W. Meaney, published by the Fund for the Advancement of Education, which surveys the results of the experiments which it and other Ford Foundation agencies have supported since 1958.[28] The report is not based on the same sort of empirical research as that reported in the McKeachie summary, and it is oriented much more to the point of view of the teacher and planner than to that of the student. After a cautious assessment of the various programs supported by the Fund, the report concludes that "by offering better instruction to more students, television impresses its users as a highly efficient method of teaching in which the advantages definitely outweigh the disadvantages."[29]

In support of this conclusion, a great many quite real advantages are cited. The one most often given by the professor is that "television makes it possible for him to give lectures that are better than any he has given before."[30] The cynic may observe that it also makes it necessary; surely there is no reason why it should not be possible. Given the time and ability to concentrate exclusively on the preparation of closed-circuit television lectures, and given adequate technical

25. McKeachie, *op. cit.*, p. 345.
26. *Ibid.*, p. 347.
27. *Ibid.*, pp. 347-348.
28. John W. Meaney, *Televised College Courses* (New York, 1962).
29. *Ibid.*, p. 34.
30. *Ibid.*, p. 21.

assistance, a first-rate lecturer and teacher ought to be able to produce first-rate television lectures. Students agreed that the quality of lectures was improved, but everyone involved in the work was convinced that the quality of the product and its teaching effectiveness could be improved still more.[31]

Most professors in the program also agreed that "television has a real potential as a replacement for the very large lecture class where many students have difficulty seeing demonstrations or asking questions." Indeed, some television teachers "believe that they can achieve, in a television presentation, a quality of intimacy and a conversational tone that are impossible to manage in a large lecture hall."[32] Again the evidence is strong that the best use of television is in the scientific and technological fields, where experiment and demonstration are of greater importance, which is not, of course, to say that it is useless in political science.

One of the serious disadvantages noted in the Meaney report and elsewhere is the tremendous amount of time required for the preparation of television lectures. The Fund's program provided that the full time of the faculty member be released for the preparation of the single course he would be offering on television; while the course as offered could no doubt be used to supplant lectures by other staff members, most such television arrangements require the assistance and participation of other members of the staff in the administration of the course, the proctoring of viewing groups, the handling of supplementary discussion classes, and other matters. This additional use of faculty time is particularly expensive while the television system is in the experimental stages. This may be seen in the description of almost any such experiment, the one in teaching American government at Iowa being a good example.[33] While many of these supporting functions doubtless can be performed by junior staff members or teaching assistants, the total cost in faculty time is appreciable and, so far as I can judge, it has not yet been measured with any accuracy.[34]

31. *Ibid.*, p. 36.
32. *Ibid.*, p. 25.
33. Clearinghouse of Studies on Higher Education, *op. cit.*, pp. 49-52.
34. One effort has been made to assess the over-all cost and economy of television instruction as well as its effectiveness: Donald W. Paden, "The Teaching of Economics Via Television at the College Level," which is included as an appendix in the Meaney report, *op cit.*, pp. 65-88.

The professors giving the television courses also reported some important reservations. Most of them regretted the loss of personal contact with the students, which is not much relieved by putting a few of them in the television studio. Similarly, they regretted "the lack of opportunity for immediate feedback of student reactions, classroom discussion, and questions," and this lack was considered "a very real handicap and disadvantage, both by the students and by professors."[35] Freshman and sophomore students particularly balk at the television classes, feeling that though they get to know the professor, he does not get to know them. The results of efforts to remedy these deficiencies by special discussion classes in addition to the television lecture, by "talk-back" facilities during the lecture, and by other means, apparently have not been very successful. Indeed, "these facilities are not much used unless deliberate efforts are made to stimulate such use." Still more important, such facilities immediately become obsolete once the lecture is transferred to film or video tapes.[36]

The basic difficulty is that we do not yet know just how television can be most effectively used in the classroom. Everyone seems agreed that it offers a tremendous potential, especially in view of mounting enrollments, but the experiments thus far conducted do not show that it can provide teaching of the standard we hope to attain, or even maintain, and it is not yet by any means certain that it will result in a substantial saving of faculty time. The fact is that we really do not yet know what to do with television. Warner G. Rice suggests that education is abandoning the old ideal of Mark Hopkins on a log, and is turning to a brilliant professor at one end of a coaxial cable and 5,000 students at the other.[37] But we are far from that at present, and whether we ever get there is still highly speculative. The great question of television teaching is not whether faculties will be automated into technological unemployment, but whether it can be used to achieve the objectives of university education in the coming decades.

Interestingly enough, there are very few reports on experiments

35. Meaney, *op. cit.*, p. 25.
36. *Ibid.*, p. 26.
37. Warner G. Rice, "Efficient and Effective Teaching," *Current Issues in Higher Education 1956*, Proceedings of the Eleventh Annual National Conference on Higher Education (Washington, D.C., 1956) **p. 17.**

using regular filmed or taped lectures supplemented by small-group discussions. This would appear to offer an even broader opportunity, in political science as elsewhere. For, by abandoning the live lecture, it becomes possible to use lectures prepared elsewhere, to set up "lecture exchanges" among universities such as those already in existence among a number of institutions in central Texas, where a growing number of taped lectures are already available and can be obtained upon application.[38] Alvin Eurich has suggested that we could film a number of lecture series by giants like Reinhold Niebuhr, Mark Van Doren, Harold Urey, and Arnold Toynbee, so that they might teach successive generations of students.[39] In point of fact, Walter Prescott Webb was engaged in just such an enterprise and had it about half-completed at the time of his death. The series is being continued by his colleagues at the University of Texas and, when completed, will include many of the world's greatest living historians, including Toynbee.

The use of such "permanent" television lectures in political science is open to the obvious objection that some of them will get quickly out of date. But this surely does not preclude their use, or their frequent revision. One such series, of course, already is available, namely, the first-rate "Continental Classroom" series of lectures and interviews by Peter Odegard of the University of California at Berkeley. A number of schools have already devised ways of using the Odegard series for course credits, to say nothing of the vast numbers of interested citizens who have enjoyed and benefited from it. Peter Odegard has probably done more to improve the public image and standing of the academic political scientist than anyone since Woodrow Wilson. It may be useful to record here that the Odegard lectures are now available in 160 half-hour units in black-and-white 16-mm. sound film from Encyclopedia Britannica Films, Inc.

Independent Study

There is a great deal of talk in educational circles and in the educational literature about reducing the load of the faculty and the

38. A partial list is included in Meaney, *op. cit.,* pp. 52-53.
39. Eurich, *op. cit.,* p. 15.

strain on the educational institutions by having students do much more independent work of their own. There is much good sense in some of these proposals, but they can easily get out of hand and defeat their own purpose.

No country in the world bases its university system on as many contact hours between professor and students as does the United States. This may well be a by-product of our long-standing commitment to provide higher education for the masses rather than merely for an elite. But the result is our seemingly inextricable involvement in college "courses" of a set number of hours in which the professor meets his students, for either lecture or discussion, for something like a hundred hours spread over about nine months. As enrollments grow, something will have to give. Just what is not yet clear, but the problem is far from hopeless.

One way of meeting it is merely to cut down on the number of lectures and/or class meetings and thus reduce the number of professors that the present system calls for. As Henry Steele Commager observed several years ago, the time of the student "now spent going to lectures and preparing for course examinations can be more profitably spent in the study or the library."[40] This device would work better in subjects like political science than in many others. Surely there is no magic in forty-five class meetings for each three-semester-hour course. Another means of doing the same thing would be to cut down on the number of courses we offer. Most large departments of political science are still trying to adorn themselves with at least one specialist in virtually every specialty in the field, which means, of course, that each must give at least one course in his specialty. Along these same lines, we might save a tremendous amount of time and labor—for faculties as well as administrators—by reducing the amount of unnecessary impedimenta of university life. I mean things like attendance-taking, ten-minute quizzes, daily assignments, registration procedures, and the ancillary non-educational functions in which every university abounds—perhaps even grades, credits, and courses. We simply do not need to nurse our students as we do, and if we put them more on their own, it probably would result not only in a saving of faculty time but in a better education for the students

40. Henry Steele Commager, "The Problem Isn't Bricks—It's Brains," *New York Times Magazine,* Jan. 29, 1956, p. 67.

as well. As it is, students come to a university to "be educated,"
rather than to educate themselves. As someone has said, they throw
themselves down in front of their teachers like a pile of boards to
be turned into furniture. Ultimately and fundamentally, the problem
of growing numbers can be solved only by putting more responsibility on the students themselves, whether we do it by televised lectures,
independent study programs, or something else.

We already have done some of this for the better students, presumably on the assumption that they will learn more that way. A
great many universities have adopted "honors" programs, "independent study" programs, special arrangements of all kinds for the gifted
student that let him work on his own.[41] What remains to be done
is to apply this same principle to greater numbers of students, just
as far as their abilities will enable them to profit from such an arrangement and just as far as it has the effect of conserving and not wast-
ing faculty time.[42]

This last point is serious. The assumption in much of the discussion of independent study is that the student works by himself and
thus does not require the time of the professor. So stated, there
seems to be nothing wrong with the proposal. But in my own experience, an independent study program takes *more,* not less, faculty
time than the existing course system. Virtually every such proposal
depends on faculty supervision, consultation, weekly tutorials, direction of research or reading programs, the reading of reports, essays,
or research papers. The peril is that the need for this kind of faculty
participation, if multiplied by additional students, will wreck the system. If by "independent study" is really meant *independent* study,
it can be a means of both improving education and conserving faculty time and energy. But I have two serious reservations about it.
First, I am very skeptical about the saving in faculty time, and,
second, I do not believe it would be effective with the average (or
below-average) student in the large state university. These reservations do not constitute insuperable obstacles. The basic proposition
that students are going to have to rely increasingly on their own

41. See George R. Waggoner, "The Development of Programs for the Superior
Student in Large Universities," *Educational Record,* XL (1959), 319-325.
42. A useful report that is oriented not only toward the superior but toward
the ordinary student, and which contains an extensive bibliography, is that by
Winslow R. Hatch and Ann Bennet, *Independent Study,* New Dimensions in Higher
Education, No. 1, U.S. Office of Education (1960).

efforts and devices is surely sound. The problem again is how is it to be put into effect.

Closely related to the student's independent study is the question of how much of his time he spends independent of study. The large university offers an unlimited number of distractions, out of which some students virtually make careers. Carried to excess, such extra-curricular activities obviously hinder a student's education. But I am not one of those who looks down on such activity per se; I should not be the least bit disappointed if all our present generation of students turned out to be intellectuals, but I should be very disappointed if they turned out to be hermits. I plead only that a far greater portion of these activities be given an intellectual flavor. We have far too many beauty queens, elections, "ugly-man" contests, chowder-and-marching societies, intercollegiate athletic passions, committees on nothing that do nothing, and general hoopla. A faculty, and particularly a political science faculty, could do a great deal to direct some of this frenzy into intellectually profitable channels.

The problem of the large university on this score is perhaps greater than that of the small college, for it is impossible for vast numbers of students to share in common the intellectual experiences of the classroom or lecture hall. And since student conversation tends to center on shared experiences, it concerns itself mainly with dormitory and social life, athletics, and other non-academic matters. How this can be overcome, I do not know; it may be inherent in the large university. Stephens College tackled it by setting up a required television course consisting of "brief lectures viewed by students in small faculty-led discussion groups,"[43] and then craftily scheduling it just before lunch so the discussion would carry over into the dining halls.

One objection to the large university, which will be heard increasingly as enrollments mount, is that it is "so big" that the student tends to "get lost" and does not get as much faculty attention as in the small school. In my view, this is very much overstated. Students, like other people, form associations and small circles of friends and acquaintances within the larger group. It is doubtless true that the student in the large school has less contact with the faculty than in the small school, but this is compensated for by the greater variety of opportunities and by the presence on the campus of a greater

43. McKeachie, *op. cit.,* p. 347.

variety of students. If contact with fellow beings is one adventure in education, then there are far greater opportunities for such contacts on the large campus. The presence of graduate students, the multiplicity of schools and colleges within the university, the rough and tumble of large university life, offer an educational experience that is not afforded in the smaller institution. Which is to say that as the smaller institutions grow larger, they will derive perhaps unexpected advantages from the extracurricular side of student life—if only (an important "if") they can keep it under some sort of control.

The Use of the Faculty

There is one sort of reform that nearly every university should and could attempt, and that is to provide the teaching faculty with the time and assistance necessary to enable them to do their job properly. The widespread assumption that what a college teacher does is teach is laughably naïve. What he does is try to fit his teaching into the other demands upon his time. Some of these are perfectly legitimate demands; some are of his own doing; some cannot be avoided. But there is not enough concern by the university to relieve him of those that are irrelevant, unnecessary, and wasteful of his talents.

The first of these competing demands is that he is expected to to carry on an active research program. Some do and some do not. Research is a fundamental function of a university faculty, and those faculty members who do it well should surely be encouraged to do it. But we may have to reassess this research function as student numbers increase. Research is time-consuming, as is good teaching, and the plain truth is that a great deal of what passes for "research" is a waste of time. What is worse is that the quantity (rather than the quality) of research, or, more candidly, the quantity of publication, has become the most important single criterion in the measurement of faculty competence.

Thus, the real measure of academic success is not success as a teacher at all, for the simple reason that teaching competence is difficult to measure and can seldom be tangibly displayed. Academic success and promotion may be based on several other things, but the principal criterion is a public record, which is produced chiefly by publications. Ambitious universities want their faculties well-known and what makes a faculty well-known is, to a very great extent, the record of its publication. Hence, that is what is rewarded. The effect on the young teacher is obvious. If he is ambitious, he conducts himself in such a way as to achieve such recognition and rewards. His teaching is undervalued, never assessed, and disregarded almost entirely when it comes to promotions. He is under very considerable pressure to devote his energies and concern to other things.

The demands on faculty time, however, go far beyond research and teaching. Another real drain is the multiplicity of administrative and committee chores that fall to every faculty member. No doubt, most of these tasks have a justification, historical if not contemporary, but too many of them constitute a mere shuffling of unimportant papers, the filing of useless records, the preparation of soon-forgotten reports, the inevitable paraphernalia of increasing bureaucratization. Universities, like other large organizations, have a tendency to become increasingly formalized. And faculties, composed too often of eggheads and eccentrics, cling jealously to meaningless prerogatives which drain their time and sap their energies no less than do their unwanted administrative functions. Anyone who has ever sat through a faculty committee meeting can scarcely help being amazed by the spectacle of so many high-powered brains being concentrated on such unimportant problems with so little being accomplished. It has been estimated that approximately one-fifth of faculty time is devoted to committee work.[44] But surely this misrepresents the case; the administrative tasks of the faculty member, whether performed in committee or individually, must altogether take more nearly twice that.

There are other such demands, as well, that drain away the teacher's teaching time: lectures to the public and to organizations, radio and television appearances, conferences, and the many "public relations" functions the faculty are called upon to perform.

And the man who is the best teacher is quite likely to be the man who is best at these other things. Indeed, as his reputation as a teacher grows and spreads, to that same extent the other demands on his time are multiplied, to the point where he has little time for teaching. He gets by, and if he is clever he does a competent, or

44. *New York Times Magazine,* Oct. 12, 1958, p. 10.

at least passable, job. But the hurried glance at the curling, yellowed notes before running off to class is scarcely to be dignified by calling it preparation.

My point is not that these other things themselves are unimportant, but, rather, that they interfere with the ability of the faculty member to devote himself to teaching. And as the teaching task grows greater, we are going to have to rethink the extent to which these other matters can be accommodated in a teaching faculty's program. Quite clearly, a great many of them cannot be avoided, and the curtailment of some would impair the university's teaching function itself. But what must be done is to provide the faculty member with the means of doing his varied tasks (including the teaching task) more economically and effectively and with less waste of his time on trivialities. Typically today, he has virtually nothing in the way of clerical, secretarial, research, or academic assistance, except a limited share in the services of a department "secretary" who must serve the entire department staff. Consequently, the faculty member spends far too much of his highly skilled and not-so-highly paid time in such chores as filing his clippings, keeping records, typing his own letters, and sharpening his own pencils. For want of adequate facilities and assistance, he spends an absurd amount of energy doing things that waste his time and talents. The provision of adequate help of this sort is a minimum requirement if we expect him to perform satisfactorily his ever-burgeoning teaching task.

Real teaching—the kind of deeply concerned teaching that produces good education, the kind of teaching that will become increasingly difficult at best as the number of students grows—that kind of teaching requires patience, preparation, and endless reading, a willingness to read endless essays, reports, reviews, and term papers, and the guts to assign them, knowing they must be read; endless conferences with endless lines of students. That kind of teaching takes endless time. And there are very few teachers, in large universities or small, who are willing to spend such time. Indeed, there are very few who have it to spend.

This paper has dealt more with problems than with solutions, more with the "challenge" than with the response. The basic difficulty is that, though we are beginning to perceive the nature and size of the problem, we have not yet thought up the solutions. A good bit of research on the possibilities has been done and is being done, but the results are not yet sufficient to show us the way. Even so, there is plenty of concern, and the flood is almost upon us; the next decade or two will produce some real changes in the pattern of university education.

We neither can nor should change our whole teaching system overnight. We shall no doubt shift increasingly to television, filmed lectures, teaching machines, and independent study. But the use of these devices will vary from school to school and the change cannot come all at once. For the vast majority of schools, and for most political scientists, there will be no closed-circuit television, no programmed instruction, no breathtaking innovations, but a continuation and adaptation of methods with which we are familiar. In all candor, it seems to me that the challenge of numbers in political science will be less demanding than in many other fields—for example, in languages, English, and the laboratory sciences. We must modify our techniques as best we can, and if we are smart enough, we will be able to figure out ways to make more effective use of our faculties and facilities. Just what shape the reforms will take in political science is far from clear. But reform is in the air and in the census figures, and it will be exacted from us, willy-nilly, by the challenge of numbers.

EARL LATHAM

The superior student

When John Marshall began to write his biography of George Washington, he started the five-volume work with the voyages of Columbus. It is not necessary to start quite so far back in a discussion of the superior student, but it is useful to establish at the outset some of the characteristics of the habitat in which he is to be found. It is an assumption of these remarks that institutions vary from each other, that students vary from institution to institution, and that the sum of local variations may be described as the culture of the campus. But before considering some of these variations, it might be of some value to say what I think are some of the common characteristics of the learning situation in colleges and universities. Although there are millions of college graduates in the country, and although they no doubt received excellent educations, a disconcerting number are alike in this—that they are without clear recollection of what college is like; and the more vigorous among them who have made careers as professional alumni entertain certain illusions which their own experience should have belied.

The first of several fallacies cherished by some alumni, rich donors, and minor trustees is the Trilby fallacy, in which Svengalilike teachers dominate narcoleptic students, and make them sing socialism, deficit budgets, nuclear disarmament, and other refrains out of harmony with the chorus of orthodox opinion. The real error in this view is not that these songs will never become big hits, but that the professors dominate the students. Mark Hopkins and his famous log and Mr. Chips are both passé in the college of today; and although students come to like some teachers and heed well their words, this is a far different thing from the absolute mastery of the mind that the cliché of the "master" professor presents. Indeed, the submissive prostration of the student to the teacher would be some cause for thinking rather that the student needed psychiatric help than that the teacher had succeeded in fascinating his patient by force of resistless domination.

In my experience, the college student of today perceives the faculty generally as an aggregation of men to be respected, from whom something can be learned, who represent authority *in loco parentis,* who, like father, can be manipulated and sometimes misled, who are cherished for their whimsy, avoided in their wrath, and who set standards of expectation that the student usually will try to meet, unless the standards are inhuman, in which case he takes another course. Some students are certainly more responsive than others, but this is a long shot from the assumption that the professor in American universities and colleges controls the opinion or even the behavior of the students with Jovean command. Some of our colleagues from abroad, where caste has comforts that are more generally available here without high rank, sometimes create "schools," acquire disciples, and conduct the academic enterprise as though it were a monastery and they were the abbots. But the American professor normally expects less than prostration, works to make himself as clear and informed as he can be in his subject matter, and generally supports free trade and not monopoly in the traffic for the attention of his students.

Companion to the illusion of the professor as mesmerist, is the fallacy of the sausage, in which it is supposed that students come to the college as empty vessels, to be filled with bits of this and that. To the contrary, their basic attitudes and values already have been set—for life—by their families, and the college is not likely in four years of interrupted attention to change these deeply imbedded predilections. It is well known in politics that young people, voting for the first time, tend to vote as their parents do. This is normally at age twenty-one, when they are *leaving* college, after seventeen years of life with father, and three hours a week for one semester with the professor who, it is assumed, can lead them astray. When students seem to depart radically from the ethic of the family in which they were brought up, the reason usually is to be sought in the family in which they were brought up. Sons who wish to break away from the influence of the family got the original idea from the family. The same opportunity would exist if the young man should elect to spend his time in military service instead of college study.

Although the student brings his basic values to college with him, and although his pristine personality structure was built in the cradle and before, this is not to say that college is without influence, else it would exist only as a baby-sitting service for teen-agers of good fortune. The colleges—the liberal arts colleges, that is—are engaged, when they are at their best, in an important intellectual enterprise— the uses of the mind and its development, with special attention to the subjects of knowledge and the process of knowing. Military and other vocational schools, and schools devoted to the indoctrination of the devout, place other values, said to be absolute, ahead of the free use of the critical faculties; but the liberal arts schools cannot be faulted for reckless relativism. As Justice Holmes once said, "The test of certitude is not certainty," to which one may add that the quest for certitude is rooted as certainly in a faith that it can be found as are the claims of dogma that it has been.

So, it can and does happen that the values the student brings to college with his trunk get some competition from others he did not pack. If he makes a change, however, it is not the college that makes the transformation; only the student can make the transformation. When there are other definitions of reality than those thought true by the family, it is the student himself who will choose what he wishes, determine what he believes, and come to the conclusion ulti- mately that he cannot help but believe. The process by which this occurs is not a litigation between parents and professors; it is an in- terior dialogue within the student in which he speaks all the parts.

This leads to the third illusion, the fallacy of the danger of read- ing books. The alumnus of an Eastern college returned to his campus to acquaint himself with a new experimental course for sophomores which required the students to judge between the alternatives of cer- tain public policies, both historic and contemporary. Because of his outspoken conservatism, he was asked to give a lecture presenting his views on the need for new legislation regulating labor unions, which he did with great vigor. In the question period after the lecture one of the students asked him, "Sir, since businessmen enjoy the right to form corporations and other organizations of their own choosing, isn't it fair that workers should have the same right?" The answer to this question was, "Mister, what books have you been reading?"

When I was a small boy, my Scottish great-grandmother once counseled me that "Reading rots the mind," and in this dictum she was supported by the authority of Thomas Hobbes, who said that if he had read as much as his critics, he would be as stupid as they. But Hobbes and great-grandmother notwithstanding, the case for the censors is hardly supportable and need not be argued. It is a persistent metaphor of the censors, however, that minds can be "poisoned" by books, which invade a healthy mental and moral system, disable it, and cause it to die.

Books may be wrong, tedious, dull, scandalous, inept, superficial, one-sided, tendentious, pretentious, or trite. They may bore, but they cannot kill. It is the function of the teacher to supply guidance through the literature, to identify what he thinks is worthy and what he thinks is trash, to invite the student to consider his judgments, to encourage the reader to appraise an author and his work in the context of the whole body of thought and writing to which he presumes to make a contribution, to set out on an inquiry into understanding with the student, and to stimulate his awareness of the whole range of opinions on any subject. The teacher does not control the student's reactions but he can help to set in motion a process of reflection that will enable the student to decide for himself what it is he wishes to accept.

It is doubtful that anyone who has had experience in teaching can recall ever having heard an alumnus say of a teacher, "He poisoned my mind," or "He gave me dangerous books to read." Even William Buckley, who does not seem to have enjoyed all aspects of his life at Yale, has not said that he was corrupted by exposure to books of which he disapproved. It is always someone else who is threatened by the toxins of teachers, and who may become "poisoned" by the experience.

And this leads to still one more illusion—the fallacy of the good teacher. Although alumni may not admit infection from teachers of whom they disapprove, they often cherish a boisterous conception of the "good teacher," which, however, is not always flattering to the smiling winner of this accolade, for he gets remembered for the wrong things. Too often he is the one whose jokes the grad remembers at his fifteenth reunion, although, for the life of him, he cannot recall a detail of the course he took. He remembers where the students sat but not where the teacher stood on the subject matter of the course. Teachers must necessarily be humble: they have worked their way through four years of college, strained and worried through graduate school, earned doctorates, written books and articles, acquired some small and grudging recognition from colleagues elsewhere, labored to master the intricacies and subtleties of difficult disciplines—only to be remembered as the man who made that funny remark about Eisenhower, or Adlai Stevenson, or the dean of the college, or was it someone else?

A national news magazine recently had a cruel kind of fun with the teachers of certain courses at Yale, Harvard, Texas, North Carolina, Wayne State University, Princeton, Michigan, and Northwestern, courses in which it "is almost impossible to fail." These courses, given by eminent men, were crowded with students with a taste for Slavic folklore, opera appreciation, iconography, abnormal personality, and home emergency health problems, and a distaste for term papers, final examinations, lectures, reading, and even attendance. I remember a course attended by approximately 250 students in which a yearly feature was a lecture on one of the naval battles of World War I, and the average grade was 86. The lecture was a great emotional experience. Gunsmoke filled the air, the walls were awash with brine, and students left with seaweed in their hair. Everybody remembers the lecture on the battle, but few can remember who was in it, where it took place, or how it came out. In the main this kind of instruction is entertainment, not scholarship; Chautauqua, not learning; an enterprise of the tent, rather than the study.

The good teacher is one who has knowledge and who is recognized and respected for it. But he must also be able to communicate it, for the essence of the teaching relation is communication. Is not "education" a leading forth? In communicating his knowledge and judgment, it is pleasant if the teacher is also charming, interesting, and lovable, but it is more important that he be creative, clear, and comprehensive. Everything else is bonus. One of the best teachers I know has, to my knowledge, never said a funny thing about Rousseau, but he has illuminated the understanding of numerous undergraduates who found it difficult to make sense out of the "general will" until they heard it expounded.

The office of teacher is the post of honor on the campus, and the good teacher perceives himself as the hub around which the whole academic enterprise turns. This is the "line" to which all else is "staff," or stuff. If there is no effective communication between teachers and students, the root purpose of the college is vitiated, and the voyage of the mind never gets far beyond the dock.

There is one other respect in which campuses tend to resemble each other. This is the similarity of outlook of the administrative managers of the campus—the multitude of officers and functionaries in the campus bureaucracy—for whom the Whig establishment is the political ideal. This conception assumes that there will be no crises if prudent management foresees the trend and prevents them from occurring. There should not be much drama in the quiet governance of the college system, and not much decisiveness. No policy should be very radical or very conservative. It should always manage to be something in between. Few matters will be really solved. They are just dealt with, and the "solutions" are always partial. In this respect there are probably few differences among the campuses of the country. This is not necessarily to disparage the Whig policy, for the impulse to do so should be restrained by recollection of the painful insecurities of administration and faculty alike where effort has been made to try to be radically different from the pattern.

But if there are unities in the learning situation of students, there are also diversities, and the culture of the campus is one of these. Even where the Whig spirit guides college administration, campuses vary from each other according to the ethnic, social, and economic composition of the student body, and according to the patterns of the local mores. Within recent time, I have visited several campuses that are strongly different from each other in these respects: Amherst (to start), the University of Florida, Harvard, Cornell, Wooster, Swarthmore, and Morgan State Teachers College in Baltimore. As the social composition of the campus varies, so do the values, that is, the local agreements on what is important, the preferred styles of undergraduate behavior, and so on; and these set conditions that influence the education of students, superior and average.

It would be invidious to characterize specifically the social structures of these several campuses but it is clear that they vary. For example, two have some kind of religious coloration although none indoctrinates in any creed. Two are state schools, and two are private universities in the Ivy League. The requirements for admission vary from the automatic acceptance of three-quarters of the high school students in the state who wish to attend, to the rejection of three-quarters of all the students who apply. The very rich and the very poor are not distributed among these seven schools with anything like an impartial hand. One is a school primarily, although not exclusively, for Negroes; another is a school which Negroes find it very difficult to enter at all. When we talk about the superior student, it makes a considerable difference whether we place him in one academic setting or another.

The element of "desire" is a characteristic that may serve to discriminate among the superior students at various institutions. The superior student at a Negro college, for example, has different drives from those of the superior student at a state university in the South or at Harvard. For him a college education is perceived as an instrument for the attainment of quite clear ends, and his motivation is likely to be strong and sustained. In a state university in the North at which I have taught, the superior student was more likely than not to be a lower middle-class boy or girl with a strong vocational or professional interest in a college education as a means of social ascension. Many of them worked at factory and other jobs when not on the campus, and the night shift was paid better by the hour than the faculty. The life chances of students at universities and colleges of low social composition tend to be different from those whose students expect to be given access to the resources and posts of command of the society as a matter of course. The superior student at the first place may find that he needs impulses of energy and capacities for endurance in the face of discouragement that are not charged to the personal resources of students in the second place.

The problem for the superior student at upper middle-class and upper-class academic institutions is exactly the opposite—he does not have an intensive drive for material advancement, social elevation, or personal development. By and large, he already has it "made." Attendance at college for him is often merely a function of his class. He goes to college because everybody he knows goes to college, and it would be unthinkable for him not to do so.

For some such, the campus is perceived as Theater, in which the student is one of the actors, with a role to play and a script to follow. He thinks of what he does as a "performance," and, in public, he is always on guard or on stage. Teachers and students are sets of actors in the same production, separated, literally, by the proscenium of the platform or the desk. The object of the role is the successful presentation of self; reputation and appearance are the techniques for a successful presentation. Marks, grades, and other signs of approval constitute the scores by which gains and losses are counted by the student player. These are the campus equivalents of the critics' notices by which dramatic productions live or die.

In this view of the campus as Theater, the faculty, as has been remarked, is also a troupe of performers. They make a successful presentation of self when they too receive good notices among the students. The measure of the success is the number of students who elect to take the course; bad notices can close the show, although the tenure rules, happily, prevent dismissal of the cast. Mimesis, it is thought, is the principal skill of the teacher—the exhibition of copies of appearance where nothing is real.

Where this view of the academic enterprise prevails, the superior student is sometimes not fully free to involve himself in learning to the utmost of his capacity because, as a student, he is inhibited by the social pressure of other students. He may not, for example, wish to be seen studying, and pretends that he is going to the movies when he is in fact going to a hideaway in the library. Or he cannot let it be known that he is going to the house of the professor to talk about his work or about any other intellectual concern. He may make believe that he does well in a course without cracking a book when he has spent weeks to master the material. Or he may not talk up in class because he will be thought by his peers to be a "turkey," an opprobrious word of uncertain meaning.

With these remarks about the learning situation in colleges and universities, and with some thought about the differences among the schools in mind, perhaps the eye can move from the setting to the gem it encloses. The superior student should be a superior person— that is to say, he should be endowed with other talents than a skill to score high on intelligence and aptitude tests. He should have attributes of will, desire, personality, and character that enable him to develop his intelligence, to attain a high degree of personal organization, and to make effective use of his intellectual talents and skills in his relations with others. He is not the mere grade-hunter, nor the lonely creature who lives in freakish isolation from his peers, nor the student with a small skill in taking examinations for which he prepares by filling his head the night before and emptying it the next morning on paper.

The element of desire is always present in the superior student. Or, to put it another way, although not all students with desire are superior students, all superior students display the characteristic of desire. They must have high intelligence, but they must also want to do something with it. The desire need not be for material advantage nor social ascension. There are, happily, institutions where intellectuality is the highest value in and of itself; and where both faculty and students strive to meet and match standards of quality that always recede as they are approached, for the best is never too good, nor the individual utmost, enough. And students who feel this way about themselves may even be found in institutions where the local mores discourage intellectuality.

Professors cherish the able student who shares for a time a partnership in goals to which the teacher has devoted his life, if it is clear that the interest is curious, generous, uncontrived, spontaneous, candid, and committed. I think of two like this. There is the student on his way to Yale law school, and a career at the bar, who became interested in the process by which Thomas Dewey bade farewell to the American people in 1950, shoved his lieutenant-governor, Joe Hanley, forward as his successor in Albany, changed his mind, and then shoved Joe Hanley aside in his haste to return to the American people. Interviews with the parties in the comedy led to an honor's thesis that was good enough to earn a *summa*. The entire project was made to succeed by the full investment by the student of great resources of intelligence, enthusiasm, and personal effectiveness. And for a second example of the superior student who is also a superior person, there is the graduate student right after the war who took reading courses in public administration theory, showing up breathless and always on the run, clad in an Army shirt, blue jeans, and canvas shoes, who thought that he might like to enter journalism or the public service, and who because he was both able and full of desire excited the compassion of his instructor who offered to help him start his career in journalism. The instructor asked the student which paper he was interested in and, when he said the *Washington Post,* was told that it might be possible to get him a job there. It turned out, however, that the young man was not interested in working for the paper; he was interested in buying it, for the frog in blue jeans was really a prince in disguise. As it happened, the young man did not go with the *Post.* Instead, he went with a newspaper in the Middle West as a reporter, was the despair of the paper's accountants because he let his checks accumulate, and eventually became a United States senator.

Professors come to share part of the lives of their good students and, although their participation after graduation is purely vicarious, identify with the student they had for awhile, and watch his subsequent career with special pleasure. In fact, the professor with good students is one of the blessed of the earth. The students are always the same age, and although the teacher grows older, the people with whom he spends most of his life do not. And they are among the best of the land, not that they are merely a fortunate minority, but because they are a fresh and vigorous population, forever renewed, endowed with gifts of mind and manner, winners in a competition to get into college in the first place, and bound to be among the leaders of society when they finish.

There are certain arrangements that experience shows help superior students to fulfil themselves, and certain kinds of program and emphasis about which I am skeptical. As to the first of these, the following examples are drawn from the field of political science, where all my experience has been. The superior student, first of all, is worth the special attention that an honors program will give him. Of notable quality are the honors programs at Harvard and Swarthmore, where the superior student is encouraged to do as much independent work as time and other limitations allow. It is possible at Swarthmore for such a student to elect not to write a thesis, and students who so elect may miss a valuable creative experience, which all undergo at Harvard. On the other hand, the comprehensive examinations at Harvard are not in the control of outsider examiners as they are at Swarthmore and other places, and the student who has survived an examination into his qualifications by strangers has met a test that assures him of comparability with the stiffest and most objective norms available in the discipline he has entered.

The comprehensive examination in the student's discipline ideally forces him to relate the particulars of various courses to some central whole and requires him to overcome the limitations of the useful but artificial packaging that the division of complex subjects into courses produces. If he can learn to see that sewers and hydrants and the Congo and Montesquieu and Marx and foreign aid and *Marbury* v. *Madison* and the *ombudsman* and John Wise and the national party convention are all related to each other in some profound way—that they constitute a comprehensive entirety as do the surfs and deeps of the sea—he has recovered some sense of the unity of knowledge which earlier centuries knew about, but which we may have forgotten. Of course, four three-hour examinations in the spring of the senior year are not by themselves going to make Leonardos of the young, but the effort to see the entirety in the particular, the universe in the atom, is a rigorous mental discipline, of which the comprehensive examination is merely a stage and not the conclusion. Comprehensive examinations, alas, are not always ideal, and some tend to ease the students' way in some fields in which he is not quite as much at home as others. Political theory is harder for some students than for others, and custom in some comprehensive examinations in this field of political science has guaranteed the appearance of a question that involves some combination of Aristotle, Plato, Machiavelli, Hobbes, Locke, and Rousseau. But perhaps the custom is not without its justification. Anyone who is prepared to be examined on all aspects of the work of these philosophers knows something about political theory.

In most places, one supposes, it is the preparation of an original and creative work of writing that constitutes the special task for the superior student, and it is in working with good students on their theses that a rich and fruitful intellectual relation can be established between teacher and student. For the work of the thesis combines discovery, reflection, and craftsmanship in which the professor points out the likely places to dig, the student considers what he has found, and both co-operate in the technical skills of presentation. It is a species of intellectual search and seizure in which the student, armed with the warrant of his professor, opens doors he never saw before and discovers goods of which he hitherto lacked possession. The warrant of the good teacher, like that of the careful judge, describes with some particularity the place to be searched and the thing to be seized, and it is a defective warrant only if it lacks probability.

The proper preparation of an honors thesis can be the most stimulating and rewarding single effort the student may have in college, and many have said so, when it was all over. In political science there is almost an infinity of subjects to explore, as there is in any substantial learned discipline, and although most theses will serve primarily to demonstrate some new aspect of the familiar, the aspect in fact *is* new, and the presentation of it by the student is unique to him. In this sense, honors theses are always original and creative.

It is probably true in most colleges that the students do not get enough experience writing substantial papers in their four years. It might not be too much to require a substantial paper throughout the college in one or two courses in each half-year. It is a little depressing to find even superior students in their last year struggling with the difference between "will" and "shall," perpetrating such curiosities of spelling as "seperate," producing such barbarisms as "analyzation," and showing themselves to be unfamiliar with the mysteries of topic sentences, paragraphing, and punctuation. But occasionally there is a rewarding accident like the invention in one paper of the word "diselected." The language has needed this word for a long time.

Honors programs may make use of special seminars for superior students, in which they prepare a number of shorter papers and contribute thereby to the instruction of each other. It helps if the instructor has a fairly demanding conception of the "seminar," which comes in a profusion of styles. Although seminars ought to be places of creation, many of the creations called seminars must have been begotten by artifice and not nature. It is especially useful when the instructor has set a theme—broad or narrow—and the students contribute their energy to the exploration of phases of the theme, all adding to the common store of information and ideas, and all discussing the matters of the seminar in a free exchange. Such seminars can be useful in helping to accomplish the same objects as the comprehensive examination, and under promising conditions: for there is time in a seminar, as there is not in an examination; the preparation for the seminar can be specific and in focus, and the development of the interconnections of knowledge can proceed by discussion and exchange.

A familiar idea in connection with superior students is the concept of independent study, and good things are justly said of it, but the concept requires some clarification. If the study were literally independent—turn them loose in the libraries—the college could be run by the dean and the librarian, if all the students were superior students, and the dean, it might be added, were a superior dean. Correspondence courses, five-foot bookshelves, and the like are all do-it-yourself kits for the improvement of the mind, but they are never likely to replace the school or the college, or the need for guidance and supervision. So, the question has to be asked about independent study, "Independent from what?" It may mean freedom from some of the course requirements that apply to the generality, presumably on the assumption that the student, under the guidance of an instructor or tutor, is advanced enough to do special work. If it means, however, that he can do better for himself in the stacks and the study than he can in the classroom, it is a reflection on whatever takes place in the classroom.

Reading courses are a form of independent work in the sense that they cover matters not covered in the classroom, or they set the student off upon an investigation of his own, relying upon the teacher for advice as to starts and stops, and counting upon his availability for conversations about the material as the student progresses. Such reading courses have an attractive plausibility about them as educational devices—and the impression is a warm and gracious one of student and teacher under a tree talking about the apple that fell on Newton's head, and proceeding thence to the Second Law of Thermodynamics, the quantum theory, the increasing relativity of human knowledge, man's groping in the modern world, woman's groping in the modern world, men and women, boys and girls, and so on until it rains, and the instructor goes home and gives the student from one to three credits. But what holds the superior student, or any other, for that matter, from spontaneously reading whatever he wants? Who holds him back from doing what ought to come naturally? Why is it necessary to give any student credit for reading the short stories of O. Henry, or the works of three exponents of existentialism, or the role of tanks in World War II? Except for graduate students who want a light patina of information about some problem for which they already have an understanding background, reading courses are not a substitute for, nor even very much of a supplement to, regular course offerings and hardly deserve extra credit.

A better procedure for enabling the superior student to do something original, creative, and comprehensive is a combined major that puts him deep into the subject matters of cognate discipline. There are some natural combinations that political science can make with economics, and with philosophy and literature. The work in two disciplines can come to a focus in a thesis that requires the skills and insights of both, such as (in a combination of political science and economics) the politics of the corporation, the formulation of tax policy, the political and economic consequences of public policy in any regulatory field like railroads, securities, air transport, and the like. The affinity of philosophy and political theory is close and constant. The political novel draws a small but steady interest among the more lettered of the brethren in political science. Combinations of political science and sociology are extremely fertile and interesting. It would, however, take a really superior student to do justice to the possibilities that such combinations would provide, and even the top students usually are content to stay with one discipline, while maintaining a polite interest in others.

But although a horizontal extension of the scope of the superior student into allied disciplines is difficult to achieve, the enrichment of his understanding in depth is possible, through certain kinds of field work. Among these is the internship in a governmental or political office. Amherst has had such a program for selected students since the end of World War II, long before it became such a fad that Washington is now viewed by thousands of students as the summertime equivalent of Fort Lauderdale, and the scepter of power has come to rival the beer can and guitar as a symbol of status.

Where the internship is regarded as an educational opportunity and not merely as a gratification of the glands—governing can be fun!—the student enters into another dimension of learning. The office cannot take the place of the classroom but it can supplement it by providing contact with events that the books write about. And from this contact there comes a kind of learning by inadvertence which supplies a context within which the more public events can be better understood. The work done by students—the superior students—in such offices, especially those on the Hill, often has value in itself. For example, the student may get to perform the research on and do the writing of a speech on disruptive competition by the Soviet Union, which his senator will give on the floor of the upper house. Or he may write a policy statement on changes in the Taft-Hartley Act which will find its way to the White House. Or the student may be taken to a national party convention where he works for his man in the Byzantine strategems of factional maneuver. Even when he merely works sixteen hours a day for a week with all the office staff in a crash program to clear the arrears of correspondence with constituents, he learns something about the political process.

There are advantages and disadvantages in small colleges for the superior student, and there are special advantages and disadvantages in the large university. In the small college there are the containments of a tight social compression, which may inhibit the public expression of intellectual interests. There is more social space in the large university, which can be hospitable to a larger number of more varied types of interest. On the other hand, the small college does usually provide for easier and more constant association at close range between teacher and student. We all have heard of the university star who was so busy that he put his lectures on tape to be run for the students during his absence in Washington. When he returned he found his tape recorder going all right, and in every student seat there was another tape recorder to receive the lecture.

Because of his accessibility in a small college, the teacher sometimes may fall into the trap of being a "pal," who exchanges professional dignity and standing for the doubtful reputation of being a "good guy." Although he regards himself as one of the boys, the boys see him only as one of the men, although somewhat underdeveloped, and captive to fickle favor. He can run around with the coaches and fling his limbs about at pep rallies, but he defaults his professional responsibility in a pathetic comedy. He will be most effective as a teacher when he remembers the distinction between the men and the boys and when he deals with the latter with both command and compassion. Where this occurs, as it does with most of the faculty, the benefits of a small college for the ordinary student as well as the superior student are enormous.

The student at a rich upper-class small college in the East, whatever the income bracket of his father, is already highly privileged, and privilege has its corruptions for the superior student. Some young men of high promise and great innate ability have been led by the excessive attention bestowed upon them, and by the notoriety of acclaim in a small integrated community, to suppose that the world is like their cell and have assumed manners ungracious and impervious. The number is not many, and the same transmogrification doubtless occurs elsewhere, but more than none is too many, and it is with sadness that the faculty views the misshapen character that hothouse security has grown. The cynical among them will feel that their profession is as useless as a life of social work among the rich, but new students are always coming along, and the discovery of fresh promise sweetens melancholy and restores zest. Happily, most superior students are pretty well adjusted or know how to cope with their tensions, and few suffer from what may be thought of as pre-Copernican personalities, grossly egocentric, in which the individual sees self as center, free from an objective and external social system with controlling laws.

The culture of the campus is sometimes like that of the penitentiary, populated by involuntary inmates, largely anonymous, clad in a uniform garb of chinos and tennis shoes, who wear numbers on their sweaters, forecasting the year of their release. But no custodial institution, college or prison, is in fact a mere table of human numbers, and within each of the uniforms is a student who wants to be seen as a person. It is perhaps easier in a small college to discover and recover the individual behind the front of masking appearances than it is in a large university, and the disclosure is a benefit to the whole community. In a small college, then, there are comforts—and stimulations—that are a function of the very contiguity that can be destructive of an occasional superior student—for the faculty it is fresh discovery, and for the student, the warmth of recognition and fulfillment.

The student with special gifts should have a setting that will encourage him to develop them, which is why the culture of the campus is significantly influential in his growth, as it is for that of all other students also. But there is a rage in the country for special programs that would isolate the superior student from his classmates, about which I have considerable skepticism. It is my feeling that any school that can control its own admissions ought not to segregate students in this way. In some big state universities, there is doubtless a case for creating a "general college" to take care of the lower half (or whatever fraction may be chosen) of the students whose levels of ability keep them from being competitive with the good ones. And for some members in the upper half of such a separation, as well as for students in colleges which can control their own admissions, I can see a case for advanced placement where college requirements have been satisfied in high school or preparatory school. If this number becomes substantially high, the increase is symptomatic of some lag in the general development of the college curriculum, which may not be keeping pace with acceleration in the high schools and other preparatory schools.

But otherwise—these exceptions aside—I do not favor the distinctions implied in a "superior student program," and I certainly deplore the establishment of special organizations to promote them, with the usual appurtenances—executive directors, associate directors, executive boards and committees, brochures, foundation funds, conferences, annual reports with tables of statistics and pictures of superior students and the wise promoters who chose them. The recent annual report of one such group shows how smart the organization was but somewhat less about how the superior students it supported fared in comparison with all the others it did not support. Thus, one out of every five supported held major student leadership positions on the campus—president of the class, editor of the undergraduate newspaper, and the like. I think it rather more significant that 80 per cent did not become campus leaders. Only two out of three of those in the top category of seeded players made honors. What happened to the other 33⅓ per cent? Even on the basis of academic ability—the criterion that made them eligible in the first place—for as many as one-third to fail to get honors indicates that the selection process itself may be faulty, or that other influences after matriculation turn the superior student from the paths predicted for him.

The eligibility of students for honors work and other such distinctions in college should not depend, it seems to me, on the basis of grade differences of students before they come to college. Once students are in college, some will do better than others, and will want to do more and somewhat different work from those who are less gifted or less ambitious. Their needs can be taken care of in programs like those already mentioned—the basis of selection, however, would be performance in college, not schools attended before college. Eligibility to do special work in college should be established by proof of ability in college to do special work.

But even when eligibility for certain forms of advanced study is established, I do not think that the superior student should be institutionally segregated from the others. To be sure, he will do some work that the other students will not do because they have not qualified. This is also true of football players and chemistry majors. But in most of their work the superior students should share the academic experiences of their classmates. The superior students have something to give to those of lesser gifts and something to learn from them. It is not a kindness to insulate those who have been pre-tested, cellophane-wrapped, and marked "bright" from the humanizing contact of common associations with fellow-students. One of the things they can learn is that brightness is not a category of the computers, but that it is a human attribute affected by elements of desire, character, and experience, and the more they can learn about other people. the better they will understand themselves. They might even learn something they did not know at all—like the celebrated physicist of a decade ago who learned about the depression back in the early thirties when somebody told him about it.

In the main, the excessive stir about special programs for superior students leaves me, as it finds me, with pulse normal and respiration steady. Although, as said earlier, the academic enterprise is more highly organized and professional than Mark Hopkins or Mr. Chips would relish, it also was said that learning is primarily a matter of teachers and students. A certain amount of structure and order is necessary in the formal organization of education, but it is all too easy to compromise the basic relationship of teacher and student with administrative pedantry—the clutter of rules, credits, controls, procedures, and special devices that overorganizes and stifles. The superior and the average student will be better served by an increase

in the number of superior teachers than by the construction of more
procedural apparatus. Since example makes abstraction more readily
recognizable, I should like to illustrate certain qualities of superiority
in both teacher and student from my own experience.

I think of three teachers I have had who, it seemed to me, had
special qualities, of mind and address, and from whom I gained
special insights. The first was Charles Pelham Curtis, Jr., a Boston
lawyer who substituted in a course in American constitutional law at
Harvard while the regular professor was on leave of absence. He
taught me that constitutional law was one of the social and human
studies, that it involved real people as well as impersonal rules of
jurisdiction and conduct, and he communicated a zest for what he
was doing that he invited the class to share. As a junior, I thought it
was wonderful that he received a post card every Christmas from a
man whom he had helped to put in the penitentiary at Atlanta. Justice
Holmes in one of his letters to Harold Laski, mentioned Curtis in a
somewhat offhand way, but his teaching, and his later writing, especially his book entitled *Lions Under the Throne,* fully justified the impression he made on students as a man of serious thought, sensitive
perception in the subtleties of the law, with gifts of style in speech and
writing and of human warmth as a teacher, who saw in his class not
an amorphous group but a company of persons.

The second was Charles H. McIlwain, in the history of political
theory, for whom Manegold of Lautenbach was as real a person as
Fiorello H. LaGuardia. It was because of his enthusiasm for the
Patristics that his students read all the volumes of Carlyle's history
of medieval political theory, and did not think themselves put upon.
Although he never got as far as the eighteenth century in the chronology of political theory, he was a masterful expositor of what went
on before, especially the constitutional controversies of seventeenth-
century England. What a beginning graduate student got from him
was a sense of scholarly craft and professional distinction, and a feeling of total commitment to study, an encouragement by example to
reach the utmost in intellectual attainment, and then to feel unsatisfied
that one's utmost was not better than it was.

The third of the professors I remember with the warmest regard
for the influence they had was Benjamin F. Wright, Jr., former president of Smith College and now professor of political science at the

University of Texas. It was not merely that he seemed to see in me virtues that were utterly invisible to anyone else, and are still largely hidden from mankind, but he supplied standards of critical judgment that could discriminate between the palpable and the immanent, that could distinguish between the solids and gasses of scholarly output, that was both antiseptic and humane. To put such a tool in the hands of a green graduate student was like putting Occam's razor in the hands of a baby; which if it sometimes cut off the head it was trying to shave, nevertheless guaranteed that the surfaces it left were free of unnecessary encumbrance.

I think of three students also who have been especially satisfactory. All of them are now teaching political science at major universities, but they all had one characteristic in common, however different their backgrounds and personalities. The common characteristic was educability. The first I had as a graduate student at the University of Minnesota in a course in administrative law. He had the expected virtues of the serious graduate student: diligence, comprehension, and curiosity, but he also yielded the impression that he was somehow absorbing what he read and heard, and making it a part of himself. There was an incorporation of the material that could have persuaded the instructor that he was actually contributing to the building of an intellectual body, providing a sustenance that was being converted by intellectual metabolism into muscle and tissue. The student was not a disciple nor a dependent; he sat at the center of his own gravity. He took what he needed and passed up the rest, and all without the neurotic anxieties about place and opportunity that make some graduates insecure.

The second was a graduate student at Harvard right after the war, a GI who had flown artillery observation planes, whose field was political theory and whose specialty was French philosophers of the anti-Enlightenment. He came to think better of empirical approaches to the study of politics than he had been brought up to believe, and developed methods of study that have pioneered the investigation of the behavior of legislative bodies. A kind of calm clarity illuminated his understanding. He not only did not need to be told twice; often he did not need to be told once—because his intelligence, like Univac, made necessary connections with electronic speed.

The third was a student at Amherst who went on to graduate

work and teaching and writing. He was a highly individualized student who resisted the social pressures of his peers and spoke his mind with great force and wit. He often was embroiled in some local controversy of less than nuclear portent, but seemed always to relish the encounter. His skill at debating was as fearsome as the swordsmanship of the man in the James Thurber cartoon who sweeps off the head of his antagonist and cries, "Touché." But he was also responsive to instruction, was encouraged to see the natural symbiosis of politics and sociology, and did an honors thesis on the political theory of the Harvard Business School which drew praise from a distinguished sociologist at Columbia University.

It may be noted that there is another characteristic besides educability among the three people described. This is the feeling that each of them received something that he wanted and could use, and has used in his subsequent career. For the relation between the instructor and the superior student is at bottom an exchange—something is offered and something is received. And it is in the transmission from one academic generation to another that the professor finds his own fulfillment—not in the platform theatricals of the classroom, not in the routines of exposition, examination, and grading, and certainly not in the play life of the students—football, dances, and the empty artificialities of student government. The fulfillment is found in the conveyance of an incorporeal hereditament, as the law books say— an intangible value which passes from heir to heir, and enriches all who possess it.

M. MARGARET BALL

Teaching women

Given the amount of public and private soul-searching which has taken place in the last few years on the subject of the education of women, it was probably inevitable that any serious discussion of the teaching of political science should concern itself, at least in passing, with the teaching of political science to women.

Two different lines of thought pertaining to the education of women have predominated in the recent past. One, with which I have little sympathy, has relatively slight bearing on the teaching of political science. According to this particular school of thought, women, marrying before or shortly after graduation, inevitably stop thinking during their first post-graduate decade because of the demands of home and family. Men, in contrast, continue to think after college, however remote their actual employment from their undergraduate training. The Q.E.D. is a demand for a kind of education for women which, presumably, will enable them better to bear what life has in store.

This line of argument overlooks a good many pertinent facts about today's women. A good share of them, far from being tied to crib and stove, are either employed or expect to be employed outside the home for some or most of their adult years. In June, 1961, for instance, there were over 25 million women in the civilian labor force of the United States; three million of them had children under six years of age. [1] In the same year, 13.3 million of the employed women of the country were wives; that is to say, 33 per cent of all married women in the United States were employed in that year.[2] We are told by the Director of the Placement Office at Wellesley, moreover,

1. U.S. Department of Labor, Women's Bureau, *Facts on Women Workers* (Washington, D. C., July, 1961), p. 2.
2. U.S. Department of Labor, *Fifteen Years After College* (Women's Bureau Bulletin 283; Washington, D.C.: U.S. Government Printing Office, 1962), p. 1.

that the majority of college women today not only expect to look for jobs upon graduation, but actually obtain them.[3] The accuracy of this statement is reflected in the fact that of the Wellesley class of 1962, and as of November, 1962, 128 members had embarked on further study; 188 were employed; 15 others wished jobs; and only 18 indicated that they did not desire employment. The activities and plans of the remaining 20 were unknown.[4] College graduates not only want but take jobs on graduation, for a longer or shorter period, whether married or single. Some, widowed or divorced, find it necessary to earn a living in later years. Others, married, feel a need to embark on activity outside the home when their children no longer require their constant care. Obviously, married women are more likely than not to withdraw from the labor market, if formerly employed, during the child-bearing years. Not all return thereafter to employment outside the home. But to base an argument for a radical change in educational patterns on the assumption that most women must stop thinking because of domestic duties for at least ten years after college is surely absurd.

Even, however, if the premise were demonstrably correct, the argument would be far from sound, insofar as it is directed at the present pattern of liberal arts education for women. It reflects serious confusion about the nature of liberal arts, as contrasted with vocational training. To criticize education in the liberal arts on the ground that it does not prepare adequately for the vocation of being a housewife is totally to misunderstand the purpose of something which is by definition non-vocational. One might as well argue that an Amherst man's major in English literature is of no use to him in selling automobiles—or in being a father, or a member of the county Republican committee—as to argue that a liberal arts education for women falls down because it does not prepare directly for the job of being a wife, mother, or member of the local community. Indeed, in Michael J. Arlen's amusing parody of some of the recent sentiments voiced by women graduates of liberal arts colleges, one George W., described as vice-president of an investment trust, laments that although an English major in college, he had not " 'even *seen* a Spenserian stanza' in seven years." His major plaint, however, is that

3. Joan Fiss Bishop, "College Women, An Increasing Force in the Labor Market," *College Placement,* XIX (Dec., 1958), No. 2, 22.
4. Memorandum from Mrs. Bishop to the author.

he feels "out of touch with things" that his wife and other women are able to discuss with ease![5]

Whatever the merits or demerits of this particular line of argument, it has little to offer us in the context of teaching political science to women except, perhaps, the thought that something else, not political science, should be taught to them instead.

The second line of thought, presented with increasing frequency in recent years—with a number of very articulate college graduates swelling the chorus—takes quite a different point of departure. Admittedly in possession of at least some leisure, these alumnae are deeply concerned because they have found it impossible to relate what they learned in college to the sort of person they either are or would like to become. Without seeking to exonerate America's institutions of higher learning wholly of responsibility for their dilemma, one is entitled to wonder how much of the problem is properly attributable to the liberal arts education to which most of them were subjected, and how much is to be laid at the door of their own inability either to adjust to their current status or to make constructive use of the leisure time which *is* available to them. One might note in passing the recent statement of a Smith alumna, author and mother of five:

I don't know what has gone wrong with life for the modern woman, but I don't think it's going to be useful to find the world at fault. I think it is a mistake to begin with the premise that domesticity provides an uncongenial atmosphere in which a woman's mind wilts and her abilities atrophy. I know it happens, but I don't know why she lets it.[6]

Nevertheless, at least some women do feel frustrated by it all. Where the frustration arises largely because an individual feels that she should not enjoy doing what she obviously does enjoy doing—such as going shopping instead of reading Sophocles, or preferring bridge to Brontë—educational institutions cannot do much for her. But where the individual wants to become something that she is not, and needs additional training to attain her goal, there is a good deal that the institutions might do—although there is not complete agreement as to either what they ought to do or how they ought to do it. Several interesting programs for "re-treading" college graduates for

5. "College Education—Is It Wasted on Men?" *Glamour*, April, 1962, p. 167.
6. Cynthia Propper Seton, "There's an Alternative to Sulking," *Smith Alumnae Quarterly*, LIV (Winter, 1963), 93.

future activity are already in existence; more may be expected to develop if the demand for this sort of assistance increases.

Whether the blame for the current dissatisfactions of certain women graduates should be attributed to the individual or to the pattern of education followed in the individual case, the existence of a group of this sort does raise some questions which may be relevant to the teaching of political science to women. Not least in importance, perhaps, is whether women whose undergraduate interests have moved them in other directions should be required to take work in political science.

Leaving aside, then, the general problem of education for women, let us move to the matter of teaching our particular discipline to women. In doing so, we are assuming the existence and legitimacy of the discipline, and we assume that it is taught to women, among others. We are not concerned here with whether something else should be taught to women in preference to political science, or whether women should go to college at all. (We have all encountered students who should never have wanted to go to college, should never have been admitted, and should terminate the experience at the earliest opportunity. But that is beside the point.) In assuming the existence and the legitimacy of the discipline, however, we are entitled to ask whether the sex of the student does, or should, make a difference in either what is taught or in the teaching method. But in attempting to find a sensible answer to this question, in a period in which neither the intelligence of women nor their interest in the state of health of the society in which they live is any longer questioned, one must make some further distinctions. The fact that some students are men, and others women, will not, by itself, get us very far.

The study of political science may be embarked upon at the undergraduate level either as a form of pre-professional training or as a part of an education in the liberal arts. At the graduate level, it tends to assume the character of professional training, undertaken because the individual wishes to enter politics, work in some capacity having to do with government agencies or policies, teach, write, or do research.

Whether male or female, persons embarking on work in political science as pre-professional or professional training have the same type of interest and similar types of goals. As employed professionals, the same demands, in terms of competence, are made on women as on men. (Indeed, the demands on woman professionals are still likely to be greater than on men, since women are still in the position of "breaking into" a field which for a great many years may have been thought of as an exclusively male area.) No one, as far as I am aware, has argued that the training of women professionals should differ from that of men. Whether the man or woman will actually reach his or her chosen goal is always somewhat uncertain. Admittedly the degree of uncertainty is greater for the woman than for the man; it is also at least to some extent less subject to her own control. But the vocational problems which the woman may encounter after the advanced degree is in hand are not generally regarded as a reason for giving her a different approach to the subject matter of the discipline. At most, they may be used as a reason for discouraging her from embarking on graduate work in political science at all. But we shall return to this point later.

It is where the undergraduate has not elected political science for professional reasons that the question arises as to whether a different approach should be developed for women than for men. On the ground that most women college graduates, tied to crib and stove for ten years after graduation, will not have time to think, Professor Barzun has argued that women should be taught in courses that "stress principles rather than facts, using the latter chiefly as illustrative instances to be fully explored, rather than as working information to be remembered in after life."[7] Many women students—and men students, too—would heartily endorse this approach, although perhaps not for Professor Barzun's reasons. Indeed, it may be true that in many undergraduate courses today there is too much emphasis on facts and too little emphasis on the conclusions to be drawn from them. There is a weakness, however, in an approach that puts information too far down the scale of values, especially, perhaps, for the young woman swamped by domestic duties. Such an approach may have a tendency to encourage the uncritical acceptance of other people's "principles" or the holding of once-valid "principles," in changed situations, as unthinking prejudices.

At the opposite pole from the school represented by Professor Barzun are those who ask whether the unutilized or inadequately

7. Jacques Barzun, *Teaching in America* (Boston, 1945), p. 250.

utilized time of women who are not fully employed either inside or outside the home, in contrast to their hard-working husbands, might not be channeled into constructive community service if either more or a different type of preparation were made available to women undergraduates. Perhaps implicit in this query is an assumption that a specialization of function is taking place (or might well take place) in modern marriage which continues to leave the primary responsibility for supporting the family to the male but permits him to transfer part of his older responsibility for the welfare of his community to his wife. However that may be, a number of thoughtful people, pointing to the valuable work done by the League of Women Voters, for example, have wondered whether colleges and universities could prepare women better for effective community service roles than they now presume to do. This raises two questions, in brief: (*1*) whether most or all women should be required to take some work in political science; (*2*) whether the work that the non-major in political science is likely to take in that department is properly geared to anticipated future need.

Although there are those who would disagree with me on this, my own inclination is not to impose a required course in political science either upon all undergraduates or upon all undergraduate women. The presumed virtues of such a course are too likely to be offset by student resistance to the requirement.

One may very properly question whether the beginning course in political science—which is the course most likely to be affected by these suggestions relating to approach—does an adequate job of fitting future voters, regardless of sex, to assume the responsibilities of citizenship. Without attempting a survey of college or university catalogues, I would hazard that most institutions regard this as one of the important tasks of the beginning course. Whether it could be better performed in some course intended for students (male or female) who do not intend to take further work in political science is at least an open question. The profession has yet to solve the perennial problem of a beginning course which seeks to serve the ends both of those intending to pursue further studies in political science and of those who do not.

Most universities would find it difficult either to segregate women from men in the beginning course or to offer a special course, open to women only, for students not intending to take additional work in the department. Having a fairly vivid imagination, I can hear the type of comment (from both men and women students) that would be made if this were attempted. Women's colleges, of course, could introduce such a course, if it were considered desirable, on a segregated basis, without the necessity of trying to develop an explanation of why the course was deemed desirable for women but not for men. Universities, on the other hand, could easily institute courses for the non-continuer on a *non*-segregated basis, using the opportunity to experiment with better training for citizenship than the beginning course may now provide in view of its usual connection with a developing major.

That one could operate along these lines seems evident, but whether one should do so is less certain. Basic training in civics is now given, reasonably satisfactorily in most areas, in the schools. I doubt whether very many political scientists are or should be interested in giving a college level civics course at the expense of the integrity of the discipline. Whether one could put together something that one would be happy to call political science and which would do a better job than existing base courses for women not anticipating a career based on a political science major, I do not know. Certainly both thought and experimentation would be appropriate. At the present writing, however, I am inclined to believe that the woman who has a firm grounding in the elements of political science has more to offer the League of Women Voters and other civic organizations than the woman who has not. Indeed, if training for community service for married women not otherwise fully employed is what is needed, one might well advise one's otherwise unfocused undergraduate women to major in political science, and to take related work in economics, psychology, and sociology. Within the political science major, the woman oriented toward community service might well be encouraged to pay special attention to state and local government, political parties and pressure groups, urban renewal, problems of metropolitan areas, and so on—although it should be remembered that the League of Women Voters is also concerned with national and international problems. A woman so trained would be a blessing to the local league in any community in which she found herself, unless, of course, she proved, as a result of her training, to be too liberal or too conservative for her particular segment of suburbia, in which case she had better turn from politics to other forms of social and community service.

I have long argued that women students would do well to acquaint themselves with the elements of state and local government on the ground that these are areas in which women, during their child-rearing years, are likely to be able to be most immediately effective. I have argued the point, indeed, with several generations of Wellesley students. But it was only this year, after we had had Professor Donald Stone at Wellesley as Murray Seasongood Good Government Lec-turer, and after we had changed the name of the course from "Public Policy in State and Local Government" to "Political Problems of Metropolitan Areas," that any marked increase in course elections was perceptible. Where the credit belongs is unclear. Professor Stone was certainly persuasive. Students had become acquainted with a new instructor. But I shall always be inclined to think that the change in title was also a contributing factor. A rose may be a rose, as Gertrude Stein somewhat repetitiously maintains, but to suggest that it might be an orchid instead sometimes enhances its sales appeal! However that may be, Wellesley students in the past have tended to be more interested in national and comparative government, inter-national organization and relations, public law and theory, than in state and local government. And it must be admitted that women have as legitimate an interest as men in the problems of war and peace, as well as in the major problems of national policy.

Assuming that what one teaches women is political science and not some watered-down version of this or that, are there peculiarities of the female mind, character, or role which suggest that they should be taught differently from men? As far as I am aware, there is no longer any controversy—or at least overt controversy—over the potential of the female mind. Certainly those of us who have taught the women who have been able to gain entrance to institutions where admission is a highly selective process have no doubt of women's ca-pacity to learn. Women in universities of this type, I am informed, tend to rank high in comparison with men students according to what-ever tests may be locally in use.

The questions which *have* been raised relate to intellectual pre-dispositions or personality factors. It has been suggested, for example, that women tend to be conscientious about doing assignments, are excellent at assimilating facts, but are less interested in theory than their male contemporaries and find it difficult to think conceptually. Although I have occasionally taught men in summer school, my own experience has been largely limited to teaching women of the highly selective group admitted to Vassar or Wellesley. I am therefore as distrustful of my own conclusions as I am of those who have less hesitation in generalizing about women. For what it may be worth, however, my experience supports some of these generalizations, denies the validity of some, and is inconclusive on others.

The women students with whom I have worked have been exceedingly conscientious, on the whole, about doing assignments and about laying the foundations upon which any rational discussion of issues or principles must rest. Some, however, have clearly shared the preference of some of the males of their generation for the "general picture" whose frequently fuzzy outlines make a mockery of any real attempt at either analysis or evaluation. Of their excellence (in comparison with men students) in assimilating facts, I am unable to judge, although I have sometimes been disappointed in the results of examinations designed to test performance in that respect. On interest in ideas, I can only contribute the fact that the courses in history of political thought, and the courses in philosophy, are among the most heavily elected at Wellesley. On the ability to conceptualize, the evidence is less tangible, and here again I lack any adequate basis of comparison with men students of similar intelligence and background. I might add that in an advanced course in problems of American foreign policy, to name but one course, Wellesley students have demonstrated both creative imagination and an ability to think logically. The only further sidelight that I can give on this matter of qualities of women, as contrasted with men students, is the comment of a man doing graduate work at Stanford conveyed to me after I had returned to the East at the end of a summer session at that university: "I never worked so hard for a B in my life!"

I strongly suspect that much of what the good student (male or female) comes out with relates not only to the conscientiousness of the student but also to the extent to which the instructor stimulates really searching and imaginative discussion—and the extent to which classes are small enough so that discussion can take place at all.

A comment frequently heard in the women's colleges, as else-where, is that women are less likely to challenge the instructor, less likely to fight for their own ideas and interpretations, less willing to "stick their necks out," than are men students. This seems to be basically true, although some women deviate from the norm. Whether this is an inherent quality of the female personality, I do not know. It has occurred to me, however, that in some of the colleges with high-ly selective admissions policies, women students tend to be too well brought up to consider it polite to challenge their elders. If so, it is perhaps a matter of class culture rather than nature of the female. Whatever the cause or causes, where this situation is found, a good instructor will make it clear that he welcomes challenge, and that he considers the classroom a more than appropriate arena for the clash of ideas. One of the best teachers of women (or men) in my experience, Louise Overacker, for many years professor of political science at Wellesley, excelled in this respect. A staunch Democrat teaching a course in political parties (among others) in which the majority of the students were generally Republicans, her students will long remember her not only for her insistence that they know the facts before presuming to interpret them, but also for the contro-versy which she encouraged in the classroom. In contrast, a poor teacher is likely simply to bemoan the passivity of women, unless he happens to be one of those characters, beloved by himself if not by his colleagues, who considers mute acceptance an appropriate tribute to his own unquestioned wisdom.

A comment which one occasionally hears from women students is that they find discussions in which men students participate a good deal more stimulating than those in which only their female classmates take part. There may or may not be some confusion about the nature of the stimulus here, but what is disturbing about this kind of statement is the failure to recognize that if any discussion is to be stimulating (in universities or out of them), much depends upon the kind of contribution which the individual members of the group, whether men or women, are prepared to make. I am inclined to think, although admittedly on the basis of no scientific evidence whatever, that there may be a connection between this attitude toward all-women discus-sions and the attitude which demands that the instructor make an effort to be stimulating and to draw his students out—the attitude that someone or something outside the individual student owes it to her to create conditions in which she may be disposed to exercise her powers to the maximum. What sometimes seems to be an excessive preoccupation with the self, and with one's own reactions, in the present generation of students—not, perhaps, entirely unrelated to the current vogue of existentialism—may well be a contributing factor. I should be interested to learn whether teachers of men encounter anything of a similar nature.

Paralleling this desire for outside stimulus and frequently coming from the same group that voices that need, one finds rebellion against the required acquisition of information in connection with formal courses and a demand for an increase in independent work—not only for the ablest students, but for all students. Rebellion against traditional methods of instruction, however, appears to be shared equally by both men and women. In part it appears to be a desire for more individual "discovery" in the learning process, but an experience of "discovery" in which one or more instructors are present to share the experience, to help guide the process, and to applaud the results. But that this is not the whole story, at least at Wellesley, is demonstrated by the existence of the WISO (Wellesley Independent Study Opportunity) program. This program, developed entirely at student initiative, has made it possible for interested students to return before the opening of college in September, live in a dormitory, and use the library for completely undirected reading or for research on any topic in which they may be interested. While the number of students participating in this program is not large—it has recently run about thirty a year—it does indicate that at least a few students are sufficiently interested in really independent work to take advantage of such an opportunity.

Women students, like men, enjoy the opportunity, when available, of relating their studies to practice. The Wellesley-Vassar Summer internship in Washington has been very popular in both institutions.

Are there any problems in teaching women other than that of a tendency to passivity, noted above? Problems that arise simply out of the fact that they are women? Some, perhaps, but not very important ones for the most part. I do remember an incident which occurred during my first year of full-time teaching, in the mid-thirties, when Professor Emerson D. Fite at Vassar rushed into Professor Mabel

Newcomer's office in a somewhat perturbed state. "A girl in the front row is wearing shorts. Please do something about it." Miss Newcomer sensibly declined, indicating that the girl was Mr. Fite's problem. What he finally did about it, if anything, I have forgotten, if I ever knew.

Women students do occasionally get into highly emotional states over the pressures of work or other demands and problems of the society in which they are endeavoring to become adults. But I am told that this is also true of men students. What the comparative figures might show, if they exist, I do not know.

Should women be taught differently from men because of their sex, or their future role in society? I raised this question casually with a number of Wellesley students after being asked to prepare this paper. A few were sufficiently intrigued by the question to ask, "How?" Most, it was apparent, considered the question to be quite unworthy of sustained attention. In no case, I admit, did I pursue the matter sufficiently to get any real discussion either of why the question might be raised or possibly approaches which might be designed especially for women students. But these students, it was obvious, were not anticipating any sort of living intellectual death in connection with the marriages which most of them, I assume, expect to contract. I might add that their lack of interest in this question should not be taken as a passive attitude toward their whole learning experience at Wellesley. In other contexts, it is more than evident that the students at Wellesley (or some of them, at any rate) are critical of teaching methods in various courses and disciplines. But their basis of criticism has nothing to do with a consciousness of their sex or of the kind of life they hope or expect to live after college. They were and are concerned as students, but not as *women* students.

Active or passive, critical or quiescent, good women students may be a joy to teach. They actually read a good share of what one asks them to, as a basis for class discussion, and have little or no difficulty either in assimilating data or in generalizing on the basis of evidence. At least at Wellesley they are not intimidated by documents or other source materials and accept as routine that they should be as familiar with these materials in their sophomore or junior years as some universities expect them to be at the end of the first or second year of graduate study. (Lest I draw too rosy a picture, I should concede that not all students are equally proficient at these things; after all, they are women, not angels—ministering or otherwise.) One should not intimate, of course, that these qualities are possessed only by women students. They result in part from, and are conditioned by, the existence of small classes, the presence of good library facilities and of librarians who believe that books and documents are to be used rather than preserved, the local level of expectation in respect to student performance (whether student or faculty), and, above all, by the availability of instructors who believe that while research is important, their main job is to teach.

Who should teach political science to women, assuming that women are taught apart from men? The only possible answer, in my estimation, is, people in full command of the subject matter of their respective areas, who know how to teach, and who do not look down on women as students. Practical experience in government is an asset in teaching women as it is in teaching men, but not, obviously, a requirement.

In short, the person who is a good teacher of anybody is a good teacher of women, provided that, if male, he does not suffer from any form of arrogance which prevents him from devoting the time or attention to the teaching of women that any student, male or female, has a right to expect—or which tinges his lectures or handling of class discussion with a condescension which, immediately felt by any perceptive student, impedes the learning process. If good teaching involves the sharing by teacher and student of the excitement of learning, as I think it does, neither arrogance nor condescension has any place in it, whether the students be men or women. The arrogant teacher can be learned from, of course, but the experience is not only likely to be an unpleasant one; it may also serve to discourage further inroads by the student into the discipline. A good teacher of women (or men) does not *have* to be exciting, provided that the students have a will to learn and the instructor knows his field, but it helps. And the professor who yawns at his own lecture (as I once got caught doing), is justly subject to criticism.

Does all this mean that a beginning teacher, or an experienced teacher undertaking to give a course in what for him is a new field, should never try to teach women? Of course not. Women may occasionally knit in class if the practice is not frowned on by the instructor, but I have never known one to attack an instructor with a knitting needle. What every good teacher knows, and every beginning teacher should be told, is never to bluff with either men or women students. The bluff, if called, deprives the instructor of the respect of his students for the duration of their contact with him. But students more often than not will happily go along with the instructor who says, in effect, "This is a new area for me. I know something about it, but not as much as I should like to. If you want to stay while we all learn more about it, fine; if not, you would be well advised to withdraw now." I have never had a student withdraw for this reason—at least not that I know about. But women may be more tactful than men!

I have indicated above one type of man who ought not to teach women—the man who looks down on women as students. Another type who ought not to teach women is the kind of man who can never forget that his students are women. The reason for this is obvious. Sex is a fine thing, but it does not belong in the classroom, or in the relation between faculty member and student.

A third type of person who ought not to teach women is the man who craves adulation, especially from the opposite sex. The reason here is also obvious, but different. Probably the major occupational hazard of the teacher (man or woman) is that of developing what I have sometimes called the "god-complex." I refer here to the danger of coming to regard oneself as infallible because one is always teacher in the relation between the teacher and the taught; because one is insufficiently challenged by one's peers. Women students are perhaps more prone to admire an able teacher—or to give some expression to that admiration—than are men students. And such evident admiration can have a very bad effect upon the instructor who lacks either a sense of humor—or a wife—to puncture excessive self-satisfaction before he is overcome by it.

Apart from these points, it does not matter in the slightest whether the people who teach women are men or women. Women students learn equally well from both and can be equally bored by either. It is the quality of the person and his capacity as teacher that is important, not the sex of the instructor. Most women's colleges, incidentally, employ a fair number of men on their instructional staffs—not, I think, from any desire to balance the sexes, but rather because they operate on the perhaps peculiar policy of trying to find the most fully qualified person for the job, regardless of sex, when openings occur.

Do women students share the foregoing view that it does not matter whether their instructors are men or women? Or do they prefer to be taught by men? Or by women? Student registration in courses at Wellesley would tend to substantiate the position that it does not really matter. While the evidence at hand cannot be evaluated scientifically since students rarely, if ever, have the possibility of totally free choice between identical courses taught by men and by women, and since other factors also clearly play a part in the choices made, it suggests that the subject matter and the quality of the instructor are the most important elements. Some women students, however, clearly do enjoy taking courses with young men who are willing to discuss the subject matter with them at length outside of class. But even in these cases it may well be the closeness of the generations and the instructors' willingness to devote time to them, rather than the instructor's sex, which is determining. And some of the most popular courses are taught by older men and women.

In the estimation of some of their instructors, women students, like men students, sometimes prefer the "exciting" instructor to an instructor whom, better versed in his field, they may consider dull. But poor judgment is not a monopoly of women students. And in general, women students appear to be just as astute as men students in assessing the quality of potential instructors.

Perhaps a word about teaching in a woman's college is in order here. Because of their small size, in comparison with most universities, the women's colleges are generally unable to offer the number and variety of courses in political science to be found in the larger universities. This means, obviously, that the individual who teaches political science in a woman's college must be master of more than a minor segment of the discipline. He must be competent in the material covered in the beginning course as well as in at least two of the fields in which political science is generally divided for Ph.D. examination purposes. The individual who is so highly specialized that he is competent to teach only in the area of the legislative process in the United States, for example, is of limited use to most women's college departments of political science. The same is true of the area specialist who knows little about anything but Asia or Africa.

Most of the women's colleges, I believe, have the practice of virtually requiring that all members of the staff participate in the teaching of the beginning course. They consider this course much too important to be entrusted largely or entirely to inexperienced instructors. One pleasant result of this attitude, from the standpoint of young instructors, is that the latter may well have more of an opportunity in a woman's college than they would in a university to teach advanced courses in their fields of primary interest. The young instructor is not likely to find, in short, that all of the interesting advanced work has been pre-empted by tenure members of the staff.

On the other hand, the individual who wants to do nothing other than teach in a very narrow field of specialization would do well to avoid the women's colleges, or indeed any small college. If, however, he is willing to view his specialization as something that fits into a larger whole, and if his paramount desire is to teach rather than to devote most of his time to research or to the direction of graduate students, the woman's college has a great deal to offer. In these colleges the student load is small enough to permit frequent contact with students outside as well as inside the classroom, and the modest proportions of the social round permit the individual to whom research is also important to get on with it. College libraries are not meant to compete in numbers of volumes with those of the large universities, yet their resources are frequently impressive. The interlibrary loan may easily supplement local resources, moreover, and the absence of pressure to teach in summer school permits the instructor, at his own desire, to tap the resources of university libraries during the summer months.

But to return to the woman student. Should she be encouraged to do graduate work in political science or not? Or should one encourage only the ugly ones (if any) on the assumption that their matrimonial prospects are poor, while discouraging the pretty ones in the conviction that graduate work for such as they is bound to be a waste of everybody's time?

There was a dearth of women candidates for college teaching positions throughout much of the 1940's and 1950's which suggests that either young women had lost interest in teaching political science or that the graduate schools were discouraging women students from working in political science, or both. A recent study by John B. Parrish notes the increase in participation of women in the doctoral programs of American institutions of higher learning between 1900 and 1930, reaching a peak for all fields in 1932 of 16.8 per cent. This was followed, he found, by a marked across-the-board decline in the ensuing thirty years. After analyzing the decline, he concludes that it was very largely attributable to "a voluntary shift in preferences" related to a changing pattern of marriage and family planning.[8] Whether the reported decline has been arrested, or conceivably reversed, in the 1960's, it is too soon to say. My impression is that good women candidates for teaching positions are again becoming available (if perhaps in lesser numbers than in the 1930's). I also find it heartening that eight members of Wellesley's class of 1962 have embarked upon graduate work in political science, in addition to the roughly comparable numbers of members of recent earlier classes which have moved in the same direction. Given the present pattern of early marriage, however, from which these students are not exempt, it seems likely that the completion of the doctor's degree—if indeed it is completed—will in most cases be accompanied by matrimony. It also seems likely that if the professional talents of these women are to be used, prospective employers will have to accept them as the married women that they are or will become. As one of my colleagues put it several years ago, "The day of the dedicated old maid is over." Women seriously interested in professional careers no longer feel it incumbent upon themselves to eschew matrimony for career reasons. Nor, in our present affluent society, will many highly trained married professional women find it essential to work for economic reasons. If the reserve of talent which they represent is to be made fully available, we shall have to come to terms with the married woman to an extent which society has not yet sought to do.

Quite apart from what women trained in political science as undergraduates may aspire to by way of graduate work, whether they should be encouraged to embark upon it in the field of political science depends to a considerable extent, one would assume, on employment opportunities for holders of advanced degrees. The fields

8. "Professional Womanpower as a National Resource," *Quarterly Review of Economics and Business,* I (Feb., 1961), 55-59.

theoretically open to women are numerous, and include college and secondary school teaching, government, work with private organizations, writing or editorial work, and research—among others. The extent of the real opportunities in these areas depends, however, on the willingness of those making appointments to select candidates on their merits instead of on the assumption that women are necessarily poor long-term employment bets and are therefore to be avoided.

In the teaching field, women have found little difficulty in securing appointments as teachers of social studies in the secondary schools. In the women's colleges, in recent years, there have been more openings for competent women than there have been women to fill the posts. In the universities, opportunities for women have improved, but appear still to be not as good as in the women's colleges. Some universities, including Duke, have welcomed women to their departments of political science. In a number of other universities, one suspects that it simply does not occur to appointing officers that a woman might be designated. The chairman of the appointing department writes to the chairmen of departments in other universities, as he has always done, in terms of "We have an opening for a man to teach. . . ." The party of the second part interprets this literally, and in accordance with time-honored practice, overlooks his better women graduate students in making his recommendations. Of course if the inquiry stems from a department in a woman's college, the party of the second part will bring out his women graduate students for inspection, very often failing to note that he has equally qualified, or better qualified, men to dispose of. I have sometimes wondered what would happen to the profession if appointments to the universities and the women's colleges were made wholly without reference to sex. On the whole, it seems unlikely that the heavens would fall!

We all know that women political scientists sometimes marry, and that having done so, they sometimes have children. We also know that babies sometimes arrive at times which are not altogether convenient for employers. If we really thought about the matter, we would concede that this phenomenon can cause as much inconvenience to a women's college as to a university. On the other hand, a number of women professors have managed to raise fair-sized families without strain on their departments. (One young friend of mine has had four children without in any way burdening her department;

indeed, the sum total of her absences from class was substantially smaller than those of a young man in another department who fell victim of pneumonia.) What I am arguing here is that women who are intelligent enough to secure advanced degrees are frequently also bright enough, and responsible enough, to manage their personal lives in such a way as to meet their professional obligations without trading on the good nature of their male (or old maid) colleagues. This is perhaps an individual matter. My plea, if any, is that departments view it as such, rather than in terms of what any married woman colleague (or woman colleague who might someday commit matrimony) would inevitably be expected to let the department in for.

While I am on this particular tangent, perhaps I might be allowed a word to those women who have professional aspirations—particularly in teaching. Any political scientist who happens to be a woman, if she is not a fool, will keep the chip off her shoulder. Nothing is more boring, or harder to live with professionally, than the woman who fancies—especially out loud—that every time that she fails to receive what she considers her due, it is because of her sex. True or not, and it often is not, it can be deadly. What is more, any woman who is reasonably intelligent and has a sense of humor is likely to discover after a few years that she is being included in gatherings to which her professional merits might not entitle her—simply because in our supposedly egalitarian society, there must be at least one woman on the board, or committee, or platform, and that she is regarded as the least objectionable woman available. Some of the opportunities thus gained, in brief, make up for some of the opportunities lost on other counts. One further point: women who have really serious professional interests should learn (if it is not ingrained) to be "gentlemen" in their professional lives; the professional scope for women who insist on trading on their femininity is slight.

Outside of college teaching, the picture for women trained in political science, and holding advanced degrees, is reasonably bright. Offhand, I should say that there is no reason to discourage able women from doing graduate work on the ground that they are likely to be unemployable after the degree is obtained. They may find it more difficult than men of comparable ability to find congenial employment, but opportunities are there.

What happens to women trained in political science as graduate or undergraduates after their training has been completed? As far as I know, there are no nation-wide figures which would give useful information on this point, although I may be in error here. I do happen to know that of young women receiving B.A.'s in political science from Wellesley in the last twenty-five years a number have gone into the teaching of social studies in the secondary schools; a number have gone into editorial or allied jobs (one is editor of *Current History* in a period in which that periodical is doing a more useful job than ever before, and two are working for the Carnegie Endowment for International Peace in getting out *International Conciliation*); some have gone into newspaper work or write for the "slicks"; a number have taken jobs in government at various levels; some have found jobs with the United Nations or the specialized agencies; and a great many are active in PTA's and the League of Women Voters. Still others, of course, are doing work utterly unrelated to their undergraduate studies, if indeed they are employed.

Of Wellesley women who have done graduate work in political science in recent years, two (both married) are currently teaching at Wellesley; two others have done so in the past; one is working with one of the European communities; others are preparing for college teaching. One student who followed her B.A. with an LL.B., having worked for the Massachusetts Attorney General for a period, is now doing research under the auspices of the Russell Sage Foundation. (This one has three children and reads papers for me in her spare time.)

I do not offer the foregoing hit or miss picture of what some women who have studied political science at Wellesley have done as indicating that these women are superior to others (every institution of standing which has trained women in political science could equal or improve on my list). Nor do I present it as an exhaustive indication of what Wellesley women have done or are doing. I offer it simply as suggestive of the fact that in women so trained there is a reserve of ability and talent upon which society can draw in its own interest provided that it will open the door more widely to talent, even if female, and keep it open.

Should women be taught political science? Of course. But not because of any spurious specialization of function which divides the human race into those who support the family (men) and those who are responsible not only for the rearing of children but also for the preservation of the nation's culture and the welfare of the local community (women). In our changing society, responsibility for all of these things must be shared, in varying degrees, by both men and women.

Should women be required to take political science? I doubt it, and certainly not if I am the one who might be required to teach it. I cannot imagine a worse fate, personally, than having to teach a course that people take because they have to.

Within what framework should women be taught political science? In the first instance, I should say, within the framework of a liberal arts curriculum. If I may quote from the 1950 inaugural address of Dr. Margaret Clapp, President of Wellesley:

Liberal arts education is a discipline—intellectual, moral, spiritual—which should enable the intelligent man or woman to make the best of any of the environments into which circumstances throw human beings. We cannot tell whether our college graduate will become a housekeeper and/or schoolteacher, scientist, or artist. We do not know whether she will live in the East 60s, a Wyoming ranch-house, a Polynesian mission station, or an ECA office in Paris. We cannot foresee the emergencies she will face. We cannot promise her wealth or even a good income. But we can give her a liberal education; we can equip her with the power to think, which is the handle to which any skill can be fitted as a tool. We can provide her with spiritual riches. Granted that the liberal arts have little specific vocational or so-called practical value for a wife and mother, or for a husband and father. They do have value for the whole life of each one of them and they do have value for society.

JOHN M. GAUS

Practical experience: a memoir

Mirabeau is reported to have said during the French Revolution, "A testament. What is a testament? It is the will of a man who has no longer any will, with regard to property which is no longer his property" (quoted by Lord Shaw, in his *Letters to Isabel,* New York, 1922). A retired teacher, invited to discuss his experience as a teacher in such a way as to be "informative, provocative, and inspirational," may, after the moment of elation at the flattery of the invitation, turn mournfully to the application of Mirabeau's remark to his own situation. His listeners or readers may well say that his classroom strategy and tactics no longer exist, as his classroom has vanished and can have no existence in the classroom of another, in another time and place. And be it remembered that it is not only in the classroom, but the study or office, or at a casual meeting at the cafeteria or in the corridor, that teaching is done. How often when one sees a former student years later does he remark, "I remember something you said"—and he gives some statement that you rack your mind in the effort to recall, but which somehow has lingered on in his mind and been given importance there! So at the start of this effort at appraising some aspects of many years of teaching political science I must warn that I shall be dealing with very elusive and subjective things.

Yet the fact that this book has been gathered suggests that its contributors accept also the view that some of this experience of each of us is capable of being examined by others in exchange for their experience, and from it all some experience may be made useful to others. In my experience, most college teachers are, at least on the surface, skeptical of this. They sniff out quickly a threat of the invasion of formal courses in preparation for college teaching. Even a personal and unorganized interest such as I have enjoyed in the

memoirs of college teachers, or the reading of the history of college
education such as Rashdall's history of the medieval universities or
the great flow of histories of particular American colleges and universities that have come with the centennial celebrations, is perhaps
not widely shared. I have not found many kindred spirits among
my colleagues anywhere with which to discuss this dubious interest.
But there may be some who have discovered in such writings that
they have allies over the centuries and in the creators of their present
institutions who, being dead, can yet speak to them, encourage them
of a Sunday evening before they plunge into the hard tasks of Monday morning. You will recall how Sir William Osler would write to
his former students, some of whom might be struggling with the
burdens of a country practice in a remote prairie village, to read not
only the books and journals relevant to the immediate problems of
practice but those of the pioneers and discoverers. On my humbler
level I have found such correspondence one of the great satisfactions
of teaching, and I am grateful that this continues.

What is our job as political scientists? While I will attempt
to answer this for one political scientist—myself—by giving some
sampling of my work from episodes in my experience, I will first and
briefly place that work, as I see it, among the tasks which have
evolved in society generally and in our country in particular. I think
we are called to analyze and interpret the needs of all of us for
government beyond that of the family and more intimate face-to-face
groups. Forces beyond the home, beyond "the fences of the farm"
or the shop or the store or the "firm," may be harmful or limiting to
the desired and legitimate desires and hopes of these basic groups
that constitute mankind. Among such threats are physical disorder
and unjust conduct; the catastrophes of war, famine, disease, mass
unemployment, fire, flood, or drought; the more subtle consequences
of change, unanticipated and unprovided for, from the application
of new knowledge and ideas to our physical and social arrangements.
To counter-coerce these coercions, to guide change into the least
destructive and most useful channels, we need some general agreements as to the ends we desire to achieve, honest and competent
agents to act for us (for remember, we are beyond the face-to-face
participation of the family circle or the shop or the farm), and procedures to be followed, "due process," if you will, in legislature and

court and administration, which will best achieve the public house-keeping with least suppression of the legislation, adjudication, and administration that goes on hourly in the face-to-face life of the private household, farm, or firm. The costs of these coercions of change may be heavy—as with those we of today witness in transportation, population growth, and distribution, the relations among national states, automation, the quantity and quality of water supplies. And they affect different people so differently that in any effort to deal with them controversies arise, thus adding new coercions in the resulting conflicts of ideas and "isms" and the physical instruments of destruction invented to be used in them.

To serve people by helping them to understand these threats to their private lives or the equal possibilities of enrichment, personal growth, and development, and protection from catastrophe is both a necessary and dangerous task. Every resource of history for knowledge of origins and past experience, of literature with its insights into humanity, of economic and social diagnosis, of individual and social psychology, and of the way social theories get formulated, becomes a part of our life work. But our focus in our own job is upon our particular sector of what I like to term the public house-keeping, the supplement to and framework of the efforts of us all as persons and members of families and other face-to-face groups to help anticipate the consequences of the coercions that press upon us. In very general and abstract terms this is my idea of my job as a political scientist. In what follows I have tried to illustrate the teaching of this, as well as what I have learned about it from others and from my own experience in various institutions and courses and programs. And from the discussions of other participants in this book I have learned things that I wish I could have put to use in these experiences long ago.

We are rocked, gently or violently, by this ebb and flow of coercion and counter-coercion. John Dewey, in his *The Public and Its Problems,* discusses this agitation in terms of what is private and what is public that requires diagnosis if we are to see what leads people to use government. I have found this a book valuable in teaching political science, especially when the student is sent to the newspaper and to direct observation in a place familiar to him of these forces at work. He can be aided to identify what Felix Frankfurter (in his

The Public and Its Government) called "the raw materials of politics."
He is then the better oriented and equipped to turn to the question
of whether and in what way, with what procedures calculated to
invite fairness and integrity, public policy and the devices of government may be needed to protect and facilitate the lives of individuals,
families, and corporate enterprises and associations.

I perhaps bore you with this elementary statement of my conception and approach to government. But it affected—I hope controlled—my teaching experience within the limits of my ability and
knowledge and personality. Such a conception of the relation of
change to people in a place, with consequences for good or ill, requiring diagnosis by them of generally obscure and complex problems, and the initiation or selection of reasonable adequate policies
and competent agents to refine and apply them, to me, made the
job of teacher important. I was paid to collect and clarify data,
select and interpret it, but also to stimulate my students to do this.
I was older than they, and presumably with more experience in and
knowledge for the enterprise; but they could have, or could be encouraged to have, some observations of what goes on in their own
area of experience in family and neighborhood. We were thus engaged in something of a joint enterprise, but one in which I had a
major responsibility for its success in better equipping them to
diagnose the political aspects of life.

It is no wonder, then, that before I entered my classroom I had
some serious moments with myself—if I could keep some time, even
if a very little, free to consider how best to use the coming meeting
to perform my task as I have sketched it so briefly. In meeting a
class at the beginning of a year, semester, or term, I have sometimes
said that we would be meeting together such a number of hours.
How could we make best use of that time together? What part of
our materials could best be presented, discussed, supported by
selected illustration, and supplemented by the individual conference
and papers and examinations? I usually announced that my wife and
I would welcome them at our home Saturdays at four for coffee and
cookies—or at other times that might be mutually arranged. Sometimes I then have brought off the shelves some books, such as an
early edition or an item of particular relevance to our discussions,
and have indicated that browsing in a secondhand bookstore has

dividends beyond the pecuniary, or in defiance of it. A good bookstore with both new and secondhand stock, is more valuable to a college than most departments.

I have usually scheduled some open office hours at various days and hours through the week to make it reasonably possible for any student to come in, and I all but enforced some individual conferences by inviting a conference on written work assigned early in the course and withholding information on the grade until such a meeting. My aim in such conferences was to raise points that seemed to me to indicate a good job and to indicate weakness and how one might do a better job. I found students grateful for having their papers read and a chance given to discuss them instead of having them disappear into the mystery of grading at the end of the course with no conveyance of the teacher's opinion and advice. Where the number of students was so large that I had the help of a reader or teaching assistant, I would arrange the written work so that I would read something from every student as well as papers which the reader felt I should read for their special quality or because in some way he was uncertain of the paper.

Particularly with larger classes, but also with seminars generally, I used mimeographed materials. With the seminars these materials were the agenda for the meeting, plus a reference to new books or articles, new reports on current developments, and quotations to help point up and make relevant the seminar discussion. Often a memorandum would include newspaper items that indicated contradictions to positions taken generally in the community or in the class. For such materials and other provocative items I drew much upon the urban communities in which I was living or the village and my native region in which in later years I lived in summer and now live. This village is in the high hills of upstate New York, in farm and forest country. One sees at first hand the problems of water supply, sewage disposal, location of paved roads, changing land use, school districting, financing of the old and newer public services, and the integrating of the policies of local, state, regional, and national levels of government—even international, as in the distribution of power from Niagara and the St. Lawrence Seaway.

The full impact of the changes in the distribution of people by age, place, and employment is upon us in this country. And all this is occurring in a population drawn from every corner of the earth, every color, every creed, every nationality, even many tribes in a pre-national stage. There is also the intermingling of people on farms and in villages, of city and suburban people who have moved out to villages or open country and commute to their city jobs, and rural people who are employed in cities. Here are the raw materials of politics and political science, and it is possible to make students aware of them by the weekly newspaper account, for example, of a fight over the school budget with its grants from the state for special purposes, or from the federal government for the "impacted areas"— meaningful term—when such impact brings new population of a race or creed different from the older mixture in the community.

In this highly subjective and personal but quite unoriginal effort to initiate students into their life-long education and career in citizenship, two specific devices have given me particular pleasure and profit. For example, in a course in American institutions at Harvard, I asked for papers in which the students would appraise the extent to which De Tocqueville, Henry Adams, James Bryce, and Frederick Turner threw light and gave meaning to the story of their family's life in this country. An interesting by-product of this assignment was that often members of the family, challenged by the student's questions, would themselves help to make the inquiry a means of bridging the chasm between generations, loyalties, and outlook upon life. The other device I hit upon from reading, some twenty-two years ago, the novel *Storm,* by George R. Stewart, in which the hero is a storm that develops in the Pacific, strikes the West Coast, and challenges all sorts of people and institutions to anticipate and attempt to meet its consequences—the weather bureau, power and telephone companies, the highway department, the Sacramento Valley flood control administrator, farmers, department stores. Here were portrayed people confronted with the coercions of catastrophe and acting to counter-coerce through various agencies and agents. I assigned it as required reading after the discussion of regular reading of the course had been completed, on the eve of the post-Christmas examination period, with the announcement that a required question on it would be included on the final examination. I asked, as part of that question, that they relate various episodes in the book to aspects of public administration we had discussed in the course, such as the discretionary powers of the weather bureau and other officials or the extent to which education and training could anticipate the problems on the job.

Finally I asked them whether the assignment should be retained, and if so whether the book should be read early in the course and discussed in the classroom or left to be read at the end of all class meetings. The replies on the examination have invariably been for retention with perhaps two negatives out of several hundred students who have registered their views. A very large majority have voted in favor of leaving the reading to the end, although a small number have expressed the wish that it might be read early and discussed in the classroom. Many students have written in answer, or told me, "Reading this novel showed me for the first time what this course was all about!" But here is a queer aspect of the teaching experience. More than once this book was read and the subsequent examination written in January days when the press and radio were reporting heavy snow storms in the Sierras, the blockage of the highways through the passes, and at least twice the snowing in of the crack transcontinental trains. Yet this telling example of how nature copies art, as Oscar Wilde once said, almost never was drawn upon in student answers, in spite of the effective use of such episodes by Stewart in his novel to illustrate the challenge of catastrophe to highway and railroad crews. This is a chastening experience to a teacher —it cuts him down to size, and shows him that at the very points at which he feels his methods and materials have been effective in stirring the student to weave the academic into the personal, and both into the life of the nation, he sees them kept separate—or rather, only one has been noted, perhaps because the pressure of preparing for an examination does not permit the mind to wander from the printed page.

I have also used some form of regional study by the student of his home region. I did this first as a young instructor at Amherst in the freshman course in social and economic institutions, a good deal influenced by boyhood interest in my home region, by experience in a settlement house in which there was emphasis upon the city neighborhood as a society, and where I became acquainted with the ideas about regions of Patrick Geddes of Edinburgh, and by the experience of studying under Frederick Jackson Turner. His studies and ideas of sections in American history—the interplay of people of varied origins, in various physical environments as one of the clues to political and other cultural expressions—stimulated my teaching and fed my feelings for my country and its landscapes and cityscapes. I thought that if one could send a student to looking at what he might conceive to be his native region and asking him how it had come into being, and whether it had some character expressed in literature or the arts, or some peculiarities of political or economic policy, he might get more insight into the more general views to be derived from texts and other class reading. When I went from Amherst to Minnesota, residence in the twin cities, colleagues and programs of the university, some travels in the hinterland fed and confirmed this interest. I could see the point of Turner's reference to the view of the Italian scholar Loria that to understand the earlier nation-building in Europe one must go to the new lands where the process was now under way. At Wisconsin I used the regional study on the captive sophomore class of the Experimental College, each member of which was required to submit a regional study, preparation of which began at the closing of the first year, devoted to a study of fifth-century Athens, and extended through the second year; and I later used it in our American civilization major there that cross-sected departments in the junior-senior years. I returned to a modification of this device in a course in the general education program at Harvard to which I have referred ("Some Interpretations of American Institutions") in which the general readings I already have mentioned (De Tocqueville, Bryce, Turner, Adams, and Myrdal) were supplemented briefly at the end by readings from a list of books about various regions from which each student could make appropriate selections.

My appraisal of this experience is that the most important means of teaching, so far as the courses and programs I have mentioned here are concerned, are reading and writing. You must help the student to read carefully the material you have selected for your joint enterprise and to write clearly about it. I would include in reading, not only books, but also the landscape. Every advance in student status calls for a step up in the quality of reading and writing.

I think that for some of my courses, those relating particularly to the United States, I should have focused the work more sharply on the Constitution as a continuing expression, through selected relevant cases, of national ideas in action, determined for the time being in a concrete and practical way in legislative and administrative measures and written decisions of the Supreme Court. It was only late in my teaching that I came to realize such a use of the Constitution, partly because of the appraisal of the work in the second year of the Experimental College, that on nineteenth-century America, by Alexander Meiklejohn, chairman of the college, and partly because I began to see how the logic and trend of my teaching in certain of my courses pointed to it. In the decisions of the court, the particular event or episode is related to principles that have been given a special and superior status in the Constitution. To orient the varied materials in a course to this fundamental fact of our government may help to prevent diffusion of content and stimulate in the student a sense of personal and civic responsibility.

During the period of my teaching there has been a good deal of study of and experiment with introductory courses drawing upon content and personnel from various departments of a general group such as the social studies, sciences, and humanities. In part these "introductory" or "orientation" courses were a reaction against the rise of specialization by departments that in turn had been a reaction against the older comprehensive courses such as moral and natural philosophy. In part, also, there was concern that larger numbers of students were coming to college who did not have a professional objective in mind and not much notion of what a college was about. It was thought that a sharper challenge than the traditional course designed to lead the student into advanced departmental work might be attempted. An early example was the freshman course in social and economic institutions, first given at Amherst in 1915-1916 by Professor Gettell, a political scientist, and Walton Hamilton, an economist. I think it was in the next year that the deservedly famous course in contemporary civilization, also I think for freshmen, was begun at Columbia College. At about this time President Lowell was getting a program of divisional organization, distribution of programs beyond the field of concentration, and tutorial work for selected students under way at Harvard. I had a brief taste of the work of tutor at Harvard while a graduate student there in 1919-1920, and during the next three years was an instructor on the staff of the Amherst course while also teaching courses in political science. I remember well a stimulating day we of the staff had with John Coss, the head of the Columbia program. From 1923 to 1927 I participated in the development and teaching of the orientation course for freshmen at the University of Minnesota while a member of the department of political science there. This was a course of two terms, assigned respectively to man in nature and man in society. We of the staff were drawn from several departments—botany, philosophy, political science, psychology—and we each taught our sections through the entire two terms and thus were working hard to keep up with our students in fields unfamiliar to us. At the Experimental College at the University of Wisconsin, a semi-autonomous unit within the College of Letters and Science given the privilege and challenge of trying out content and method, integration was in part sought through the focus upon a period and "civilization" in each of the two years. The student lived in two quadrangles of a new dormitory group, and the staff of advisers had offices in a wing of these quadrangles. There was strong emphasis on the relation of the adviser (faculty member) and his advisees, especially in the criticism of the weekly student paper. There are aspects of this program akin to that at Bennington College, with whose history I have had the privilege of being acquainted in the planning stage and later as a trustee. The Harvard general education program, instituted at the end of World War II and now under review by a faculty committee, is in some ways a reflection modified by place and time of earlier movements there and elsewhere.

I have mentioned these experiments because political science has been and will continue to be a participant in such efforts since political scientists are not only members of departments but of divisions and college and university faculties. All such experiments are controversial, but a brief general review of them is relevant to my appraisal of my own experience.

First, each experiment is deeply influenced by the peculiarities of the institution in which it takes place and the situation there at the time it takes place, at least as much as by the general intellectual influences among the universities and those interested in higher education at the time. Thus the orientation course at Minnesota cannot be understood unless one knows something of the philosophy of the late Dean John B. Johnston. Bennington College was initiated in large measure by an unusual group of thoughtful parents concerned for the kind of higher education, especially in the East, available to young women and who sought professional advice. That Robert Leigh (I may point out that he was a political scientist!) was Bennington's first president has meant that it is a different institution than if he had not been. That a new—and first—group of dormitories for men was just being opened at the University of Wisconsin at the time of the proposal for an experimental college at the University of Wisconsin under the chairmanship of Dr. Mieklejohn recently invited to a professorship of philosophy there by the new president, Glenn Frank, affected the life of the college. And it follows that the diffusion of ideas from one of such projects throughout the academic world is possible insofar as it rests upon general educational concerns of the time and the unpredictable chances of personality and the whims of communication, yet is rarely or never brought to snug harbor in any particular institution. The honors-tutorial system of Harvard or Swarthmore is not that of their model in Oxford. To borrow is to guarantee risks for the better or the worse.

Yet the risks may better be run, if there is a strong indigenous desire by an informed and thoughtful local group that some new measures should be undertaken. Here an experimental and limited new program may avoid wholesale expensive change and massive resistance by the persons who are relatively satisfied and entrenched. I think that a major value of experiments, if they are permissive and semi-autonomous, is that they make growth possible even when an opposition will cite the additional cost financially and in terms of their recruitment of some of the more lively and pioneering members, generally younger, in the "establishment" departments and colleges. Ironically, a real cost comes when the program established to loosen and ventilate an existing educational institution and its policies, and to get around some crucial course and its ruler that have become a liability, becomes itself rigid and conventional. Few institutions have done as I understand Columbia College has decided to do—drop a famous experimental course because the conditions which brought it into being are no longer present. But in general, again, and in specific examples with which I have had some experience, such experiments are therapeutic and limit somewhat the power of vested but out-of-date programs and persons.

If you are thinking that this discussion has led us away from the teaching of political science, I may remind you that it was a political scientist, Charles Merriam, who had a major part in the founding and development of the Social Science Research Council, which reflected on its level the same groping in the 1920's for collaboration across existing department lines and a recognition of the need for an encouragement of new content and method. And I was interested to note in the essay entitled "The Current Meaning of Behavioralism" that its author, David Easton, views this search for "integration of the disciplines," and "the idea that the understanding of man in society would be immeasureably enriched if some way could be found to draw the social sciences together in a basic unity," as one of the major currents of thought and action that has created the behavioral sciences. The development of political science, like government itself, is "an endless adventure."

We have a good tradition among political scientists for pioneering not only within the central substance of our subject but also in collaboration with our neighbor colleagues. The remarkable group who eighty years ago created the school of political science at Columbia University included John Burgess, one of the first to give courses in political science. The group also contained historians, economists, sociologists, and philosophers and was to influence greatly the work in these fields throughout the United States. These men founded the *Political Science Quarterly,* whose services have been and continue to be so important to us all. The prestige of the school drew graduate students from all over the country. The fact that several of its members, for example, Burgess, Clark the economist, Osgood the historian, and Mayo-Smith the sociologist and statistician, had been students at Amherst at a time when Julius Hawley Seelye was professor of philosophy and later president has been noted by them and others as significant. Seelye's teachings were not only in his classroom but in his fostering of what was then called the "Amherst Plan" of student self-government. And President Seelye played an influential part in public affairs in the Commonwealth and as a member of Congress to which he was elected as an Independent in a period of bitter partisanship.

The influence at the University of Michigan of President James B. Angell, who had studied at Brown under Francis Wayland, and of the Cooleys; at Wisconsin of John Bascom, a graduate of Williams, two of whose students, Charles R. Van Hise and Robert M. LaFollette were to collaborate in the development of the university early in the present century; and at Minnesota of William W. Folwell, a graduate of Hobart College—these influences illustrate the importance of the qualities of these men whose education had been received in small colleges. They had the vision to see the challenge of the state university, most especially in regard to the public services. We will do well to acquaint ourselves and our students with them as we appraise our responsibilities as political scientists and shapers of institutional policies and programs in our time. When we complain of great enrollments, the increase and specialization in knowledge and inadequate resources, we may, in studying them, become at once a little humble and freshly inspired with the "morning wishes" of our intellectual and professional ancestors. Their stories throw light on present debates over the participation of the teacher in wider policy-making and content and method of instruction within university walls and in public and civic services and problems outside. In Van Hise's view, the campus extended to the borders of the state—a view rejected by many of his faculty.

I have tried to illustrate from my own experience or relatively close acquaintance some efforts in the past forty-five years in which political scientists have attempted to advance the quality of instruction and focus it better on what seems more relevant in the light of changing conditions. While claiming the benefits of such participation, I would not minimize the costs. There is a cost in time, energy, and personal life generally to the teacher. This was true, for example, at the Experimental College at Wisconsin, and it was and is true at Bennington College, and I am sure in all such ventures.

It is true also of similar efforts made by the individual teacher to improve his own courses. But I think we sometimes overlook the potentialities of the course, so rooted in our American system, in borrowing other ways of organizing instruction, such as tutorial systems. A reduction in the number of courses, linked with the use of the resources saved in providing more writing and advising within the course, may be wise strategy and also wise tactics. We often think and speak of great teachers as "great personalities," unique almost to the point of isolation. But those teachers whom I have known or studied with and would call great or rate highly in some way have been so in part because they wove into their classrooms and studies lines that led us to other ideas and experience, both contradictory and supplementary. The arrogance, even sadism, that sometimes seems to accompany a vocation of words and paper-work, and a relationship of power to make or break the career of younger people by examinations and grades, or the wounding use of irony, is not present in the great. They will make of their own courses what we lesser ones must hope to achieve by other means of integrating resources. So the sensible first move in the introduction of a new program should be a careful search for ways in which the innovation can draw upon the existing course resources as assets. The two-civilization program of the Experimental College at Wisconsin, for example, was dependent on supplementary course resources "on the Hill" (that is, in the regular course offerings of the departments in the College of Letters and Sciences) and for particular students, such as those in pre-medicine, these were indispensable.

Experiment in the grouping of smaller units within larger university communities continues. There are examples from Harvard and Yale on the East Coast to Claremont in California and the new University of California at Santa Cruz (where the head, Dean McHenry, is a political scientist). I note the placing of faculty studies in the new student houses at Michigan State University, and the co-operation among four institutions, Smith, Mt. Holyoke, Amherst, and the University of Massachusetts in the Connecticut Valley. I have even dreamed of the possibility which I once saw in actuality of fraternity and sorority development in this direction, somewhat as the medieval hostels at Bologna, Paris, Oxford, and Cambridge evolved into semi-autonomous corporate colleges. I treat here superficially a factor of institutional life not especially a responsibility of the political scientist, but offering, in my experience, rich opportunity to him. And it is an aspect of his responsibilities as a faculty member. While some people discourage such interests as harmful to his "getting on in his field," this depends in part also on the fact that to some institutions in search of staff such interest is an asset, even a requirement.

The attitude of a department chairman and a dean toward participation in experiment and innovation in teaching on the part of teachers, both in encouragement and in advice based on longer experience and in greater knowledge of the total situation in the institution, is important. Since this is a personal memoir, I may properly record my gratitude for the advantages I had, especially in the critical earlier years of teaching, from President Meiklejohn and Professor Gettell at Amherst, Dean Johnston and Professor Cephas Allin at the University of Minnesota, and Dean Sellery and Professor Ogg at the University of Wisconsin, in positive encouragement or the practical facilitation within the complex operations of the institution of my activities. I had in my professional life during these years also the help and encouragement of Charles Merriam of the University of Chicago. Their own part in some of these activities ranged from active leadership and initiation to perhaps genial skepticism, which they never permitted to qualify a personal friendship or improvement in salary or status. I may say with the Psalmist, "The lines are fallen unto me in pleasant places; yea, I have a goodly heritage."

That my inclusion of the experience in teaching political science in relation to the neighboring fields and general institutional relations is relevant to our theme was pressed upon me by two letters I received within a week (on March 17 and 22) when I was completing this essay. They were from friends who are successful teachers of political science and also have an unusually responsible relation to policy-making in their respective institutions. One is thirty-seven years old, the other, fifty-one. Neither knew that I was engaged in preparing this essay, but they knew from having studied with me in the past something of my interests, and we have now and then corresponded as they know I am grateful for keeping in touch with some of their thinking. A few passages which I will quote seemed to me relevant to my discussion here.

The younger friend gives me some general observations about teaching political science based on his experience in organizing and directing a new program:

First, much of our graduate education in the social sciences is an utter waste; it produces neither scholars nor moral men. This new empirical neo-scholasticism is quite sterile. For example, I have a staff member (whose field is not political science) who holds a Ph.D. from a respected institution. He is an utterly contemporary being. I sometimes feel he was born in 1963. . . . He is incapable of handling ideas. The technique has become the whole of "science," which, in his mind, will save the world.

Allied to this "professional" outlook is a basic disregard for the problems of this society. In his mind, the only significant problems are disciplinary, and, worse yet, methodological, and the only significant people to know are those who can help one get a leg up. . . .

Second, the dominant social science models, by stressing equilibrium as a major concept, are producing either trivia or justifications of the status quo. I feel that this is a great disservice to a society that is in a bad way. The very people who ought to be, because of their training, questioning the customary modes of thought and action have no inclination to go to the battlefield. . . .

Third, I now believe that at least part of our salvation, as a society, lies in motivating young people to serve, not to be ministered unto. . . .

What kinds of educational experiences can make political men out of technicians? What are the limits of trying to re-educate administrators who have been on the firing line for a while? How can one create an intelligent lay backing for risk-taking professionals?

And now from my older friend:

There is no doubt that with our rapid growth [in his university] we are losing a sense of community and, perhaps, of institutional purpose. Perhaps we must set up some neighborhood communities within the university—to use the lingo of the city planners.

I feel, also, that our own discipline is losing some touch with social problems. I can't say that I am opposed to the new model-building, statistical approach to things, for I am sure that these people are going to find some knowledge that we can use. I am opposed to the abandonment of what we used to call social engineering and to the effort to substitute methodology for mature judgment.

I quote my two friends because they have provided me at this particular time unsolicited contributory evidence relevant to three aspects of the experience of teaching political science which I have chosen to discuss here. Over two of them I have perhaps lingered too long: that which is, so to speak, oriented to the traditional classroom and course and that which reaches out within and across the institution. Adjustments across department and even divisional lines, are perhaps illustrated now for some by what is termed the behavioral approach. Forty years ago, such topics as a science of politics, international relations, and public administration were comparable themes. Eighty years ago there were the pioneer creators to whom I have referred. And there is also, as my friends record, concern for the institutional conditions in the structure of faculty-student organization and relations that may affect the quality and motives of its members. Directly or by implication my friends have recognized a relation of the political scientist to political science beyond the walls, so to speak, as in the education of public servants or research on and participation in "social problems" and "social engineering."

The teacher of political science may himself be employed in the public service, whether administrative, legislative, or judicial, or so closely and actively concerned with public matters as to cause people to think of him as much for this as for his teaching. The place of education for the public service in the college and in graduate schools has been so debated and written about that there is not a cranny left in which I can plant any new seed. The first report on the subject by the American Political Science Association came when I was a college student, and my political science teacher, Raymond G. Gettell, was on that committee, but I do not recall any discussion of the subject among us. At this time, the Training School for the Public Service, a joint creation of the then relatively young New York Bureau of Municipal Research and Columbia University, was under the direction of Charles A. Beard. But I knew all this only after I had graduated from college and gone to the South End House in Boston and met there Morris Lambie, a graduate of Williams College, who gave me a job on the Massachusetts Salary Standardization Study Staff he was directing. He had been at the training school, as had Luther Gulick, who was also working at the state house then for a legislative committee planning a budget system, about which he shortly wrote his doctoral thesis for the Columbia degree. Since that time when I had the rare and valuable privilege of studying the ten thousand paid positions in the Massachusetts civil service and the classification of them, I almost always have been concerned with the subject, whether in the public service or in teaching positions. I always have had a strong bias in favor of the importance of personnel and budget processes in the larger process of government in my teaching. I have returned at times to participation in government at all levels on a part-time and usually consultant basis. In my teaching I have participated in the pre-entry education of public servants in various special programs as well as in my general courses. And I have also participated in post-entry education for public servants, within a university as at Wisconsin and Harvard, in extension classes at Wisconsin, and in government agencies such as the United States

Department of Agriculture and the Social Security Board. I always enjoyed having students in substantive fields of administration enrolled in professional schools come in to my courses—natural resources, city planning, education, journalism, for example—because it gave us an opportunity to search for the questions and problems common to all as a joint enterprise. A practical gain to me was the warning to suppress any tendency toward overemphasis on techniques as against function and purpose, whose needs must be served.

I will attempt to make some generalizations from this experience. You may find them both platitudes and evasions. And I begin with both when I say that whether a political scientist does or does not participate in public service depends on that individual and his circumstances and not upon a general division between theory-centered or vocation-centered types. Such reasonably respectable theorists as Hobbes, Locke, Burke, Bentham, and Mill were pretty deeply engaged in various kinds of public service. And Hobbes is reported to have said of other learned men about the king who scoffed at him that, "If I had read as many books as they, I would be as stupid as they are."

I think that the political scientist has so important a job as teacher that his decision to participate should be oriented to it. Will it jeopardize his relations to his students and his colleagues in such a way as adversely to affect his teaching? At one time when I was serving part-time in a public post, I began to feel that in spite of the value and objectivity of the work I was doing, some of my students and colleagues probably felt that what I said in class or did in matters of university policy was colored by my association with the political leadership under whom I was serving in a staff position, but having to deal, and properly so, with policy matters. At such a point, a choice should be made. I have known men who could, in such a post, project the integrity they possessed and the power of their wisdom and knowledge across the waves of controversy. Outstanding among these was one, a friend and colleague of mine, who, since he is dead, I will name—Edwin Witte—because he illustrates how much it is the person and not the general rule which should govern. He was Wisconsin-born, a graduate of the university, with graduate doctorate from its distinguished department of economics and in a distinguished special field of labor economics. After research posts in national and state industrial matters, he became the head of the Legislative Reference Library of the Wisconsin Legislature. His industry, knowledge, and penetration were great. What is more, every legislator of whatever party could come to him for advice and technical assistance on their legislative proposals with absolute confidence in obtaining it with no color or prejudice behind his words. He taught courses in his field in the department of economics, and the course in state government in the department of political science. When Franklin D. Roosevelt appointed a Cabinet committee to prepare proposals for an unemployment compensation and related social security measures, my colleague became its executive director. The number of public posts he held during the Depression and World War II was large but grounded in his field of knowledge and experience. During these years he was chairman of the department of economics part of the time and a professor whose courses were greatly respected always. Yet his door was open, and a student received a warm welcome and was embarrassed only by the knowledge of a great number of other waiting students and a distraught secretary outside the door.

A teacher will find, or should find, rich resources for his teaching and research in his public service. Here again dangers lurk. It is a temptation to hint at importance in high places, or to make the interpretation under the heady brew of being chosen to even a minor princeling's throne. I suspect I have sinned in this manner. But against this I place the gratitude I have for the privilege of experience in the public service, both for substantive knowledge especially valuable to one working in a relatively new academic field, and for friendships with some remarkable men and women in our public service. I think, for example, of William A. Jump, late director of budget and finance in the United States Department of Agriculture, whose long career service and extraordinary qualities akin to those of Edwin Witte's—industry and integrity, for example—made his apparently casual comment, as one talked with him about the events of a budget hearing, an opening of a new vista on government.

So with me, experience in the public service has meant more than additional data concerning government. It has taught me to put alongside reading in medieval administrative history observation of something like universal principles at work in the household of the medieval ruler and the executive office of president, governor, and mayor. I have enjoyed teaching the history of Western political thought and American political thought. Not a little of that enjoyment was that even my own humble experience could make Plato's classification of personnel, or Burke's speech on Economical Reform, more meaningful to me, and I hope, to my students.

Post-entry education for public servants, to which I have referred, is part of the general subject of education for the public service about which so much has been written in the past fifty years. Some of these writings and conferences on the subject have been influential and have helped to clarify the peculiarities of our American situation. I think of the writings of Leonard White and George Graham and the discussions and reports of the University of Minnesota conference. We have to bring into relation the factors in American society, systems of government, college and university obligations and opportunities, and relevant foreign experience. Our experience since World War II, not only in civil and military public services but also in education and in economics and professional institutions, has been receiving much study. There is, for example, the article by John J. Corson, who is surely one who has given much thought to these problems, based on wide and deep experience of the current situation "Equipping Men for Career Growth in the Public Service," *Public Administration Review,* XXIII (March, 1963). The opportunities available for both pre-entry and post-entry education for the public service in this country have increased and become varied far beyond the dreams of any political scientists of the first two decades of this century. And much of this development has taken place within the governments—which the political scientists who pioneered in this field helped to bring about.

Here again I have not found that participation in this section of teaching political science was opposed to my general academic or intellectual interests, even within the special topics of the public service itself. A current manifestation of the same concerns and problems that were present at the University of Bologna when it helped prepare for the staffing of the medieval papal chancery, at the University of Naples in the preparation of the medieval emperor's staff, or the German universities in the preparation of officials for the cameralist policies of early modern Germany is surely not only respectable for the courses in public administration today but relevant to courses in comparative government or political theory. And a knowledge of the palace school of the Ottoman emperors might have enriched our understanding of international relations.

For some years I had an evening extension class in public administration at the University of Wisconsin's then extension center in Milwaukee. The membership was almost entirely from the municipal, county and state civil services and from the several regional offices of national agencies in that city—the forest service, for example. I enjoyed this experience, and I was taught much by the members of the class. I was often skeptical as to whether I was able to give much in return to men in their thirties and forties, for the most part, whose previous education had been in substantive fields relevant to their careers and who came to a class that met from 8 to 10 P.M. after a day's work. They were presumably more likely to be giving what time they could or wished to further work in subjects relevant to their posts. Books assigned or recommended were available on special shelves at the excellent public library, the head of which, a member of the class, had been the municipal reference librarian of the city and knew a great deal more than I did. But to do the reading meant at least another evening for members of the class.

I learned, however, that these men were at the stage of their careers at which their duties were widening from the more technical ones of their entrance and apprentice years to include relations with the public, other agencies, and their counterparts in our interrelated system that includes city, county, state, and national agencies. And they were reaching out toward greater understanding of the social changes in population, land use, and technology, whose impact on their fields they were observing daily. I found also that there was often perplexity and confusion as to lines of authority and changes in organization that then (the 1930's) were frequent. The very fact of my position as a teacher, assigned to study these questions and familiar to some degree with relevant problems in government, made me at times helpful to them in seeing themselves in the larger setting of a changing government in a changing world—within my personal limitations, which they humorously accepted. In this respect I was reminded of an earlier experience in the Amherst classes for workers, an enterprise jointly conducted by a committee of the Amherst faculty and the Central Labor Union of Holyoke, Massachusetts, in 1921-

1923. The members of the class were chiefly craft workers in the paper and textile mills, some of whom were active in politics and all of whom were older, some much older, and with far more experience with the life of a city and industry than I had. But here again there were the assets—the privilege of my assignment to study, compare, and interpret some general aspects of American government and the changes affecting it that were taking place, and some special acquaintance with available sources of information useful to them, that, again within my personal limitations, made me useful.

Now I grant that both groups were unusual in their qualities. The Milwaukee Civil Service, for example, was then, as I judge it still is, one of the finest in the country, and the regional United States officials were also excellent. The Holyoke group was a live one, with a tradition of civic interest. And I grant that my recollection and estimate is colored by the friendships I formed among these men, which I still cherish over this long span of years. Both classes were given as an addition to my full teaching schedule on the campus of the University of Wisconsin and of Amherst College, respectively, and required some travel and a long evening. You may ask whether the equivalent time and effort should not have gone into research. I incline to the defense that these endeavors helped to make what research I was doing more relevant to my conception of what I as a teacher and a political scientist and a faculty member should be doing in my time and place. I suspect, however, that the real determinant was the nature of my temperament.

I have referred to the increasing interest in public service education and greater and more varied opportunities whereby those in the service may receive in-service education or assistance in continuing their education through fellowships, grants, and leave arrangements. There was much of this at the University of Wisconsin, beginning early in the present century, where an excellent state civil service had many members recruited from the university students who would continue with graduate work at the university on a part-time basis facilitated by the presence of the university and the capitol in the same city. Examples of recent developments of programs directed to, or at least inclusive of, public servants on leave now multiply. With one of the programs at Harvard University Graduate School of Public Administration I had some experience of great value and enjoyment. On the initiation of the late John Black, professor of economics with special experience in agricultural policy, a program was instituted whereby a group of fellows selected from agricultural extension personnel spent a year at the school. Their programs were arranged to assist them to understand better the economic, social, and political factors affecting agriculture and the resulting challenges to public policy. They were generally of an age and stage in their careers at which their work related less to the technical substantive fields in which they may have majored than to general policy and directive responsibilities. They were officials whose superior officers had marked them for posts of greater responsibility. The program was financed largely from special foundation grants. It was succeeded by another grant-aided one for officials in national and state natural resources agencies such as the United States Forest and Soil Conservation Services, the Geological Survey, and state conservation departments.

One seminar was the central point of integration, initiated and administered first by Professor Black and then Dr. Ayers Brinser. There were also participants from other units or departments of the university, such as the Harvard Forest, the law school, and the department of government. I had the good fortune to participate in the program and seminar and had most of the fellows in my own seminars: the planning process in administration and public policy and administration. I witnessed at first hand the development of some teaching arrangements that I found very valuable. I can make this judgment the more freely because the responsible creator of them as the natural resources program evolved was Ayers Brinser, and from him, as also from Dr. Hugh Raup, a botanist and director of the Harvard Forest, and Dr. Ernest Gould, an economist on the forest staff, and others I had my prejudices challenged and my imagination stimulated.

The most important devices to me came at the start of the year. The fellows reported two weeks before the fall semester, and, with such of the participating faculty as were able in that busiest of periods, went to the Harvard Forest, located in Petersham in the forested uplands just east of the Connecticut Valley and about ninety miles west of Cambridge. The headquarters building there contained a dormitory, library, and eating facilities, so that the ten fellows and perhaps three participant instructors, in addition to the resident forest staff, could be together. For three of four days there were evening discussions led by the staff, opening up the general objectives of the program, and focusing upon some intellectual problems that would then be illustrated in some field visits in the forest the next day. The relating of natural science observation to implications for the economy and public policy, the cost of holding ideas of one generation of scholars beyond the discovery of new knowledge that undermined or seriously qualified them, began to set a tone for the year with a group who were enjoying the friendly atmosphere that a forest setting and autumn air gives.

With these field observations in the forest and the afternoon and evening discussions as a base, half- or full-day expeditions in station wagons began, to visit various landscapes and particular farms or forests within a short distance. These visits were arranged in co-operation with the owner or operator, the extension or other public service, whose local agents would be present to help in the exposition of significant factors.

The second week came to be devoted to a longer journey, with overnight stays on the road. The field trip included visits to farms, state and national and privately owned forests and parks, agricultural and forest research stations, and pulp and paper industries in northern New England—Vermont, New Hampshire and Maine—including coastal areas, the Green and White and Border mountains, the dairy and poultry regions, and in the farthest north, the potato areas of Aroostook County, Maine. The arrangement for visits, including meetings and discussions with operators, administrators, and research staffs, as well as the routes and time schedules had been prepared by Dr. Brinser during the previous summer on "dry runs," and accommodations reserved. About fifteen persons, ten or eleven fellows and four or five from the faculty participants, made a group which was small enough to gather about a discussant-host, and varied enough in background to give a tang to the discussions en route and in the evening.

A valuable feature in the preparation for and conduct of the trips was the fairly lengthy guide prepared by Dr. Brinser, a mimeographed copy of which was at hand for each member at the earlier meetings at the forest. In this, historical and descriptive comment on the landscape along the planned route and geared to the mileage somewhat after the fashion of the WPA guides helped to prepare for the discussions at the stops along the way, whether briefly at the roadside or at greater length with a farmer in the field or an official at an experiment station or industry.

One result of this early initiation into the program for the year was that when we met in Cambridge seminars, whether the central one for the members of the program or our own seminars in the first week of the university fall term, we had had two weeks of close association, including the weariness and trials and humor and kidding of a longish, tough trip on the road.

One of the hazards of all adult education is the adjustment of people from everyday life to the peculiarities of attitude, language, and intellectual and emotional environment of academic institutions and practices, even in a single evening class a week. There is an additional hazard when the faculty participants in a program built around a central theme are drawn from different departments and jurisdictions. I cannot claim that the arrangements for the opening two weeks of this program, which I have described inadequately in this brief compass, enabled us to avoid completely these hazards. In my experience they did create a valuable sense of corporate enterprise. This was further supported by the fact that some of the topics for seminar study and reporting related back to places, problems, and personnel to which we had been introduced by the field trip, and the comradeship of the road was revived in the hospitality of the Brinser home.

I am grateful that the latter years of my teaching included this opportunity to participate under these ideal conditions, in an educational program with public servants at that strategic point in their careers at which they are moving from preoccupation with substantive fields to the relating of them to wider public responsibilities. This has been, in general, the characteristic line of recruiting of our career executives. We forget that we have had a career service in our country. It has been a natural evolution from early days when West Point was established and engineers were trained, through the development of the land-grant institutions and state universities and the proliferation of higher education generally. The idea and practice of giving to the career officials in substantive fields additional post-entry education to equip them better for staff and general administrative positions probably originated in the military and naval services and has spread more recently and with far less support to the civil services. In this latter move, political scientists have had, and I think should continue to take, an important part.

Three characteristics of modern government make this mutual participation by scholar and official important in the study of our institutions and the impact of change upon them. The first is the presence all through the process of government of discretionary powers, guides to the use of which are only partially provided in constitutional and statutory law. The second is the permissive and facilitating element—as against the coercive—in much governmental policy, so that for policy to be effective many citizens and professional and economic organizations must be given, and must give in return from their experience and knowledge, opportunity for making essential contributions to that policy. The third is the complexity and technical nature and interdependence of the problems dealt with. All these create dangers of abuse of power, too limited an outlook, and failure to provide a better accounting of costs and consequences fatal to the best use of our resources. We have to help ourselves in this situation through improvement in our political, party, and legislative institutions, but also in the development of the capacities of our administrative personnel. Both tasks are basically educational, and political scientists have a place in supplying diagnosis and interpretation which are central to our calling.

As I conclude this memoir of my own experience in teaching political science, I would record my gratitude for the happy association with my colleagues in both faculty and public service, as well as association with those of other places and times that has come through my reading.

CHARLES S. HYNEMAN

Some crucial learning experiences: a personal view

Something like deathbed repentance set in on me a few years ago. I have in recent years scrutinized my objectives and my performance as teacher more severely than had been my custom. This led to a few do-hereby-highly-resolves, and perhaps to some more or less scared girding up of the loins. In any event, when I entered upon my last decade of active professional life, as fixed by the retirement policies of my university, I announced a new policy. I told the dean of my college that I had up to now devoted myself mainly to the development of subject matter, that during the final decade of my teaching I proposed to devote myself wholly to the development of young people. I had in mind a significant change in my activities.*

The change contemplated in my statement to the dean was one of emphasis. No doubt everything that makes a noticeable impact on the college student contributes to his development. Surely every enrichment of his understanding of the world he lives in is an important step in his advancement to maturity. Development of the subject matter which is the content of a college course is an important means—an essential means—for equipping the young person to advance his interests, keep his brother, and find pleasure in living. Enlargement of the cargo of knowledge is, however, only a part of the gains that the young man should acquire from association with the older man. The college experience should be one of examining positions; of making an inventory of value holdings; of confirming, reshaping, and rejecting premises; of enlarging vision and sharpening

---

* It ought to be said right now that this paper is going to be brashly autobiographical. The editor said that this is the time for testimony to personal experience and for presentation of personal conviction. I respond in the spirit of the instruction; talking about myself comes easy for me.

focus; of throwing off old habits and fixing new habits of working and thinking; of developing know-how for getting evidence, evaluating evidence, and extending evidence by reasoning; and so on. The teacher who brings imagination and stern demand to a course which is primarily concerned with conquest of an important subject matter is bound to quicken the student's progress along these many lines of growth. There is a danger, however, that these other gains will be too greatly subordinated to the ordering and storing of the supposition, belief, and dogma we call knowledge.

We have long realized that some courses contribute more than others to these other-than-knowledge objectives. We insist that the student take a laboratory science, not just because we want him to acquire a more accurate view of a segment of nature, but because we want him to appreciate if not master the scientific way of examining a bit of reality. A course in logic may not be required by college policy, but teachers in all departments point students to that course hoping that their abilities and habits of reasoning will be improved. My principal adviser in undergraduate days sent me to the economics department for the same reason. He had a low regard for the accounts that economists give of the world they study, but he thought I would profit from having to maneuver propositions about as economists maneuver them in a course called Principles of Economics.

In our own discipline, political science, I think we have generally believed that two courses provide special opportunities for contributions other than adding to the store of knowledge: the course that examines the classic writings and the course in American constitutional law. What gains the student will realize from either of these courses, in addition to the cargo of knowledge taken on board, must vary according to the teacher.

Courses in "political theory" are widely criticized for failure to realize their distinctive potential. A concern to have the student learn as much as possible about what the great men said, it appears, has led to reading of summaries and critiques of the classics rather than the classic writings themselves. Opportunities to show the student how the great man defined a problem, set it up for examination, and developed his inquiry are lost in the rush to have the student learn what the great man concluded and where his conclusions stand in an array of conclusions reached by a company of thoughtful writers. In sharpest contrast to this, I understand, is the experience of a young man who studies with Professor Leo Strauss. I have heard from graduate students who have sat at his feet that all of the class meetings may be devoted to intensive scrutiny of a single writing of one man, and that a few score rather than a few hundred pages of the classic document supply the materials for a semester of analysis. It is my understanding that students of Professor Strauss are carrying this method of intense documentary analysis into their undergraduate courses. Judgments will vary as to what utilities are made available and as to the gross value of those utilities to students in courses taught in this manner. There can be no doubt that objectives which have been labeled Straussian bring a great deal to the political science curriculum which is not provided in courses almost wholly concerned with accumulation and comparison of the conclusions arrived at in a number of classic writings.

Perhaps objectives vary as widely among teachers of American constitutional law. I recall a conversation with a faculty colleague at the time I assumed responsibility for a course in constitutional law at the University of Illinois. The department had a course called the American Constitutional System which covered everything from the calling of the Philadelphia convention to the latest decision of the Supreme Court. I thought then, as I do now, that it is good for college students to know about these things. They ought, insofar as possible, to relive the national experience. They ought to learn about the causes of unhappiness during the period of the Articles, and how historians have related that unhappiness to the form of government; the interests that were aggrandized and the interests that were repressed in fixing the character of the new government; the questions of documentary interpretation which arose over the years, the arrays of interest and the arrays of force that stood back of alternative interpretations, and the resolutions of conflict which were achieved by the adoption and announcement of particular interpretations; the restriction and the elaboration of the Constitution, viewed as particular events and as flow of history; the content of documents and the critical statements of historians and lawyers. All of this you and I may view as a cargo of knowledge appropriate for a course in American constitutional law and count it a sad fact that the teacher of constitutional law never finds it possible to fix more than a small part of this knowledge in the heads of his students. Equally, we can agree that if the teacher is determined to maximize the amount of knowledge taken on by the student in this course, other gains readily attainable in the study of constitutional law will have to be sacrificed.

This brings us back to the conversation with a faculty colleague at the time I joined the faculty of the University of Illinois. The course, American Constitutional System, packed in all of the above-cited content the teacher could get around to and not a few students told me he did a very good job of it. My course was intended for students who missed the main course. I figured (it turned out correctly) that I could do about what I pleased in my course. The conversation mentioned was with a colleague who asked what I intended to do. I replied that the Supreme Court represented authority where it is most clearly recognized in our political system, and that I thought the most important thing to be done was to cause the students to see how authority is used. I remember saying that I thought the student ought to face the question as to whether the judges were required to reach the conclusions they reached, to identify alternative lines of reasoning to those which the judges pursued, and in a few instances to write a concurring or dissenting opinion in which the student matches his own mind against that of the judge. I also remember saying that I thought it less important for the student to know what the authoritative interpretation of the Constitution appears to be than to have some appreciation of what turns interpretation could take in the future without doing violence to statements made in the past.

I remember only two of the reactions expressed by my colleague: (1) He thought I had peculiar ideas about what a constitutional law course was for; and (2) he advised me not to let the older members of the department find out what I was up to. I taught the course for seven years. I thought it was the best course I taught during my period at the University of Illinois. It is the only course I taught there which is mentioned when I run into a student from those days.

This experience in the constitutional law course illustrates a predicament we constantly face in trying to make a course carry a big load of knowledge and at the same time add significantly to the student's equipment for getting knowledge. Possibly no respected teacher of American constitutional law would say this today, but I heard it said by more than one member of an earlier generation: "I do not have time for severe criticism of individual court decisions because I need more time than I have to make the student aware of the big problems that the courts have dealt with and the main things the judges have said and done in disposition of those problems." No doubt this same idea, that knowledge of experience is more important than development of the boy, is back of the argument still heard occasionally: that the case method is not a good way of teaching constitutional law in the arts college.

The indicated next step in this presentation is an array of other-than-getting-knowledge objectives appropriate to a political science curriculum. That is a more exacting assignment than I am ready to tackle. I shall, however, name some goals for the teacher of politics that seem to me important, achievable, and in too-small measure realized because they are ordinarily submerged in the race to pile up knowledge.

Appreciation of the Nature of Knowledge and the Nature of Inquiry

Beyond question, this objective is wholly compatible with a high concern to master the literature viewed as the subject matter of the course. Even if the assigned reading materials do not further this objective, the teacher can make a big point of what we know and how little we know, how we found out what we know and why we know so little, and what seem to be most promising routes to future knowledge. A thoughtful consideration of these things, no doubt, can be mixed with an exploration of any subject matter area. But the testimony seems to be overwhelming that most courses in political science find room for very little of it, and that the cumulative pickup from all his political science courses leaves the typical political science major at the edge of this threshold of understanding.

The standout course in my own undergraduate experience was one that thrust me up against the question: what can I know and how can I find out? It was a course in the philosophy department labeled ethics, and the professor who taught it in my junior year sabotaged the intent of the philosophy faculty as fully as I ever managed to sidestep the expectations of the full professors in my younger days at the University of Illinois. The highly regarded philosophy professor who owned the course went to the hospital and the course fell into the hands of a psychologist—not just a psychologist but an avant garde Watson-behaviorist. In part, perhaps, because he was not well acquainted with the literature about ethics, but mainly I think because he had a low regard for it, the teacher opened the course by asking the students what they believed to be right and wrong and why they believed it. We never got past that question in the entire semester. I have some pretty clear memories of that course today, and one of the clearest is of combat between teacher and a middle-aged female student. The point at issue was the ground for believing that there is a state of affairs worthy of the term "mother instinct." The female student was a missionary, recently returned from China— home from the field, attending the university, and taking a course in ethics, no doubt, to replenish her arsenal for future triumphs over heathen doctrines. Perhaps the outcome of this one should be called a draw. My recollection is that the missionary quit saying that a "mother instinct" is certainly there and started saying there is reason to believe something would be found if we made further search. If this memory is correct, we may rejoice in the thought that the transfer of an item from the catalogue of knowledge to that of belief sent her back to China with her faith enlarged if not more secure.

In my own case a critical discussion turned on the consequences of lust. I recalled a statement in the Bible that one who looks upon a woman to lust after her committeth adultery in his heart and therefore ought to cut it out. I was discreet enough to wait until after class to ask for the professor's views about this, but he thought the question a good one and said it ought to be put to the whole class at the next meeting. I was not one to raise that question in the presence of a middle-aged female missionary, so I was ready with what I thought to be a fair equivalent: If the doctor tells his patient not to eat for three days, is it wrong for the patient to daydream about a square meal? I did not get away with it. We talked in class about what possibly could be immediate consequences and indirect consequences of a fervent contemplation of the opposite sex, and what prospect there is that man will ever know what price he pays for daydreams of this character.

By the time I had acquired a Ph.D. degree and begun my career as a college teacher, I had concluded that this course was the high point in my undergraduate and graduate education. It seems to me that that teacher, in that semester, shattered a crust that had lain like a blanket over my thinking. I took from it not only a new respect for evidence but a new conception of evidence, a readiness I had not had before to look at the ground on which I stood, and a new sense of how to probe into my foundations and scrutnize them. Having erected a small memorial here to this great teacher, I ought to put his name on it: Jacob R. Kantor. He won a considerable respect, especially in Europe, for pioneer writing about the impact of language structure on the development of thought.

What Kantor did for me, and I am confident for other students as well, was not the by-product of a course in ethics. He junked the course in ethics the first day, and gave us an unplanned, unsystematic introduction to the problem of knowledge. If he had known well in advance that he was to teach the course and had chosen to make it a systematic enterprise, I have no doubt his course would have done the crust-shattering job for me and in addition have given me much better guidance for extending my own inquiry into the grounds for supposition, belief, and dogmatic assertions. I shall say something later about the need for a direct attack on these problems by way of a special course in the political science curriculum.

Experience in Analysis

By analysis I mean breaking the complex problem into its components and observing how the parts combine to be a problem. This objective also is wholly compatible with a very considerable loading on of knowledge. I suppose that every course worthy of being tolerated on a college campus is a demonstration of analytic thought and requires the student to engage in analytic thought. The question raised here is whether our courses in political science give the student a sufficient number of analytic jobs of sufficient difficulty.

I have been told on a few occasions: "You are right about the importance of this. I do it in my final examinations; that's why I have no use for objective examinations." This answer seems little short of ridiculous to me. Not that it is ridiculous to require analysis in an examination, but it is ridiculous to think this fulfils the requirement. In the examination, the student is removed from his sources of information, and he is required to complete his solution in less time than is needed for a fair casing of the problem. Is it not possible that the assignment of a trying job of analysis in the examination period fixes in the student's mind an impression that the faculty thinks a quick job is preferable to a thorough job, and that reliance on memory is to be preferred above patient checking of sources to make sure that memory is accurate?

I am skeptical also when I hear a man say: "I require every student to write a term paper, and my term papers are analytic jobs." I have looked at term papers turned in for courses under a sizable number of political science teachers. No doubt there is some analysis in all of them. At least the student has to figure out how to do his job. But usually the job calls for low-level analysis, if indeed for anything that ought to be called analysis at all. Usually the task is one of describing a situation, reporting an event or series of events, and perhaps passing judgment on someone's actions. Such enterprises will be of very great value for the student if they send him on a devious search for information, force him to ponder before choosing between conflicting reports, confront him with a complicated job of arranging many pieces of information into a coherent and creditable story. But such an experience, it seems to me, is not likely to require the precise differentiation and imaginative probing for relevance which gives its distinguishing character to what I call the analytic job.

Another incident of my undergraduate days may clarify the point. A list of suggested topics for term papers by an economics professor included "The Effects of the Panama Canal on Development of Industry." I grabbed this one, thinking to make a killing by joining it to a term paper for a history course on how Theodore Roosevelt caused a revolution and stole a strip of land for the Panama Canal. I found the history paper a pushover in conception, though possibly difficult enough in execution. I read Bunau-Varilla's memoirs and other books and documents and pieced them together into a story of how somebody got what, when, and how. The paper for the economics course floored me. I remember that I was standing in the stacks of the library when it came to the front of my mind that it was not enough to know what commodities moved through the Panama Canal in what volume and to know what changes occurred in the production of commodities after the Panama Canal was built. I had to figure out what changes in kinds of goods produced and what changes in volume of goods produced could be traced to the fact that the Panama Canal was now available for goods to be moved through. I never figured out the answers. My recollection is that I filled the paper up with statistics about production of goods and movement of goods, and statements about the impossibility of finding out which set of events caused the other set of events to take place. I do remember that I got an "A" for the paper and that the professor said it was because I was the first student who did not drop the topic and pick another one when he found out what he was up against. No doubt I was saved by the fact that it took me longer than any other student to find out I was licked.

That experience was important to me, but the importance lay in my recognizing that certain kinds of knowledge are hard to get, and not in the discipline of going after and getting the needed information. Surely the experience would have been of even greater value if the professor had been available for conference and given me some advice about how to trace out obscured relationships.

Since World War II I have made the analytic essay my special responsibility. All the department faculty know that in any course I teach, in addition to answering for the subject matter mentioned in the college bulletin, the student will have to do one or more essays designed to test and improve his analytic powers. This is the case for my section of the beginning course (American Government) and for every advanced course I teach.

In the beginning course the problems are general, the assignment requiring the student to case the problem and figure out what he would need to know in order to make a good answer. The instruction sheet which accompanies the assignment may or may not supply suggested readings. Perhaps most students do a good deal of self-imposed reading in hope of finding an answer to the problem, but they ultimately conclude that they have to work it out themselves, if I have been successful in formulating the problem. One of the most successful assignments in the beginning course has an interesting tale connected with it. Senator Humphrey of Minnesota introduced in the Senate a proposal for a constitutional amendment which would make every ex-president of the United States a member of the Senate for the remainder of his life. Two of the best jobs done for me (each a freshman in the same class at Northwestern University) took a dim view of the Senator's proposal, resting their objections (among other grounds) on a likelihood that this would divide leadership within the Senate and be a hazard to the legislative program of the man currently in the White House. I brought the two youngsters together and told them if they would put their ideas together in a bang-up paper we would send it to the Senator who undoubtedly would put their essay in the *Congressional Record*. The students did their part and the Senator wrote each of them a letter of thanks, but the essay did not appear in the *Record*. After some weeks I wrote a member of the Senator's staff asking why the Senator had not printed the essay. He replied: "I asked the Senator about this and he said he concluded the kids were right about it and dropped his proposal."

Practice in assigning essays in advanced courses has varied. With few exceptions, the minimum number required has been three short essays for a one-semester, three-hour course. In some cases the assignment calls for a fair amount of preparatory reading. A couple of assignments which were used in a course in American Political Thought are printed at the end of this article.

These analytic jobs, it must be remembered, are in addition to the main task of taking on the cargo of knowledge provided in textbook (if any) and other required and optional reading, and often in addition to essays whose main purpose is to force the student to read a document (or set of documents) carefully and prove that he comprehended what he read. I would not undertake to prove to a skeptical person that there is value for all students or even for most students in the kind of exercise described above; perhaps my entire investment in a teaching career rests on faith. But my faith in this particular experience is great enough that I make it the prime justification of a course for honor students which will be described later.

Critical Study of the Great Book

An arts college dean in a university where I have taught told a group of the faculty once that he was convinced, on the basis of several years of conversations with students, that few graduates of that college had ever been asked by the faculty to read a book clear through (textbooks excepted). A little bit of rumination convinced me that I was guilty. My assignments and suggested readings consisted mainly of parts of books, magazine articles, and documents. Can we not conclude that every college student ought to read at least one good book clear through—not merely read a good book but read clear through a book which one of the faculty regards as a model of thoughtful inquiry, write a critique of that book, and discuss the critique with a mature person? Perhaps it is not necessary for each student to sit alone with a faculty member to discuss the book; some of us might settle for a two-hour session in which a half dozen students discuss the book with a graduate assistant. Is it an adequate answer to say that every major in political science should be required to take a course on the classic political writings, and that every worthy course in the classics will provide the discipline here suggested? A lot of students wander into (or get forced into) the introductory course in political science who will never get into a course that concentrates on the classics. In many places a graduate assistant meets thirty students on Friday to ask them what the professor said in his lectures on Monday and Wednesday. Might not the payoff be greater if the professor lectured on nine out of ten Fridays while the graduate assistant was getting around, in groups of six, to talk with the students for two hours about what they may have failed to find in the great book they have read and criticized in their essays?

Confrontation of the Human Being

I resist a temptation to generalize about the reluctance of the American citizen to explore the minds of his contemporaries. It is a safe bet that a large proportion of the students in college today have never had a thought-provoking conversation with any adult other than a member of the family or next-door neighbor or school teacher, or on a restricted point of attention such as why the car isn't firing right or why dentists agree that the teeth ought to be brushed at least three times a day. Conversations with my students reveal that very few of them have ever talked with a politician or office holder about what the life of a politician or public official is like and about the attributes and qualities that increase chances for getting ahead in the world of public affairs. Things I read in books and articles convince me that a lot of people we call intellectuals have never passed a good paragraph of conversation with the kind of people I grew up with in Gibson County, with the kind of people one encounters in the headquarters of the Chicago Sanitary District, with the kind of people that get elected to a state legislature. I doubt that I ever sent five students out to interview a politician without four of them reporting back: "I must have got an unusual specimen, for this fellow took an interest in me, talked very intelligently about his experience and problems, and you know, Professor, I think he is an honest man."

If anyone in this group is skeptical about Washington semesters, two-weeks internships or one-day tours of the state house, will he not agree that every political science department ought to have one course where every student will have to break the ice of timidity and reticence in a series of interviews with adults who can tell him what government and politics are like as seen by the civic leader, the political manager, the candidate for office, the public official, the administrative servant?

The Citizen's Profane Scriptures

No doubt a few hundred people, in addition to Walter Lippmann, have characterized the newspaper as the citizen's Bible. I grew up in the days of "higher criticism" and learned that casting a critical eye on the content of the Bible is not to be encouraged. The time is long overdue for injecting higher criticism of the newspaper into the political science curriculum. Much more is involved than bias on the part of publishers and editors and incompetence and laziness on the part of reporters. College students may need more knowledge about how pervasive these attributes are than they now get, but what is on my mind at the moment is the subtler question: Given the resources likely to be at their command, what can the conscientious reporter or team of reporters actually run down and what is the probability that the story they have carefully compiled has a high congruence with the events that occurred?

Earl Mazo talked about this problem in a conference I attended a few months ago. Like a few hundred other newspapermen, Mazo tried to find out by what mixture of plans and accidents it came to pass that the senator from Texas was selected as the Democratic nominee for Vice President in 1960. Mazo figured that this one is for mention in history, and he was determined to find out exactly how it happened. He was determined enough to resist repeated entreaties and threats from headquarters to get a story in before other newspaper accounts had made it stale news. He stuck it out until he had interviewed everybody he thought could possibly have authentic knowledge of how the decision was made. Paraphrasing Mazo: "Never before or since did I file a story of a complicated series of events where I was so certain that I was right and that further disclosures would never prove I was wrong." But he was wrong, or, if not wrong, too far from right for him ever to be comfortable in recollection of the experience.

I am convinced [Mazo said] that the truth as to what happens at the cutting edge of decision making can never be known if the men who make the decision think it to be of great consequence and the decision is made under conditions of great emotional strain. The principals cannot reconstruct the situation. They do not remember what they said and did, or they remember it wrongly. The reporter, invading such a decision-situation, may avoid giving an account which is egregiously wrong; he can never be certain that his story is correct where he is most concerned to be absolutely right.

I do not suggest that we need a course on how to read a newspaper and when not to read a newspaper at all. The marked discrepancy in views about the trustworthiness of the press (including magazines, radio, and TV) which I encounter in the classroom, and the intense conviction with which conflicting views are expressed, cause me to think that a guided exploration of the limits of trustworthiness is badly needed. It may be that the remedy for my unhappiness is on the shelf where they keep the courses in journalism. Still, I would like to know that in one of the courses which every political science major takes, there is going to be some hard talk and a demonstration or two which makes the student forever aware that his image of the world far away from him is always hazy and sometimes laden with mirages right where he is most earnestly assured that he is looking at reality.

The contention of this essay, up to this point, has been that we need to strike more consciously for the realization of certain learning experiences that tend to be made incidental to other worthy teaching objectives, or left to realization by chance, or ignored altogether. I have said for some of these learning experiences that it may be sufficient to hook them on to one or more courses that have as a main objective the aim to traverse an informative literature and implant a sophisticated man's understanding of a segment of the political world. Two of them, in my judgment, are wholly worthy of being made the central objective of a semester course.

The first course to be mentioned is one we do not have in the undergraduate curriculum of my own department. The second is a course which was created when I entered my reform period three years ago.

The point of concern in the first course is the nature of inquiry and the nature of knowledge. If you are skeptical about its worth or about its feasibility, you may label it "methodology" and acquire merit by dismissing it from attention. This is the way such a course was commonly identified when I taught it at Northwestern, though the bulletin listed it as Systematic Study of Politics. The course was designed for students starting their graduate work, but we let outstanding senior undergraduates get into it too.

I will not inflict a description of the course upon you. It was in part a poor man's course in epistemology. We read things like Hume's *Enquiry Concerning Human Understanding,* Cohen's *Reason and Nature,* Hosper's *Introduction to Philosophical Analysis.* It was also a poor man's course in the history of science, for we read summary treatises like Wightman's *Growth of Scientific Ideas* and reports of great exploits such as those by William Harvey and Karl von Frisch. But it was, in addition, a course for entrants to our profession, for every student wrote critiques of model studies in political science, both the theory-building kind and the theory-testing kind. I do not exaggerate when I say that I cringe a bit now when I contemplate how restricted was my own understanding, when I inaugurated the course, of the literature we explored and the problems we argued.

We have such a course for graduate students in my department and it is in better hands than my own. I think we ought to construct such a course for undergraduates, and my present inclination would be to grade it for the sophomore level. I have been told that the subject matter is too complicated for lower classmen or even for seniors. The subject matter—how do we learn and what can we know—was not too complicated for my children when they had fallen out of the high chair a time or two, and it is not too complicated for my grandchildren today when they are asking what makes an automobile run. Further, we have plenty of empirical evidence about what can be done about this concern at the undergraduate level, not only from experience in the philosophy department but from experience in political science departments here and there that have made this the central point of attention in undergraduate courses.

A further objection likely to be made is: if the entire arts college curriculum is rightly conceived and intelligently administered, every course deals forthrightly with main problems of inquiry and knowledge, and the battery of courses taken by any student gives him everything that is likely to be packed in a special course on this subject. I have been told that this is indeed the case in all respected institutions east of the territory where I have had my experience. Personal observation and testimony of my peers convinces me that generally in the Middle West, the South, and the Great West, majors in political science have not invaded that part of the library where they keep the books by Hume, and Nagel, and Bergmann, or the books by Wightman, and Crombie, and A. R. Hall. This sector of the intellectual world is not, in my part of the country, generally opened up to them by courses in the political science department or by the cumulative impact of the entire curriculum—and this in spite of the fact that missionaries trained in the East have been carrying the gospel of true intellectual interest into those parts ever since Transylvania College was founded in 1780.

If I have not been offensively autobiographical to this point, I run a great risk of being so from here on. I told the editor about a new course I have created and he said I should tell it to you.

When I notified the dean that I was going to shift my main attention from subject matter to student, he (with the advice and consent of other layers of authority and vested interest on the campus) allowed me to announce two courses that have no subject matter obligation. The point is important, at least to me. Everything I do in the two new courses could be done in the courses which I taught before, except for one fact—as long as I taught the course titled Popular Control of Government, for example, everybody in the department expected me to talk to the students about everything mentioned in V. O. Key's textbook on political parties. Now if I have to argue with the students about everything V. O. Key thought he could risk having me interpret to them with the aid of his textbook, I have much too little of their time left to guide them in a struggle with questions that interest me most, but which V. O. thought ought to be dealt with before or after or collaterally with the things he writes about. So I needed a course or two free of any commitment to content which would give my departmental colleagues occasion to raise their eyebrows if my students do not know everything that Charlie Hagan's students know.

One of the courses we created is titled: Loyalty, Sedition, and Freedom of Expression. I do not have to teach my students a thing about how to develop loyalty or destroy it, not a thing about how to root our subversion or sneak it to success, not a thing about how to secure freedom of speech and press or how to restrain them for the aggrandizement of other valued objectives. All I have to do, if it is something I have the capabilities for doing, is bring the students forward in understanding what will be found when one unravels and closely inspects a complicated social problem. More precisely stated, the point of the course last year was: How do you evaluate a governmental restraint of expression which is justified on the ground that it assures loyalty where loyalty to the nation is desired or shores up against subversion where subversion is feared?

I do not intend to offer the course, with or without credit, to this audience. A few descriptive statements should make clear the nature of the enterprise. I hold the floor for the first few weeks in what I want to be a model demonstration of how to dissect a problem and set it up for evaluation. The Sedition Act of 1798 is the specimen. With the help of the students, I try to lay out a series of differentiable acts or events and consequences of acts or events which the statute was designed to discourage or keep from coming about. They range from the immediate, observable, easily comprehended act of breaking into a jail to free a prisoner, to incitement of a determination not to pay taxes, through a dozen other identifiable things that someone might count reprehensible, to the objective which has brought the statute its bad repute—the creation (by oral or printed utterances) of states of mind which are favorable to obstruction or overthrow of government. Each of the things which the statute was intended to discourage or wholly keep from coming about can be viewed as an end-value, but each of them also can be critically examined as a contributor to or an inhibitor of other valued things. Every item in the list can be made the center of a considerable inquiry in which you ask: How could the prohibitions of the statute advance or retard the realization of the ends which the statute-makers abhorred? As you can array the reprehensible things which the statute was intended to discourage or prevent, so you can array the means which the statute adopted for effecting their repression or prevention. These are the first steps in analysis. They must be followed by search for unintended consequences and identification of alternative means. The Sedition Act may have discouraged things which John Adams and his associates would have wished to encourage, and it may have caused things to happen which they very much wanted not to happen; similarly, the unintended consequences of the statute may have included some that John Adams, or Thomas Jefferson, or you, or my students, might think wholly desirable. The search for alternative means may lead to the conclusion that a better way could have been found for achieving the desired ends, or that equally effective means could have been found which would have exacted a smaller price in unwanted consequences.

This operation on the Sedition Act of 1798 has to be completed early in the course because the student has still to do his own analytic job. Instructed by the model demonstration, he produces an essay in which he dissects, scrutinizes, and evaluates another act which seeks to aggrandize highly honored values by a means which involved some significant restraint on freedom of expression. His assignment may be a state's obscenity statute, a criminal syndicalism act of World War I, the loyalty oath adopted in a border state when Unionist and Confederate protagonists were struggling for possession of the state's government, or any of some twenty other declarations of policy and obligation that I have so far run on to, thought amenable to a youngster's analytic tools, and found time to dress up with a set of instructions.

As you might be led to suppose from the attached exhibits (problems used in another course) students are supplied with a considerable amount of mimeographed material. On the Sedition Act of 1798: a commentary on the emotional disturbances of the time, debates in Congress when the statute was up for enactment, Madison's address opposing the act and the address in support (thought to be by John Marshall), and other informative items. The problem which the student undertakes for his essay may also require some specially prepared materials. For instance, I have mimeographed a representative part of the debate relating to loyalty and loyalty oaths in a Missouri constitutional convention of 1864. I might note, finally, that I believe I am now in the course of deciding not to allow as subject for the essay any act restraining speech or press which has gone to a high court for decision on constitutionality. The students lean too much on the judgment and reasoning of the judge and tell me more about what the Constitution permits and forbids than about the choices among competing values and alternative means which analysis of the problem shows to have been available.

The dean allowed that when I came to 60 years of age, the rest of the faculty might trust me with a course which could not be audited by reference to standard works of literature. I have presumed that knowledge of my ancient origin and long subjection to the hazards of an academic environment might win from you a benign toleration of confessions that might with better grace have been withheld for release when I am out of sight.

These two assignments, prepared for a course in American Political Thought, illustrate the kinds of exercise which have been used to test and develop analytic ability.

Topic 5. *National Will versus Local Will*

Government can not please everybody perfectly, so some persons are going to get what they want and some other people are going to get what they don't want. Lucky for you if you get pretty close to what you prefer most of the time. If all but a few people are in agreement, you may think it proper for them to get what they want; the few who dissent can change their minds, put up with what they don't want, or get out. But if many want this very much, and another many are just as strongly opposed to this—in this situation you have to face the question of competing wants and competing demands of the population. The federal arrangement—in our case, national-state-local division of authority—is one style of effort to adjust public policy and governmental action to differences in demands of the population. We have had sharp controversy on several occasions as to whether, in a particular area of affairs, one policy ought to be adopted for the whole nation (triumph of a national majority) or different parts of the country should be allowed to pursue different policies (triumph of local majorities). Three problems in which this fundamental issue emerged are retention or termination of slavery, toleration or prohibition of liquor, and relations between races in public education.

Materials:

(a) *The Federalist,* Essays Nos. 10, 62, 63.

(b) John C. Calhoun, *A Disquisition on Government.*

(c) Stephen A. Douglas and Abraham Lincoln on Squatter Sovereignty. In *The People Shall Judge,* I, 727-754.

(d) The Issue of Liquor Policy (*1*) Debate in the Senate on adoption of the 18th Amendment to the Constitution, in *Congressional Record,* Vol. 55, part 6, pp. 5549 to 5587 (Speeches by Senators Sheppard, Underwood, Harwick, and Lodge on July 30, 1917). (*2*) William G. McAdoo, *The Challenge: Liquor and Lawlessness vs. Constitutional Government,* pp. 106-221.

(e) Prevention and Punishment of Lynching. Read debate on the Dyer Bill of 1922 in *Congressional Record,* Vol. 62. For content of the proposed act of Congress, read Vol. 62, part 1, pp. 604-605. For argument in support of the bill, read Vol. 62, part 2, pp. 1708-1712 (Representative Cockran), and Vol. 62, part 12, pp. 13082-13086 (Senator Shortridge). For argument in opposition to the bill, read Vol. 1, part 1, pp. 797-807 (Representative Sumners), and Vol. 62, part 2, pp. 1722-1731 (Representative Connally).

Your task:

This assignment does not call for presentation of your own views on whether slavery should or should not have been continued, whether people ought or ought not be allowed to have liquor, whether whites and Negroes should or should not be mixed in the same school. You are to write a paper about who ought to decide great questions of public policy like these. Ought such questions be decided one way to suit the majority of the American people, or should such questions be left to people living in different parts of the nation so that public policy can be different in different parts of the country? Hamilton and Madison, who wrote *The Federalist* essays, both served in the convention that drafted the Constitution. Do you conclude that they foresaw that this question of who should decide would come up? Was adequate provision made on this point in the Constitution? Was the question of how best to balance national demands and local demands fully and adequately examined in *The Federalist?* How far do you travel with Calhoun? Was he pushing a crackpot proposition, do you buy him 100 per cent, do you find him partially persuasive? Were the reasonings of Douglas and Lincoln of a quality worthy of their great reputations as statesmen? Did the arguments concerning prohibition and anti-lynching legislation produce reasoning of quality comparable to that of Calhoun, Douglas, and Lincoln? Many white persons in the South have asserted that the order of the United States Supreme Court requiring mixing of the races in public schools is an imposition of national will in an area of affairs that should be left for determination within each state. What position do you think Calhoun, Douglas, Lincoln would take on this issue? Are you now ready to set forth some statements of your own about: Under what circumstances or in respect to what kind of questions should the national will triumph, and in what circumstances or on what kinds of questions should sectors of the population be allowed to pursue the policy that suits them best? The country needs another statesman and you are as old as Alexander Hamilton was when he wrote his *A Full Vindication* (or are you under 17?).

Topic 7. *Relationships of Chief Executive and Legislature*

Materials:

(a) The Articles of Confederation; Constitution of the United States; Constitution of Indiana.

(b) *The Federalist,* Essays Nos. 47 to 51, and 67 to 77.

(c) The first great debate on the president's constitutional powers. *Annals of Congress,* Vol. 1, pp. 368 to 396. There is further debate on the same matter at pp. 456 to 485.

(d) The Senate Censures a President. This is the fight between President Andrew Jackson and his opponents in the Senate over Jackson's policy toward the United States Bank. The items to be read are in *Congressional Debates,* Vol. 10, parts 1 and 2.

pages 30-41 will tell you what the quarrel is about
      58-94 Senator Clay. Note his resolution on p. 58
      97-139 Senator Benton
      233-259 Senator Shepley
      274-289 Senator Rives
      834-836 some more resolutions by Clay
            1187 Vote on Clay's resolutions which you read on page 58
            (Jackson is censured)

    1317-1325 President Jackson protests
    1335-1365 and 1374-1423 Senators respond
    1488-1526 Senator Bibb
    1562-1581 Senator Clay again
    1640-1650 Senator Calhoun
    1663-1690 Senator Webster

If you wish to read further: (*1*) *Congressional Debates,* Vol. 11, pp. 631-689 and 723-727 (Senator Benton moves to expunge Senator Clay's resolutions from the records of the Senate). (*2*) The report of the Senate Finance Committee on Senator Clay's resolutions. (*3*) The Veto Power in Indiana. *Debates and Proceedings of the Convention for Revision of the Constitution of Indiana,* 1850, Vol. 2. The proposed section of the new constitution which is under debate is on p. 1320. The debate follows, pp. 1322-1332, 1345-1352, 1447-1448.

Your task:

This is an opportunity to compare objective thinking about separation of powers and checks and balances with the practical problems of applying these ideas when the stakes are high and men are caught up in partisanship. Hamilton and Madison, at the time they wrote *The Federalist* essays, could not know whether they would later side with the President against Congress or vice versa in contests for power. Partisanship was at its peak in the bank fight of 1834. Did the arrangements which the framers made for dividing up power, and which Hamilton and Madison explained and justified in *The Federalist,* actually have the consequences Hamilton and Madison anticipated? Or did partisanship and emotion nullify the attempt of the framers to provide a system that would stand up in time of crisis and keep public policy from going the way extreme partisans want to take it? Did you find anything you call statesmanship on the part of men who were in the center of the fight? Was the argument in Congress in 1789 in keeping with the ideas expressed in *The Federalist?* Did the Hoosiers of 1850 understand separation of powers as you do after your careful reading of *The Federalist?* What could be finer than for you to write several paragraphs on the application of classic ideas about separation of powers to effective working relationships between chief executive and legislature (i.e., relationships that result in giving the nation satisfactory public policy)? Naturally, if you respond to this call to public service, you will bear in mind that we have a much fuller network of communication throughout the population (including political parties, newspapers) than Hamilton and Madison had experienced.

ROBERT H. CONNERY

Now bring together

Today the liberal arts college faces a challenge as great as any that it has had to meet in its long history. The college is being squeezed from both ends—from the high school at one end, and from the professional and graduate schools at the other. Many high school seniors are ready for sophomore work before they enter college; some collegians are ready for graduate work before they graduate. Students may not need both the senior year in high school and the freshman year in college. And in a good college they may not need both the senior year and the first year of graduate school.

Moreover, teaching methods have kept pace neither with the caliber of the students now going to college nor with the kind of education which they should be receiving. It is no secret that textbooks are often five years out of date by the time they reach the bookstore. Much greater emphasis should be placed on the techniques of self-education and on means of bringing together into synthesis knowledge previously acquired. Today education must become continuing self-education, not the embalming of the student in yesterday's facts.

Public high schools, especially in large urban centers, have displayed marked improvement in the past dozen years. Such schools are offering, to their abler students at least, much more extensive work in mathematics and in the sciences generally, more intensive instruction in foreign languages as well as more thorough work in history and English literature. At Duke in 1956 only 20 percent of the entering freshmen had scores of 600 or higher on the Verbal Factor in the Scholastic Aptitude Test, compared with 68 percent in 1963. Some 75 percent of the freshmen scored 600 or higher on the Mathematics Factor in 1963 compared with less than half that percentage in 1956.

Another type of evidence clearly indicating both more intensive and extensive instruction in the high schools can be found in the number of entering college students who request advance placement through one or more examinations, generally administered by the College Entrance Examination Board, which will exempt them from taking courses of a similar nature in the freshman year of college. Columbia College in New York City reports that two-fifths of the class entering in the fall of 1963 requested advance placement in one or more subjects and more than half of the examinations were good enough to warrant granting the request. In a questionnaire administered to these same students in a freshman humanities course approximately one-sixth of them claimed that they had read half or more of the required reading before entering college.[1] This is, of course, no proof that the books were well read, but not many years ago it would have been astonishing if that number of freshmen had even heard of half of these authors.

Quite as important as these specific developments in the university are the more general changes which are taking place in American society. Today there is a great emphasis upon technological skills, but ours is an environment characterized by rapid change and hard-won skills soon become obsolete. There has been a spectacular increase in information, particularly in the natural sciences but also in other fields of knowledge. Society is faced with global concern for the economic and social development of the human race. All of these characteristics present serious questions for the nation's colleges. Dean Truman of Colombia, in stating some of the implications of this situation, has said "First, it is likely or inevitable that, as the education editor of the *New York Times* recently put it, liberal education will be 'swallowed up by the high school,' and that colleges will be confronted with gradual but inescapable 'obsolescence' . . . . in my judgment it need not and should not be the case in the predictable future. . . ."[2] Most of the improvements that are now taking place in the secondary schools today, he noted, are precisely what the colleges have been begging the schools to do for years. While colleges may find it difficult to adjust to the new situation, these developments at the secondary level promise to provide them with the opportunities for which colleges have long been asking.

1. David Truman, "The Changing Character of Undergraduate Education—Columbia College's Mission," Columbia *Graduate Faculties Newsletter* (March, 1964), p. 4.
   2. *Ibid.*, p. 5.

The pressure at the other end of the four-year undergraduate college is equally evident. Today more students are continuing their education in professional and graduate schools. Harvard and Columbia report that four-fifths of their graduating classes are headed towards some sort of post-graduate work. This percentage is by no means uniform across the country. But the large state universities and smaller private colleges are all feeling the effects of the prolonged educational commitment of the college population. Dean David Truman of Columbia asks "what about the possibility that well prepared students, anticipating the problem of getting into and through the graduate school, will commit themselves to an early and narrow specialization that in itself will obstruct the goals of a liberal education?" He thinks this course unlikely and that if students are given "a respectable opportunity, most of them will grasp the challenge of a liberal education."[3]

Centuries ago Plato, in laying out an educational program for "the guardians" who were to be the mainstay of his republic, summed up what should be still today the goal of the liberal arts college. Referring to the guardians he said, ". . . from their twentieth year those who have been selected shall have special privileges, and the studies which they have come across at random in their education as children, they must now bring together so that they will have a general view of their kinship with one another and with the general nature of Being."[4]

The improved secondary school, one may argue, will make it possible for colleges "to bring together" with greater facility. The changes in the secondary schools will provide some of the information, some of the skills, and some emotional maturity. The colleges then will have the opportunity to add to this fund of knowledge and develop interrelationships.

Certainly the college curriculum needs to be re-examined to assure that it contains courses at different levels aimed at explaining relations between fields of knowledge, so that it will indeed "bring together." In the past, survey courses for this purpose have been offered in some colleges to freshmen or sophomores. One suspects

3. *Ibid.*
4. *The Republic of Plato,* Everyman's Library Edition, translated by A. D. Lindsay (New York, 1950), p. 298.

with good reason that much of the content of these courses—and the textbooks that are used—are now covered in high school. But it might be worthwhile to experiment in the senior year in college with this kind of a course. This would mean involving college freshmen in pursuits which would sharpen their knowledge in specific areas and then after their interest is aroused, proceed to courses designed to bring together the segments of knowledge that they have learned through intensive studies in various fields. Reversing the order of the present day curriculum might meet an objection students so frequently voice—that the last year in high school and the first year in college are much the same both in subject matter and in teaching methods. A radical change of this kind in the college curriculum might make these later years a more challenging and stimulating experience.

Any major change in tomorrow's college, however, involves overturning a good many long accepted educational shibboleths. The whole college educational experience needs rethinking, freed from the administrative and educational strait-jacket in which college faculties have laced themselves.

The Anatomy of a Class

One dilemma that has plagued proposals for reform is the increasing size of college student bodies on the one hand and on the other hand the dogma that the smaller the class, the better the teaching. Whatever answer one gives to this problem affects college admission policy as well as the allotment of faculty resources. Teaching loads are usually determined by the number of courses a professor teaches and the number of hours he spends in the classroom. The size of a class can be increased or the size of the faculty can be enlarged. This is a dilemma, however, of our own making, since it rests on the assumption that small classes necessarily make for good teaching. Is this a sound conclusion?

There seems to be general agreement that given a very superior teacher, the student is likely to have a different kind of educational experience in a small class of a dozen students than in a very large one of 300 students. There may be, but not necessarily will be, more opportunity for discussion. Many teachers lecture even in small classes and permit little discussion. The student may become better acquainted with the teacher personally, but this does not answer the question whether he will learn more in the small class. One may even doubt whether a small class will stimulate the instructor to put forth his best efforts as much as a large class. Alvin C. Eurich, formerly Vice-President of the Fund for the Advancement of Education, maintains that "we have made a fetish out of small classes."[5]

Professor Livingston has commented at some length on this problem in his essay in this series and the discussion need not be repeated here. But one might note in passing that fifteen years ago an article in the *Encyclopedia of Educational Research* reviewed 73 separate studies of the effect of class size on learning. The authors concluded that on the basis of these experimental studies "mere size of class had little significant influence" on educational achievement. These experiments did not show that students learned more easily in large classes; neither did they show that there was greater achievement in the small classes.[6] Critics of the research that led to these conclusions no doubt would say that the examination to determine achievement was inadequate. One can readily admit that it is difficult to appraise student achievement even with the best of examinations. Yet, examinations are used for determining whether a student passes or fails a course and whether he should be awarded a degree. If examinations are valid for one purpose, they are just as valid for determining achievement in the other case. A somewhat more impressive objection to determining the effect of class size on learning is the difficulty of isolating what a student learns in a particular educational experiment. At any given time he is not only learning from one teacher in one course, but from other teachers and from his fellow students. Measuring the effect of one part of this whole experience is admittedly difficult. Even with these limitations, these experiments indicate that class size is of relatively

5. Alvin C. Eurich, "Better Instruction With Fewer Teachers" in *Current Issues in Higher Education,* Proceedings of the Eleventh Annual National Conference on Higher Education (Washington, D. C., 1956), pp. 10-11.

6. Henry J. Otto and Fred Von Borgerode, *Encyclopedia of Educational Research* (1950), p. 212; see also Earl Hudelson, *Class Size at the College Level* (Minneapolis, 1928); Laurence Siegel, F. B. Macomber, and James F. Adams, "The Effectiveness of Large Group Instruction at the University Level," *Harvard Educational Review,* XXIX (Summer, 1959), 216-226.

minor importance. The effectiveness of teaching seems to depend much more upon the ability of the instructor, the capacity of the student, and the relationship between the two. Eurich concludes that "the ratio, then, needs to be reconsidered from the standpoint of the number of effective relationships with individual students the superior teacher can actually establish regardless of the size of the class."[7]

One wonders whether the debate over class size is not archaic, and whether the issue is not how different arrangements in different circumstances can best be used to meet the needs of students. The function of higher education is not simply to give information but to bring together and add to what has been learned earlier. Consequently, one wonders whether large class lectures should not be used in some instances as well as small seminars in others. Independent study, laboratory assignments, and internships are all possible organizational arrangements, and some combination of them might provide much more effective teaching than merely small classes throughout.

Education is primarily a process of communication, but need it be two-way communication? The important thing in teacher-student relations is the student reaction. The student must react to the professor. The assumption that good teaching depends on intimate personal acquaintance between teacher and student seems to be based on the idea that the teacher is what the student studies, not the subject. Thus, if the teacher does not know each of his students personally, teaching is assumed to be ineffective. The ideal of tutor-pupil relationship on a one-to-one basis leads us to keep our classes as small as possible. Thus, the ratio of number of faculty to number of students is frequently used as a measure of the quality of a college. With little consistency, however, the reputation of an instructor is often based on the number of students who elect his course and the more the better. A professor who can build his course from ten students to a hundred is usually regarded as an outstanding success by college administrators. Students who elect the large course, however, do not do so because the class is large, but because the professor is skillful. "Great teachers are great teachers because they are wise, learned, and skillful men of good will—not because they have few students, and not because they have an intimate acquaintance with

7. Eurich, *op. cit.*, p. 13.

each student."[8] Somewhat humorously I. A. Richards advised teachers in regard to their students, "don't have a relation. Don't have one; don't."[9]

The relation of a student to his teacher, however, should be very personal. Indeed the more personal it is, the greater impression the teacher will make upon the mind and character of the student. The student's attitude towards the teacher is important, but it does not necessarily depend on the intimacy of a tête-à-tête or even the intimacy of a small class. The relationship of a teenager to Frank Sinatra or to the Beatles is a personal relationship although neither Sinatra nor the Beatles need reciprocate the emotions of each teenager. Neither do they have to know each youngster as an individual in order to exercise influence over them. The success of a teacher, like that of an orator, depends on establishing a one-way relationship between himself and members of his audience.

Suppose, for the moment, a professor knows each of his students individually when he faces a class of twenty, what does he do differently than if he did not know them? Does he give individual assignments to fit each student's needs? Perhaps he does but more than likely he does not. To be sure, with a small class he may be able to see each student in individual tutorial sessions. If he does, the quality of his teaching may be better, but it is better because of what takes place at these sessions rather than what takes place in the classroom. Another instructor might be able to give the tutorial and the results would be just as effective. There is no necessary relation between the tutorial and the student's attitude towards the professor in the classroom. The author recalls that as an undergraduate he followed the lectures of one political scientist in a large class with enthusiasm only to find the same professor a dull dog in his office.

Discovering what the students know about political science before the class begins is an entirely different matter, because it can be directly related to the content of the course. One might well ask how much does the average political scientist know about his students when he walks into the classroom? Registration data may tell him whether they are freshmen or seniors. He knows nothing about their

8. John S. Diekhoff, *The Domain of the Faculty in Our Expanding Colleges* (New York, 1956), p. 18.
9. I. A. Richards, "The Teaching Process," in Bernice B. Cronkite (ed.), *A Handbook for College Teachers* (Cambridge, 1950), pp. 3-4.

attitude towards political questions, their maturity of political thought, nor their purpose in taking the course. The teacher assumes, generally, that all his students have reached a common level of knowledge, consequently, he teaches a standard course which may or may not be of maximum benefit to his students. One suspects that some of the criticism of the dullness of college arises from the endless repetition of the same material in secondary schools and in college. The advanced placement tests to some degree remedy this situation, at least for the freshman year. More information about what his students know about political science would enable a teacher to pitch the level of his instruction properly.

Some years ago the Duke political science department, with the aid of a small grant from the Fund for the Advancement of Teaching, developed an information test in American government for students about to take their first college course in the subject. Using a similar test of the same difficulty at the end of the course, an attempt was made not only to measure progress but to determine which students should be given advanced placement. Some 10 percent of the entering group knew more about American government before they took the course than did the average student upon completing the course. Consequently, anything that they might gain from the course would not be worth the time expended. This was a clear case for advanced placement.

The whole subject of tests and their use in colleges would bear re-examination. What does a college teacher learn from the tests that he gives his students? The majority of instructors probably would answer that through tests they are measuring how much students have learned in the course. Actually, they may be measuring a student's ability to write well, to regurgitate the teacher's ideas, or to gamble successfully with a group of choices offered him. Sometimes a test measures nothing at all, and many times it has no relationship to any learning process.

Objective tests have considerably lower standing among political scientists than essay-type tests, but each is open to criticism. Part of the criticism of objective tests arises from the fact that many of them are poorly constructed. It is very difficult to make a good objective test, as any authority on test methods will emphasize. It seems much easier to pose an essay question, but actually it may be as difficult if the instructor relates the question to the answer which he thinks he should obtain and weighs in his own mind whether this answer has any relation to the goals of his teaching. All too frequently an essay question simply measures a student's ability to write well. Well constructed objective tests coupled with essay-type questions probably are the best solution. But unless the professor is prepared to answer the question "what are you attempting to do" no test will make sense. Is your goal factual information, relations between sets of facts, skill in analysis, or some combination of them? Even the best test is simply a means of measuring the degree to which a given goal has been reached.

Goals of the Beginning Course

Political scientists have spent a great deal of time debating the best way of introducing students to the discipline. What should be the content of the first course? The general assumption seems to have been that there is one and only one best beginning course so far as content is concerned. Whether this assumption is correct may be seriously doubted, and if not, much of the debate has been fruitless. It is also assumed that there is a proper hierarchy of courses that should be built one upon the other. Lindsay Rogers argues earlier in these essays that there are few, if any, courses in political science that must be taken before other courses can be understood.

Usually beginning courses deal with American government, comparative government, political theory, or some combination of these three. Actually, a very good case might be made for studying Far Eastern government or the government of underdeveloped countries as the first college course, since these would be completely new and different from anything that a student has had in high school. Whatever the decision may be about the major content area, innumerable questions arise about what government, what theories, and what policies should be studied. In comparative government courses, everything from Sweden to India is studied without any apparent reason unless it is merely to give a smattering of information, much of it repetitious, about as many countries as possible. So unsatisfactory is this country-by-country approach that some courses attempt to compare great political systems with one another—dictatorship with democracies, the presidential versus the parliamentary, etc. But this solution is bound to leave out some favorite countries and usually has very little to say about the numerous new states. When one attempts to use political theory as the basic course, the problem is where to start and what to include. Frequently, the theory course deals with the history of political ideas and becomes what has been called by an unfriendly critic a "ramble through archaic opinions." Little attempt is made to apply theory to the study of modern institutions and sometimes the "theorist tends to regard his work as a commentary upon what other theorists have said in the past."[10]

Even the traditional "American Government" as a beginning course has its problems. How much time should be allotted to the national government in comparison with state and local governments and, for that matter, should they be considered at all? What attention should be given to political behavior, to programs and policies compared to the structure of government?

Since there is so little agreement on the content of the first (and for many students the last) course they take in political science, and so little agreement on the criteria for determining what the content should be, one wonders whether the teacher's interest should not determine content. An instructor will teach best the material he knows best and will arouse greater interest in his students if he knows his subject well. Will an expert in political theory do a good job when he is assigned to teach American local government, and vice versa? This may be a challenge in some cases, but since graduate education in the United States is based on specialization, a man trained in one specialty usually will be ineffective if forced to teach a subject in which he has little interest.

Even if the course is built around the interest of the instructor, can it be a good course without some goal toward which it is intended to move? If an instructor does not know what he is trying to do with his students, how can he determine the best means of doing it? What is the purpose of teaching political science? There is a tremendous lot of factual information about government available, but there is only a little time to examine it. How much of this should be offered to college students? Indeed, does it make any difference what sets of miscellaneous facts are put before them unless the teacher has a pretty

10. S. E. Finer, "On the Teaching of Politics," *Universities Quarterly*, VIII (1953-1954), 53.

clear idea of what impact he expects to have on his students? Some
political scientists, as evidenced in the essays that have preceded this
one, state that their purpose in teaching is to show students how to
think rationally about political questions, that is, to train them in
the ability to analyze a given body of facts about politics, to synthe-
size arguments, and to reach conclusions in a logical manner. Others
have argued that political science is a humane subject and that its
purpose, essentially, is to prepare students to live a full life. Elsewhere, good citizenship has been cited as a goal, or preparing students
for participation in political life. Thus, there seems to be as little
agreement on the purpose of political education as there is upon how
to reach whatever goal may be chosen.

Cynics may well say that if some agreement on the mental functions being trained, on the methodology being mastered, and on the
content cannot be reached, it must mean that political science is not
a recognizable field of knowledge. They would maintain that an
intellectual discipline consists of some commonly accepted body of
knowledge and an agreed-upon methodology for analyzing and evaluating that knowledge, and that without this, one has at best only a
set of individual artistic experiences and at worst a hodge-podge of
emotions revolving around a number of isolated facts.

Must the methodology and the goals in an area as long studied
as political science be narrowly defined? The study of politics, in the
Western world at least, dates back to Plato and Aristotle, and as an
intellectual discipline it is as new as the last century. Is there only
one methodology that is sound in so ancient a field of intellectual
interest? Political theory may have a sound methodology which is
quite unsuited for the study of political behavior. The question would
seem to be whether each of the major fields in political science has
been able to develop a commonly accepted body of knowledge and
an accepted methodology. In listening to the debates upon the one
best methodology, one is reminded of Aesop's fable of the blind men
and the elephant. It well may be that each has hold of one part of
the whole.

If each instructor knows what outcome he expects from his teaching, and suits the content of the course and his methodology to his
goal, is this not sufficient? If the speciality and the training of the
teacher be taken into consideratiton and the goal that he expects to

attain with his students, it might be that the order in which courses are offered would differ from one political science department to another, and still be essentially sound. Indeed, some departments might decide to give little attention to a hierarchy of courses. Others might use a variety of beginning courses.

This is all to suggest that course content has relevance and meaning only in relation to the goals of the instructor. It does not seem nearly as important for the profession as a whole to agree on the goals as it is that each instructor set his own goals before he begins to teach a political science course. Without belittling the importance of content, this approach puts content in its proper relation to the larger problem of bringing areas of knowledge into relation with each other. What is important is that the instructor should have fixed firmly in mind what he is trying to do with his class. Then he can find appropriate teaching techniques to reach his goal.

Teaching: Art or Science?

Scholars through the ages have found it difficult to define a "great teacher" in any precise way. Two qualifications most often associated with a good teacher are mastery of his subject and clarity in its presentation. To this might be added the ability to engage with his students in a joint enterprise of equal importance to them both. A teacher's ability to arouse a spirit of adventure in facing the challenge of mastering what is known, or conquering the unknown, may well be the test of great teaching.

Guy Stanton Ford, who at various times was Dean of the Graduate School and President of the University of Minnesota, trying to determine what was a good teacher from the students' point of view, said:

All I can say is that few, if any, teachers are rated good by all students. Some like them long, some like them short, some prefer the mild and hesitant, some the aggressive and dogmatic, some even prefer brunettes to blonds. For an occasional successful teacher I can find no reason at all.[11]

One of the issues that goes to the heart of teaching is the age-old question of whether teaching is an art or a science. This is a well

11. Guy Stanton Ford, "Teacher and Taught," *Bulletin of the American Association of University Professors,* XLI (Autumn, 1955), 478.

chewed chestnut but some meat still remains. If teaching is an art, then it follows that good teachers are born rather than made. Thus, to improve teaching, apparently, one should resort to prayerful petition. Is one really pushed inevitably to this conclusion, or is this the counsel of despair?

Virtually all of the vast flow of books and articles coming from teacher's colleges and from the pens of professional educators consider teaching a science. Developing side by side with the science of psychology, which came into full flower in the twentieth century, and the pragmatism which starts with assumptions that there are no absolutes, no certainties, and no eternal values, the new science of education places a great deal of emphasis upon research and the collection of facts. Truth, it was argued, could be discovered through evaluating the consequences of an idea. These views have greatly altered the role of the teacher. In the view of the professional educator, it is less important that the teacher be a competent historian, mathematician, or political scientist than that he thoroughly understand how a student learns and grows, and the social environment in which he develops.

The teacher is expected to do much more than simply teach subject matter. As Woodring puts it,

he has increasingly been held responsible for the child's recreation, his social life, his emotional adjustment, and his physical health. Though progressive educators have encouraged teachers to accept this total responsibility, they alone are not responsible for the change. In increasing numbers parents have passed on to the schools responsibilities which they once accepted as their own. Parents have held the schools responsible for everything from bad manners and indolence to juvenile deliquency.[12]

As is usual with any movement, the followers push far beyond the goals of the masters; this has been true also in the progressive teaching movement. John Dewey always insisted that the teacher should know his subject as well as understand children. But progressive educational clichés such as "we teach children not subjects" and "education is life" led some educators to say that knowledge of subject matter was of less importance than other skills that a teacher should have. This change of attitude was reflected in the requirements of teachers' certificates for the secondary and the elementary schools which emphasized courses in education. Fortunately the pro-

12. Paul Woodring, *A Fourth of A Nation* (New York, 1957), p. 87.

fessional educator has not made much headway at the college level, although more and more chairs of higher education are being established. This may not necessarily be disastrous since there are many areas of college teaching that might well be studied empirically.

The other side of the debate, however, has been presented with equal force. Gilbert Highet significantly called his book *The Art of Teaching,* because he believed teaching was an art not a science. He argued that

teaching involves emotions, which cannot be systematically appraised and employed, and human values, which are quite outside the grasp of science. . . . Teaching is not like inducing a chemical reaction: it is much more like painting a picture or making a piece of music, or on a lower level like planting a garden or writing a friendly letter. You must throw your heart into it, you must realize that it cannot all be done by formulas, or you will spoil your work, and your pupils, and yourself.[13]

He maintained that it was very dangerous to apply the aims and methods of science to human beings as individuals. While their behavior in large groups and scientific diagnosis of their physical structure was valuable, scientific relationships between human beings were bound to be inadequate. Consequently, scientific teaching would be inadequate so long as both teachers and pupils were human beings.

Highet did not ignore individual differences in learning ability, motivation, and interests. Actually, he gave a good deal of attention to these differences and to suggesting ways of dealing with them. Nor did he automatically rule out all courses in education. He simply argued that the scientific method should not be the primary basis for approaching teaching.

Woodring, accepting Highet's points of view, argues further,

The fact that teaching is held to be an art rather than a science does not mean even that methodology cannot be taught. Every artist learns his methods, usually from another artist who acts as teacher. The genius will develop his own methods, but it cannot be expected that all of the more than a million American teachers will be geniuses.[14]

He points out the very fact that Highet has taken time to write a book on the art of teaching seemed to indicate that he believed that this art can, in part at least, be learned from books. Highet's book, how-

13. Gilbert Highet, *The Art of Teaching* (New York, 1950), p. 7.
14. Woodring, *op. cit.,* p. 52.

ever, is not based on scientific research, it contains no statistics or citations. Rather it discusses the qualities and abilities of a good teacher, describes the methods used by some of the great teachers of the Western world from Plato, Aristotle, and Jesus to the Jesuits of the sixteenth century and to famous modern teachers.

Does the college professor teach subjects or does he teach students? What, if anything, does this question mean? Certainly it cannot mean that teaching should be unrelated to student interest or is not concerned with the student. On the other hand, how is it possible to teach students without teaching subject matter? To return to the original question; what is teaching, an art or a science? Could it be that teaching is an art which has certain scientific aspects? Could it be that what is needed is a marriage and not a divorce between these two? Woodring sums up the aim of education in a single sentence: "in a society of free men, the proper aim of education is to prepare the individual to make wise decisions. All else is but contributory."[15] At best, colleges can do no more than provide opportunities for the individual to develop the initiative, resourcefulness, and knowledge to make the right decisions. As Diekhoff puts it "the student does not learn what the professor knows, he learns much less and much more."[16] He also learns from his fellow students, from the books he reads, from the experiments he performs, and all the extra collegiate experiences of that period of his life. A distinction should be made between the aim of education as a whole and the methods and skills which contribute to this aim. In the modern society, an educated individual must be able to read, write, and talk because decisions are based upon information and the ability to communicate with others. Yet, these are not the ultimate aims of education; they are simply ways of achieving that goal.

Henry Jules in a challenging article says "learning to learn has been and continues to be homo sapiens' most formidable evolutionary task." He thinks that the learning task has become so enormous for men that "today education, along with survival, constitutes a major preoccupation. In all the fighting over education we are simply saying that after a million years of struggling to become human, we are

15. *Ibid.,* p. 111.
16. John S. Diekhoff, *Tomorrow's Professors* (Fund for the Advancement of Education, Ford Foundation, New York, 1959), p. 7.

not yet satisfied that we have mastered the fundamental human task, learning."[17]

Unfortunately, not even the psychologists really know very much about learning. As Kenneth Spence puts it "the truth of the matter is that we psychologists have been asked to solve practical problems before we had the laws of behavior necessary to do so."[18] We do know that in the learning process "what the learner learns is confined to what he does himself. Learning is confined to the activity induced in the learner by what he sees and hears."[19] This, of course, has long been recognized by good teachers. Thus, an effective lecture is really a conversation. If it does not stir up the hearers to comment and reply, even though the reply may not be spoken, it leaves the audience unchanged and might as well not have been delivered.

In the same way a well-written book stimulates the reader to talk back. Mortimer Adler long ago, in his classic *How To Read A Book,* urged students to talk back to the author as one of the means of learning. Accepting these basic theories, what are their implications for college teaching? One question on which light might be shed is whether the students should be instructed in or led to inquire into subjects. Should they be "told" or allowed to "discover"? In a word, should education be largely non-directed and democratic or directed and authoritarian? Under which leadership do students learn the most rapidly and the most extensively? One would suppose that the answer to these questions would not only be readily forthcoming but also concise. One authority, however, reports that available research evidence fails to demonstrate that either authoritarian or democratic leadership has consistently been associated with higher productivity.[20] He reinforces the conclusion that for knowledge of exactly how learning best takes place answers still must be found. He says "when a satisfactory body of knowledge of learning in social situations is available, it then will be possible to describe the behavior which a teacher can exhibit to achieve a given learning outcome." These comments seem to cast a good deal of doubt upon the adaptability of the theory of "progressive

17. Henry Jules, "American Schoolrooms: Learning the Nightmare," *Columbia University Forum,* VI (Spring, 1963), 24.
18. Kenneth W. Spence, "The Relation of Learning Theory to the Technology of Education," *Harvard Educational Review,* XXIX (Spring, 1959), p. 87.
19. E. R. Guthrie, *The State University* (Seattle, 1959), p. 28.
20. Richard C. Anderson, "Learning in Discussions: A Resume of the Authoritarian-Democratic Studies," *Harvard Educational Review,* XXIX (Spring, 1959), 212.

education" to college teaching. Woodring, commenting upon these theories as applied to elementary schools, noted that, "The progressives demand that there be no discipline except self-discipline has done much to reduce the effectiveness of adult control but has not set the child free. . . . He is increasingly the slave of his peer group to which he has been taught he must conform."[21] Students may freely express opinions, but this does not guarantee that their opinions are any more informed at the end of the semester than they were at the beginning. The same conclusion could be reached about the results of this method in college teaching.

Expanding the Range of the Learning Experience

The author does not propose to write a textbook on methods of instruction, but rather to discuss some devices with which he has had personal experience and which might be useful to a political scientist in adjusting his teaching to the opportunities of the moment. University teaching should be a process resulting from interaction between faculty and student in which the student learns how to learn, how to think critically, how to discover, how to evaluate, and, above all, how to relate and "bring together." The methods by which this process is achieved may vary, for methods are instruments which, if blunted, we should throw away. Field trips, internships, role-playing, independent study, honors programs, and various kinds of audio-visual aids, under certain circumstances, all can be useful methods of teaching in addition to the classroom method. All of them have certain limitations. It seems pretty well established that a good teacher will employ different methods to deal with different courses and different kinds of students. Unfortunately, there seems to be a stereotype in political science leading one to assume that there is one best method which should fit all situations. Theoretically this may be true but the choice of method is a subjective judgment. The method should suit the teacher's purpose, the skills which he possesses, the material to be mastered, and the ability and interests of the class. The teacher should weigh all of these various factors and reach a decision as to which method is best.

More than a decade ago Marion Irish argued that an academic

21. Woodring, *op. cit.,* p. 25.

revolution was taking place brought about in large part by student interns in American government who were "invading the city hall, the county courthouse, the state capitals, and the alphabetical agencies of Washington."[22] She argued that the mingling of the academic and the practical was all to the good. While separation of town and gown was an ancient and honorable tradition, it did not bring the student face to face with real problems in the turbulent world outside the academic halls in the way the experience of an internship could.

This view has been questioned by Lane Lancaster who maintained that internships, like field trips, could be a waste of time. He argued that "under the influence of the physical sciences, a considerable number of students have concluded that the secret of rule may be found by studying government in action." He doubted that students would learn about justice by attending a trial, about law making by observing the legislature, or about local government by inspecting the fire and police departments. He supposed "such excursions are harmless and they are often interesting; yet I think we should not critically assume that what we say in any such cases is the whole truth of the matter."[23] Unless the student understood how the great tradition of the law developed, he would appreciate little of what went on in the courtroom.

One may suggest that a third position is most tenable: that internships, like field trips, in themselves are neither good nor bad. They may be an exciting learning experience or a complete waste of time, depending on how well planned and organized they are. To be successful requires preparation, direction, discussion, and digestion. An internship is always somewhat of a gamble and depends upon how significant the problems are that present themselves during the period of tenure in the post. The extent of the gamble, however, can be reduced by insuring that interns are assigned to offices which deal with important problems. Occasionally, interns have been placed in clerical positions where it is quite clear that they would learn very little about the major operations of government. But this criticism seems to have been more prevalent when internships first came into use than it has been in recent years. Nevertheless, the question always

22. Marion D. Irish, "The Academic Revolution," *Bulletin of the American Association of University Professors,* XXXII (1946), 472.

23. Lane W. Lancaster, "The Ivory Tower—No Vacancies," *Bulletin of the American Association of University Professors,* XXXIII (1947), 282.

should be asked whether the assignment will be at a sufficiently high level in the government to enable an intern to observe how major problems arise and how they are solved. It is important, too, that some academic contact be maintained during the period of the internship. This can usually be done by having a man with academic experience directing a group of interns, meeting with them periodically for discussion of what they have observed and how it relates to the larger theoretical problems of government. There may well be, of course, some value in simply living and working for a year in the environment of Washington, D. C., or of the state capital. This experience can hardly fail to make some impression on the student of government. But this experience can be made much more meaningful through continued academic direction. The weakness of some intern programs lies in the failure to provide sufficiently mature academic direction which would relate what an intern observes to what he has learned in the classroom.

Field trips have been criticized on the same basis as internships and perhaps with more validity. Any one who has observed the hoards of excited high school tourists that pour into Washington in the spring may be pardoned if he has some reservations about similar "field trips" at the college level. This kind of junket may have considerable value in broadening the horizons of an adolescent, but it is of questionable worth to the mature college student. Yet, a good case may be made for field trips provided they are properly planned and directed. They should not be sightseeing tours, of course, but they can provide opportunities to observe government which will make a much more lasting impression on a college student than hours spent in the classroom. Understanding the legislative process should not stop with a few minutes spent in the galleries of a legislative chamber. The opportunity to observe the work of legislative committees at hearings on bills and carefully structured interviews with members of a legislative body on both sides of the bill, followed up by conferences with pressure organizations, can be most fruitful. This is so particularly if both the most able and the least able members of a legislative committee are interviewed. To obtain this type of interview requires not only a good deal of preparation with the legislators but also with the students themselves. Generally, the persons being interviewed are surprisingly frank, not only about their own role, but also regarding their views of the strengths and weaknesses of the legislative process.

The same approach can be used in studying the judicial and administrative process. A student may learn something by sitting in a courtroom, but he will learn a great deal more by interviewing the judge and opposing attorneys. The problems of decision-making at the administrative level can be made much more meaningful by not only interviewing administrative officers but by talking with representatives of interest groups in favor or opposed to a particular course of action. All of these interviews should be followed by seminars with the students to give them an opportunity to digest and analyze what they have observed. Lack of this follow-up has been one of the major weaknesses in the use of field trips.

Neither role-playing nor gaming has been exploited to anything like its full capacity as a teaching device. To be sure, there have been model United Nations Assemblies and mock legislative sessions, but they have been weak on follow-up in relating the experience of participation to what has been discussed in theory in the classroom. What the military men mean by the terms "the critique of the exercise" is usually entirely absent. Law schools have found moot courts effective, but what professor of constitutional law has used them in political science? The details of court procedure need not be emphasized but preparing briefs and writing a decision followed by a critique should prove stimulating.

Gaming an administrative situation has all sorts of exciting possibilities. For example, reliance upon lectures is less satisfactory in the field of public administration than in any other area of political science. Undergraduate students usually do not have any personal experience with the problems of public administration. Statistics involving millions and billions of dollars or hundreds and thousands of employees are so far beyond the grasp of imagination that they mean very little. Arthur Macmahon used to say that if an instructor could simply bring an undergraduate class to appreciate the size and complexity of government activities, a great deal would have been accomplished.

Lecturing on administration or even class discussion based on textbooks omits some of the most important elements in administration. None of the struggle for power and status is present in a lecture-room. The student in the classroom experiences none of the clash of personality and the struggle to obtain personal goals that he would probably find in an administrative agency. Neither can he experience the necessity for getting along with people which some successful administrators feel is one of the most important qualities of a good administrator. Topics are discussed serially. Problems of organization, personnel, budget, etc. are considered separately although an administrator is faced with all of these problems at the same time. Thus the normal approach in teaching trends to oversimplify the administrative process.

Case studies have answered some of these criticisms and if students are assigned roles to play from a case study script, teaching can be made much more realistic. The use of the laboratory technique can be even more challenging since the student is permitted a greater degree of personal choice and does not act out a script. In the use of this method, the problem—the enforcement of a particular statute or the operation of an administrative agency—is set, students are assigned roles, and the situation is played out as a game. New elements are introduced from time to time in the terms of new orders from the executive or new developments on the part of the public. If the game can be monitored by people from the government service, it can be made instructive and valuable as a teaching device. One advantage of this method is that the instructor in creating the situation can determine what problems in administration will be illustrated and the order in which they will be permitted to arise. It may be as simple or as elaborate a game as he chooses. As with case studies, field trips, and internships, the effectiveness of the laboratory method will depend to a large extent upon the critique. This is the single most important factor in the use of any of these methods. What did you learn, what were the choices, who made the decisions? These are the questions that must be asked again and again if what is learned is to be brought together in a series of meaningful relationships.[24]

Independent study offers equally challenging opportunities. One would assume that the goal of every college student would be to learn to continue his studies independently. The main characteristic of the independent study program is that the student pursues a course of reading at his own pace rather than attending classes. This may

24. See Robert H. Connery, "A Laboratory Method for Teaching Public Administration," *American Political Science Review*, XLII (1948), 68-74.

involve a small part or, in a few cases, a large portion of his college program. One of the basic theories of this system is that it will permit the bright student to go faster and further than the average. Cutting him free from a schedule of courses will permit him to achieve this end. Unfortunately for college budgets, independent study involves some type of tutorial, and thus becomes one of the most expensive types of instruction. It is possible, of course, to limit the program to a few students, or even to put students into small groups, but a college which follows the tutorial system must expect its instruction costs to be more than those of a college that uses the lecture system. These limitations mean that independent study usually involves only the superior student and leaves unanswered the problem of how the skills and habits of independent study may be used for the average student.

The same goals might be attained by much more carefully selected readings to accompany regular courses plus publicity to arouse the students' interest in the books which are suggested. In addition, some instruction in how to go about reading a book might be helpful. The traditionally grim mimeographed outside reading lists usually given to students will not do the job. Frequently, titles are repeated on successive lists year after year, often without much thought about the reason for their inclusion in the first place.

Political scientists certainly would not agree on a list of a hundred best books in the field, but they probably would agree that any book recommended to undergraduates should be of some lasting significance and written in a style which would appeal to a college student. Some would hold for great classics, others would emphasize recent books. One means of encouraging students to read on their own would be to give greater thought to the books that are recommended to them. Certainly the list ought to include some biographies, some examples of special pleading, and some frankly partisan essays and perhaps a few novels.[25]

Libraries and book clubs have been successful in stimulating reading, at least to the point of increasing the sales of best sellers.

25. The results of the experiments with independent study guides, visual aids, and testing at Duke University are discussed in Robert H. Connery, Richard H. Leach, and Henry Weitz, "Teaching the Beginning Course in Political Science: A Report on Research in the Better Utilization of College Teaching Resources" (processed) (Durham, 1959). This report has been drawn upon freely in writing this article.

A brief descriptive paragraph on each book or article recommended in a relatively short list might encourage a student to venture forth on independent study more boldly than page after page of titles do now. Book exhibits in the libraries, attractive descriptions in language that the student can understand, and an attempt to relate the proposed reading to something which the student recognizes as a problem all might be helpful in developing the habit of independent reading.

Independent "study," however, involves more than scanning a book. Mortimer Adler's classic *How to Read a Book* really should be entitled "How to Study Independently." If a student is shown how to analyze the material which he reads and how to talk back to the author, it is possible to develop the skills necessary for independent study.

American colleges unlike those in Britain pay very little attention to the intellectual use of vacation periods. The whole educational process is looked upon as something which takes place on campus and, to a large extent, in the classroom. Vacations, at least until the graduate school, are looked upon as periods when the student will loaf or work to earn enough money to return to school. The student week-end parties during spring vacation at Fort Lauderdale and in Bermuda no doubt add credence to this theory.

One might suggest that challenging independent study guides might be used to exploit the possibilities of better use of vacation periods. Certainly the superior student would find them encouraging, particularly if he were permitted to accelerate his college studies, perhaps by achieving grades through examination for the readings he did during the summer. The average student might make somewhat less use of these possibilities, but experience with former students who have been called into the armed forces leads one to believe that the desire to continue their education, even when they are away from the campus, is more common than one might expect. Certainly, there are opportunities here to be exploited which have scarcely been touched up to the present.

There seems to be little doubt that visual aids in the form of maps, slides, and movies can be valuable learning tools provided they are used correctly. The problem seems to be to find the type that is most effective in a given situation and to solve some of the technical problems involved in making and using such aids.

There is a wide range of choice among visual aids, but the political science professor seems to have given more attention to the use of motion pictures than to any other type of visual aid. Perhaps the reason for this is that the various commercial producers have gone to considerable effort to list various types of films available and to call them to the attention of college teachers. Despite this practice, many teachers who have experimented with the use of these films have found them unsatisfactory. Perhaps the reason is that most commercial movies are made for entertainment, not for instruction. For every minute of instruction, there is ten minutes of irrelevant material intended to entertain.

Visual aids should supplement rather than replace the teacher. They should present in visual form material that the instructor is discussing orally. Their purpose is to reinforce his discussion and reach through the visual senses what the student hears through the audio senses. They should not take control of the class away from the teacher and reduce him to the status of a projector operator.

To be sure, some motion pictures, which were made primarily for entertainment, have some value for political science students. *Mr. Smith Goes to Washington* and *Advise and Consent* not only have a number of insights into the operation of Congress, but take the student into the Capitol building. *Woodrow Wilson* not only has some historical value, but may lead a student to appreciate the problems of the presidency better. Even *Seven Days in May* raises some provocative questions about civil-military relations. Whether class time should be taken to showing pictures of this type is questionable. There is an alternative which would seem to permit the wider use of such films. That would be to show them outside the class on the voluntary attendance basis as is done at the United States Military Academy at West Point. This might be one means not only of financing their showing, but of relating attendance to a more fully developed independent study program.

Such fine old documentaries as *The River* and *TVA,* dated as they may be, not only present interesting studies of government propaganda, but convey a good deal of information about the use of natural resources in the United States.

In this same group are occasional documentary films produced by government agencies, either foreign or the United States, whose major purpose is conveying information. Some of those produced by the British and Commonwealth governments are particularly useful. As with most good things, their use can be overdone, but if shown occasionally, they may make teaching more effective.

Another alternative is for the instructor to make movies of his own as has been done in the Duke Medical School. These overcome the objections that can be raised against most commercially produced motion pictures. Their purpose is solely to instruct, and if they are sound movies the professor's lecture is given at the same time that the picture is shown. Consequently, he is not replaced by another teacher. The major difficulty, of course, is lack of technical skill in producing pictures. However, this may not be as much of an obstacle as it would seem at first glance. If the motion pictures are intended to be used in large classes, the incentive for making them might justify the employment of commercial facilities. Some universities are developing their own television studios and these usually include facilities for motion picture production. Thus, in time the problem of lack of technical skill may be solved.

Moving pictures are not really necessary, however, unless the subject shown must be moving to convey the thought. Statistical tables, charts, and maps may be more effective on a slide than they are in a motion picture. Wall maps and charts and a blackboard are not of very much use in large lecture sections. In fact, the larger the lecture group, the less use these traditional visual aids are. Recent technological developments make the production and use of slides easier than formerly. Maps and charts can be blown up to large sizes so that they can be seen by all the students even in a large classroom. Modern slide projectors can be used in lighted rooms making it easy for students to take notes while listening to the lecture. Slides are cheap to make, easy to keep up to date since they can be adapted to new lecture material, and they can be made without extensive technical knowledge of photography. Indeed, slides are as feasible a "do-it-yourself project" in political science as they long have been in the natural sciences.

There are some problems, of course, to be overcome but they are considerably easier to deal with than in the case of making motion pictures. Statistical material particularly lends itself to slide presentation. The number of persons voting in an election, population movement, sources of revenue and types of expenditures, comparisons between the past and present are relatively easy to present on a slide. Philosophical ideas and political concepts are harder but not necessarily impossible.

As in the case of motion pictures, slides should reinforce an oral presentation and not replace it. The lecture itself is the important thing. It should be prepared first and be supported by the visual material. It is an unfortunate practice in government "briefing" to put an entire lecture on slides. In this kind of a presentation, the lecturer becomes merely a reader.

A common practice in business use of slides is to use humor freely to make the presentation more palatable. Unfortunately, students sometimes become more interested in the cartoons than they do in the main points of the lecture. It should always be kept in mind that the purpose of the college class is to teach, not to amuse, the students.

Slides are most effective when used in the middle of a lecture. Educational psychologists report that students' interest is at its peak during the first fifteen minutes of a fifty-minute lecture and then declines rapidly. The best procedure, consequently, probably would be for an instructor to talk without slides at first and then, when student interest begins to decline, use slides to reinforce his audio presentation. This capitalizes on periods of student interest and permits a certain repetition of the same points in visual as well as oral form. Audio-visual materials are not limited to motion pictures, slides, and wall charts. Some instructors have made good use of tape recordings, large transparencies, and various overlay devices, as well as self-operating audio-visual exhibits. The initial cost of such equipment is high and not much research has been done to determine how effective they are in teaching. Exhibits have been widely used in private business and government in the last decade. The wide-spread use of this type of equipment in hundreds of industrial fairs and international exhibits challenges universities to adopt the use of this equipment to the campus. If one were to push further into the little-known but fascinating area of subliminal perception he would find that it has not been explored for college teaching.

What will we say about political science to the able college student of tomorrow? How can we help him bring together what he has learned earlier in life and will learn in college? Will we tell him in the words of Guy Stanton Ford: "Despite all the subdivision and increasing specialization, man's knowledge of himself, of his fellow men and the world they live in is becoming more and more evidently a seamless web."[26]

Should we say that politics can best be studied by examining the history of the past, or that understanding politics can best be attained through reading the great works of literature? If we do this, we would be speaking a large measure of truth. But certainly there is something that political science can say to college students that is unique and which makes the study of the subject worth their while. Should we warn him that there is a yawning gap between political scientists whose teaching is based on empirical data and those who rest their case on the philosophy of politics? Or shall we tell him that this debate is really a duel with wooden swords? Is there really a dichotomy between these two perspectives or are they simply parts of the same thing?

Shall we tell him that far from being sterile, political science offers a field of endless inquiry and adventure? While its roots are in the past, its full growth is in the future. Far from running out of materials for inquiry the problems lie in the scope of the subject. But apart from the subject content of political science, do we not need to have a fresh look at its teachers and ". . . at the sacred cows of academia that, like other ruminants, not infrequently chew and re-chew the same intellectual cud and that do not hesitate to require the same of students, first as prep school seniors, then as undergraduate, and finally as graduate students, each time with growing boredom and resentment."[27]

We may need to know much more about the learning process and be much more willing to examine data about teaching and learning even when it comes from the pens of professors of education. Perhaps we should be less inclined to reject these data without weighing their merits. Perhaps we have to be more flexible and imaginative about teaching methods if we are to cope with more intelligent and better educated generations of college students that we will face in

26. Ford, *op. cit.,* p. 477.
27. O. Meredith Wilson, "Wisdom Is Better than Strength," in *Vision and Purpose in Higher Education,* Raymond F. Howes (ed.) (Washington, 1962), p. 154.

the years ahead. If we do accept this challenge and strive to cope with it, perhaps we will be able to say with Charles Beard, who more than half a century ago wrote,

We are certain to emancipate ourselves from the pernicious doctrine, made in Germany, that the teacher who would rise to a position of eminence with its suitable rewards must be a maker of many learned treatises; and let us hope that we shall be spared the English device which turns the instructor into a cramming machine speedily worn to worse than ruin by the necessity of forcing learning upon that large percentage of recalcitrant youths whose hearts are at the stadium or the boat race. At all events there is reason for believing that the outlook for the college teacher in the United States was never brighter than it is now; and the newly developing subject of politics will come into its own.[28]

28. Charles A. Beard, "The Study and Teaching of Politics," *Columbia University Quarterly*, XII (June, 1910), 271.

J. PETER MEEKISON

A bibliographical essay

The compilation of a bibliography on teaching political science seems in many respects to be a simple task, simple because of the paucity of books and articles devoted specifically to the subject. The problem becomes complex, however, because of the abundance of literature produced by related disciplines which has some relevance to teaching political science. One might group the references available into four categories: the formal surveys conducted under the auspices of the American Political Science Association, individual articles on teaching written by political scientists and appearing in the various professional journals, articles on teaching by foreign political scientists, and finally books and articles on the broad subject of college teaching. These four groups are described separately below with some attention to chronology within each group.

The continuing concern of the Association about the "state of the discipline" is demonstrated by five studies which it has sponsored over the last fifty years. Indeed there has been approximately one study in each decade since 1900. While not all of these studies were directed specifically toward the improvement of teaching, they necessarily have had some impact upon it.

The earliest of the Association studies was conducted in 1907 and 1908. At the second meeting of the Association, in 1905, William A. Schaper of the University of Minnesota presented a paper entitled, "What Do Our Students Know about American Government before Taking College Courses in Political Science?" Alarmed over the fact that students entering the university seemed to know little about the rudiments of government, the Association appointed a committee to determine what instruction in government was available in the secondary schools. Upon the basis of a questionnaire sent to selected high schools, the committee soon decided that the problem went far deeper than it had expected. Good secondary school instruction, it concluded, depended upon a firm basis of knowledge developed in the grade school. Civics was ordinarily taught in either the seventh or the eighth grades. Since many students dropped out of school at the end of the sixth grade, they had no instruction in civics. Consequently, the committee recommended that civics be taught earlier in grade schools and more intensively in the secondary schools. Its report was published in the *Proceedings* for 1908 (V, 219-257).

This concern of the political scientist for pre-college teaching is quite understandable. Similar anxiety was expressed by historians a quarter of a century earlier and by sociologists in more recent times. Since what is taught at the secondary school level affects what needs to be taught at the college level, these same questions have been raised by social scientists time and again in the last half-century.

The first Association study was followed by a much more extensive one in the years just before World War I. In 1910 Charles G. Haines presented a paper at the Association's annual meeting entitled "Is Sufficient Time Devoted to the Study of Government in Our Colleges?" (*Proceedings,* VII, 1910, 202-209). The discussion of this paper led to the creation of another study committee, appointed in December, 1911, to "consider the methods of teaching and studying government now pursued in American schools, colleges and universities, and to suggest means of enlarging and improving such instruction." After preliminary reports in 1913 and 1914, the committee published its final report in 1916, entitled *The Teaching of Government* (New York, 1916). Compiled with the assistance of the United States Office of Education, this report was much more extensive than the earlier one and represented the first major analysis of the discipline as a whole. The 1951 report of the Association, *Goals for Political Science,* refers to this early study as being both "modern and prophetic."

The Teaching of Government was divided into four parts: recent progress in the teaching of government, teaching civics in the secondary schools, suggested courses of study for elementary and secondary schools, and teaching political science in colleges and universities. The first and most important recommendation of the committee was that political science be recognized as a separate discipline and be given departmental status in the university organization. It should not be treated simply as an appendage to the history or economics departments. This "declaration of independence" was the most striking feature of the report. Once political science achieved independence, the committee maintained, teaching methods suitable to its objectives could be developed. The report also contained a great deal of information of historical value about instruction in political science as it existed at that time, but little of it has relevance for solving today's problems.

Nine years later a third Association-sponsored study was undertaken. The Committee on Political Research under the chairmanship of Charles E. Merriam was assigned the task, as Merriam stated it, "to scrutinize the scope and method of political research in the field of government. . . ." The committee investigated five areas: recent advances in political methods, government research bodies, legislative and municipal reference agencies, research and equipment in universities and colleges, and research carried on by social and industrial agencies in the field of government. The preliminary report of the committee, found in the *American Political Science Review* (XVII, 1923, 274-312), recommended the establishment of a Social Science Research Council for the purpose of improving research in the social sciences. Apart from this important recommendation, the long-term significance of the report centers on Professor Merriam's own section which dealt with methodology. He traced the growth of the study of political processes through four phases: (*1*) the a priori and deductive method down to 1850, (*2*) the historical and comparative method, 1850-1900, (*3*) the present tendency towards observation, survey, measurement, 1900—, and (*4*) the beginnings of the psychological treatment of politics. To Merriam, the defects of the scientific development of the discipline up to that time had been the lack of adequate methods of collecting, classifying, and analyzing data; a lack of standards of measurement; and a lack of objectivity on the part of the researchers. He urged, in essence, that political science be made more "scientific." Although the principal emphasis of this inquiry was upon research, the consequences for the teaching of political science which resulted from it cannot be overlooked. This report was the first formal recognition of what has come to be known as the behavioral approach. The impact of this approach upon the content and teaching of political science has been impressive.

The committee also recommended that the relationship of political science to anthropology, biology, geography, geology, engineering, and other allied subjects be investigated. Apparently only one of these studies was ever undertaken. This was Merriam's "The Significance of Psychology for the Study of Politics," which was published in the *Review* (XVIII, 1924, 469-488) the following year.

Two additional reports on the development of political science in Europe appeared under committee auspices in the same year. Professor John A. Fairlie gave a brief account of the development of political science in Great Britain (XVIII, 1924, 574-582), and Professor W. R. Sharp gave a similar account of its status in France (XVIII, 1924, 582-592).

A fourth Association-sponsored study followed hard on the heels of the third. Charles A. Beard at the 1926 annual meeting moved that a committee on policy be appointed "to survey the field of political science activity, to analyze the part now played therein by the Association, and to make recommendations as to ways in which the Association might be made to contribute more significantly to the solutions of the problems of government, politics and administration. . . ." This committee, chaired by Thomas Reed, published its report as a *Supplement* to the *Review* (XXIV, 1930, 1-199).

The *Report* of the Reed Committee consisted of a brief review of the discipline and a recommendation that the Association create a standing policy committee with subcommittees on research, political education, publication, and personnel. Included with the report were twelve appendixes, only one of which was primarily concerned with teaching, William B. Munro's "Instruction in Political Science in Colleges and Universities" (pp. 127-145). Over half this essay was devoted to the description of political science curricula, enrollment, teaching schedules, and salaries. The remainder described briefly the teaching techniques employed by various departments of political science. This information had been compiled from replies to a questionnaire sent out under committee auspices. Munro's principal concern was with the introductory course. He felt that "there is no reason why one should look for uniformity of method. . . ." He maintained that here much depends upon local conditions and facilities. Very brief mention was made of new methods of instruction, such as field work, undergraduate seminars, tutorials, and problem study. The usefulness of these "new" techniques was not discussed, nor did Munro offer any suggestions for improving the quality of teaching. He concluded that among the outstanding problems of political science were heavy teaching loads and scarcity of good recruits for the teaching profession. These problems he felt must be solved before any program for the improvement of instruction could be effective.

The most recent study conducted by the Association, made in the years immediately following World War II, was published under the title of *Goals for Political Science* (New York, 1951). This effort was triggered by a series of articles in the *Review* (XLI, 1947, 489-534), edited by Francis O. Wilcox, entitled "Undergraduate Instruction in Political Science." Professor Wilcox opened the collection with an article on "The Introductory Course in Government." This was followed by articles by Harvey C. Mansfield on "The Major in Political Science," James W. Fesler on "Undergraduate Training for the Public Service," John D. Millett on "The Use of Visual Aids in Political Science Teaching," and Ethan P. Allen on "The Teacher of Government."

From discussion of these papers to the establishment of "the goals committee" to make a comprehensive study of the discipline was a short step. The committee not only undertook an analysis of undergraduate instruction but also considered problems of graduate study and instruction, training for public service, and co-operation in the social sciences, generally. As the committee reported, "Our interest stems from a desire to improve the teaching of political science, but the committee rapidly learned that this requires a broad look and not the narrow one that the term 'teaching' might imply. How can one deal with improvements in teaching without dealing with goals? And once that decision has been made, the inquiry is bound of necessity to become a broad one."

The actual space in *Goals* devoted to the discussion of "teaching" *qua* teaching was limited to the final two chapters. In the section on graduate study, the committee deplored the lack of preparation of graduate students to teach effectively. The last chapter "Modernized Teaching Methods" described the use and adaptation of audio-visual and laboratory methods in teaching political science.

The committee recommended that "the *American Political Science Review* should reserve space for review of new audio-visual materials and improved teaching techniques," but only three articles directly concerned with teaching have been published in the *Review* since 1951. In "The Improvement of Teaching in International Relations: The Iowa Seminars" (LI, 1957, 579-581) Vernon Van Dyke reported on an endeavor to improve teaching through "a better understanding of subject matter." Herbert Garfinkel and James F. Tierney discussed the need for "A Coordinating Course in the Political Science Major" (LI, 1957, 1178-1182). Finally, the Association's Committee on Standards of Instruction published a statement on "Political Science as a Discipline" (LVI, 1962, 417-421) reviewing the teaching-load problem, the proliferation of courses, and the preparation of teachers.

To be sure, since 1951 at least two presidential addresses, later published in the *Review,* have emphasized the importance of teaching. Pendleton Herring, in "On the Study of Government" (XLVII, 1953, 961-974), declared that "The highest form of teaching is that in which the teacher performs as a scholar and shares with his juniors in learning his own excitement and sense of integrity in the pursuit of knowledge." V. O. Key, Jr., in "The State of the Discipline" (LII, 1958, 961-971), stated that ". . . the quality of our teaching . . . depend[s] upon the quality of the content of our discipline. . . ." Moreover, the bibliographical note by Jean M. Driscoll and Charles S. Hyneman, "Methodology for Political Scientists; Perspectives for Study" (XLIX, 1955, 192-217) gives a good survey of the literature describing the scope of political science.

In addition to these formal surveys of the discipline and the articles related to them, there have been a number of other articles paralleling the Association's efforts. These pieces by individual political scientists constitute a second category of material available. Chronologically, the earliest is Charles A. Beard, "The Study and Teaching of Politics," *Columbia University Quarterly* (XII, 1910, 268-274), in which he analyzed the revolutionary impact of the "new political science" of his day upon teaching. Other articles were concerned with teaching specific courses. Arnold Bennett Hall, "The Teaching of Constitutional Law" (*Review,* XVI, 1922, 486-496) argued for an undergraduate course in constitutional law using the case method. Edwin D. Dickinson, "The Teaching of International Law to Law Students" (*Review,* XVII, 1923, 464-476), while advocating the use of the case method, pointed out some of the pitfalls encountered by this technique. Russell M. Storey, "Content of the Introductory Course in Political Science" (*Review,* XX, 1926, 419-428), urged that the introductory course go beyond mere description of political phenomena: it should include an explanation of political phenomena. A similar position was taken by Richard C. Spencer, "Significance of a Functional Approach in the Introductory Course" (*Review,* XXII, 1928, 954-966).

The years of World War II and their aftermath gave rise to a number of other articles in the *American Political Science Review.* In "Political Science in the Next Decade" (XXXIX, 1945, 757-766), Pendleton Herring noted that "the relatively greater role that government has assumed and the more active part that students of government are undertaking in public affairs" would profoundly affect the discipline in the next decade. Indeed, this statement might explain the plethora of articles appearing during this period. These included Walter H. Laves' "The Next Decade in Political Science Teaching" (XXXIV, 1940, 983-986); Robert D. Leigh, "The Educational Function of Social Scientists" (XXXVIII, 1944, 531-539); Karl Loewenstein, "Report on the Research Panel of Comparative Government" (XXXVIII, 1944, 540-548); Landon G. Rockwell, "Toward a More Integrated Political Science Curriculum" (XLI, 1947, 314-320); Russell H. Fifield, "The Introductory Course in International Relations" (XLII, 1948, 1189-1196); Robert E. Elder, "Teaching International Relations: The Model Security Council or General Assembly" (XLIII, 1949, 95-98).

Two articles published in the *Review* during this period had teaching techniques as their central theme. Robert H. Connery in "A Laboratory Method for Teaching Public Administration" (XLII, 1948, 68-74) suggested that regular lectures might be made more realistic by using "administrative games." Operating a hypothetical government agency was said to be as useful a teaching device for students as war-games were for the military. The concern of Ruth G. Weintraub's "Audio-Visual Media and Political Science Teaching" (XLIII, 1949, 766-776) is indicated by its title.

In addition to these articles in the *Review,* two essays appeared in regional journals. In "Political Science as a Profession: From the Standpoint of Teaching," *Journal of Politics* (III, 1941, 509-518),

Professor F. A. Ogg presented his views on how the teaching of political science might be strengthened. In a more recent discussion of instructional methods, "Techniques of Teaching Political Science: The Beginning Course," *Western Political Quarterly* (XI, 1958, 125-136), Professors Robert H. Connery and Richard H. Leach reviewed a whole series of teaching techniques.

Before leaving the American scene, mention should be given to an excellent bibliography contained in Professor Hyneman's recent work, *The Study of Politics* (Urbana, 1959). A person wishing to pursue the "state of political science as a discipline and profession" will find Professor Hyneman's bibliography extremely useful.

Passing reference should also be made to materials concerned with university training for the public service or public affairs. The dual purpose of the collection of essays in *The Public Service and University Education* (Princeton, 1949), edited by Joseph E. Mc-Lean, was "to assay the personnel needs of governments and, to examine the role of the university in the education of prospective public servants." The theme of *Public Affairs Education and the University* (Syracuse, 1963), edited by Gerard Mangone, is that not only the social scientists, but all the departments of a university, have an obligation for preparing students for public responsibilities. Persons primarily interested in internship programs will find the *Newsletter* of the National Commission on Education in Politics (formerly Citizenship Clearing House of the New York University) helpful in suggesting methods for active participation in politics.

The third category of source materials consists of articles on teaching written by foreign political scientists or sponsored by international agencies. In Great Britain S. E. Finer's "On the Teaching of Politics" was one of a series of articles on university teaching that appeared in *Universities Quarterly* (VIII, 1953/54, 44-54). Professor Finer's article, like many of those published in the United States, attempted to define the scope and content of political science as well as comment on teaching. The Australian Political Science Association sponsored a conference at Canberra University in 1957 which led to a series of articles entitled "Political Science in Australian Universities," found in *Australian Journal of Politics and History* (IV, 1958, 1-93). The papers given at the conference were: "Political Studies: A Conference Report," by R. N. Spann; "Politics as a University

Subject," by P. H. Partridge; "A Comment on Professor Partridge's Paper," by B. D. Beddie; "Three and Four Year Courses in Political Science," by L. F. Crisp; "The Teaching of Comparative Government," by H. A. Wolfsohn; "The Teaching of Public Administration," by B. B. Schaffer; "A Comment on Dr. Schaffer's Paper," by R. S. Parker; and "The Study of International Relations," by Gordon Greenwood.

In view of the importance of the social sciences to orderly government, it is not surprising that even international bodies like UNESCO have given some attention to the teaching of them. A volume prepared by William A. Robson, *The University Teaching of Social Sciences: Political Science* (Leiden) appeared in 1954. The volume included a discussion of the aims of political science, relationship of the discipline with other subjects, methods of teaching, and problems facing the university professor in the future. It also contained appendixes reporting the results of a survey of current teaching methods and teacher recruitment and training in political science in the United States, Great Britain, France, Sweden, India, Mexico, Poland, Egypt, Canada, and Germany. A more general report prepared by a number of authors, *Teaching of Social Sciences in the United States* (UNESCO; Paris, 1954), included a chapter on political science by Marshall E. Dimock.

The fourth and largest category includes general works on college teaching, some of them written by professional educators, some by philosophers, and some by psychologists. The area of interest is so broad that one is faced with many difficulties in selecting those publications in this category which would be of greatest value to teaching political science at the college level. A considerable number of these works are cited below but at best the list is selective. An attempt has been made to include some of the best-known books and articles in this field together with others which seem to have particular pertinence to political science.

As one might expect, the professional associations of colleges and universities have given considerable attention to teaching over the last half-century. The Association of American Colleges long had a committee on enlistment and training of college teachers. Reports of this committee were published in 1927, 1928, 1929, 1930, and 1931 in the *Bulletin* of the Association of American Colleges. The particular topics studied, however, were broad in their nature—e.g., faculty and student education, the effect of sabbatical leaves—and they related more to general academic concerns than to solving specific problems of teaching.

A similar committee of the Association of American Universities was particularly active during the decade of the 1930's. Its reports were published in the *Proceedings* of the association. Moreover, the American Association of University Professors through its various committees has been concerned not only with tenure and salaries of college professors, but with college teaching in general. The *Bulletin* of the association frequently contains articles on this subject. One particularly stimulating well-written piece by Guy Stanton Ford, entitled "Teacher and Taught" (XLI, 1955, 476-488), analyzes the qualities of a good teacher. Two articles by political scientists in the same journal more directly to the point are "Academic Revolution," by Marion D. Irish (XXXII, 1946, 472-484), and "The Ivory Tower—No Vacancies," by Lane W. Lancaster (XXXIII, 1947, 279-285), both concerned with the practicality of internships, field trips, and political participation.

Two comprehensive reports can be found in the *American Council on Education Studies,* Series I, Reports of Committees and Conferences, "The Preparation of College Teachers" (No. 42, Vol. XIV, 1950), and "Improving College Instruction," Fred J. Kelly (ed.) (No. 48, Vol. XV, 1951). The first of these is a series of papers and discussion group reports on the difficulties involved in the preparation and recruitment of university professors. The second study group report is an analysis in some detail of problems encountered in college teaching.

An additional source of information is the rapidly growing body of educational periodicals. Only a few articles from the better-known journals are listed below, but, these periodicals and others of the same type frequently contain articles on college teaching. For example, George Raab and Alvin M. Westcott in "What Ails College Teaching?" *The Educational Forum* (XXVII, 1963, 307-312), urged that teaching in colleges receive the same critical examination which elementary and secondary education have already undergone. They maintain that only through constructive criticism will the quality of instruction be improved.

Three particularly useful articles in the *Harvard Educational Review* are T. R. Henn's "Some American Universities as Seen Through British Eyes" (XXIV, 1954, 202-221), B. F. Skinner's "The Science of Learning and The Art of Teaching" (XXIV, 1954, 86-97), and Arthur W. Melton's "The Science of Learning and the Technology of Educational Methods" (XXIX, 1959, 96-106).

Three other educational journals occasionally contain articles on teaching which political scientists would profit by examining. The *Journal of Higher Education,* published by Ohio State University, in recent issues has included essays by Harold B. Dunkel, "Training College Teachers" (XXIX, 1958, 1-7 and ff.) and John H. Rohrer, "Large and Small Sections in College Classes" (XXVIII, 1957, 275-279). In the *Quarterly* of The North Central Association of Colleges and Secondary Schools, Helen C. White's "The Scholar's Time: How It Is Best Used" (XXXI, 1956/57, 235-239 and ff.) and William J. McKeefery's "Some Observations of Effective Teaching" (XXXII, 1957/58, 325-332) are worthy of mention. The article entitled "An Experimental Comparison of Recitation, Discussion, and Tutorial Methods in College Teaching" (XLV, 1954, 193-207) by Harold Guetzkow and others illustrates the experimental concern of the *Journal of Educational Psychology.*

Occasional articles in popular journals have a direct bearing on university teaching, particularly in such publications as *Harper's Magazine,* the *Saturday Review,* and the *New York Times Magazine.* A few examples are Jacques Barzun, "The Cults of 'Research' and 'Creativity,' " *Harper's Magazine* (CCXXI, October, 1960, 69-74); "The College Scene," *Harper's Magazine* (CCXXIII, October, 1961, 121-182); Paul Goodman, "For A Reactionary Experiment in Education," *Harper's Magazine* (CCXXV, November, 1962, 61-72); Bruce Dearing, "Three Myths About the College Teacher," *Saturday Review* (XLVII, January 18, 1964, 65-67); and John Q. Academesis, "Too Many College Teachers Don't Teach," *New York Times Magazine* (February 21, 1960, pp. 14 ff.).

Research and philanthropic foundations frequently sponsor studies on education. The Ford Foundation, through the Fund for the Advancement of Education, is one such body which has been particularly active in this area. The publications of the fund to date indicate increasing concern over the quality of teaching in universities. One study, *Better Utilization of College Teaching Resources* (New York, 1957), concluded that growing student enrollment and a distinct teacher shortage would require changes in the traditional concepts of university teaching. By way of illustration, the report gave a brief description of experimental programs which various universities were conducting in an effort to surmount the problem of more students and fewer teachers. A second project sponsored by the fund provided college internships for training college teachers. John Diekhoff in *Tomorrow's Professors* (New York, 1959) reported on this program and suggested how universities could establish their own teacher-training programs. The Rockefeller Brothers Fund sponsored *The Pursuit of Excellence: Education and the Future of America* (Garden City, 1958), which, as the title implies, was concerned with the pressing need for better utilization of talent and ability in the nation's schools and colleges.

Finally, there is a wealth of information on teaching, learning, and instructing in general works on education. Many of these, written by professors of education, are presented in a language which requires a considerable knowledge of educational jargon to be easily understood. Before individual works are listed, an annotated bibliography prepared by Walter C. Eells, *College Teachers and College Teaching* (Southern Regional Education Board), should be mentioned. Since this comprehensive bibliography was first issued in 1957 several supplements have appeared. The work includes substantially all books and articles which have any bearing on education, arranged by disciplines. Another bibliographical publication which appears quarterly is the *Reporter,* Clearing House of Studies on Higher Education, Department of Health, Education, and Welfare, Washington, D. C., which contains an annotated listing of completed research in higher education.

The problems of teaching should not be considered in a vacuum but are best viewed from the broader perspective of the whole man and his education according to *Higher Education for American Society* (Madison, 1949), edited by John Guy Fowlkes. This volume consisted of a series of papers delivered at the National Education Conference in 1948. E. R. Guthrie's short volume on *The State University, Its Functions and Its Future* (Seattle, 1959) includes one chapter on the "Psychology of Teaching." *Vision and Purpose in*

Higher Education (American Council on Education; Washington, 1962), edited by Raymond F. Howes, is a collection of twenty papers by university presidents which had appeared in the *Educational Record* over the ten-year period, 1952-1962. In *Memo to a College Trustee* (Fund for the Advancement of Education; New York, 1959), Beardsley Ruml asks the question, "How can colleges faced with a rising student population provide a liberal education while maintaining high standards?" His answer is that universities must institute internal changes to accommodate this problem. One chapter is devoted to "Curriculum and Methods of Instruction."

The most exhaustive and complete study of higher education in recent years is *The American College* (New York, 1962), edited by Nevitt Sanford. Intended to be a psychological and social interpretation of higher learning, this collection of essays by thirty authors runs to well over a thousand pages in length and is extensively footnoted. The major topics, all of which relate to teaching are "the entering student, academic procedure, student societies and student culture, student performance in relation to educational objectives, interaction of students and educators, the effects of college education, and higher education and the social context."

A new philosophy of education is needed, argues Professor Paul Woodring in *A Fourth of A Nation* (New York, 1957), because of expanding school enrollment. A large part of his argument centers upon a re-examination of the traditional methods of training teachers. Robert T. Kelly, in *The American Colleges and the Social Order* (New York, 1940), took a different approach. He included one chapter reviewing some of the past attempts at "The Improvement of College Teaching."

The "superior student" is another subject which has received considerable attention. The theme of *They Went to College Early* (Fund for the Advancement of Education, Report No. 2; New York, 1957) is that students with proven ability should be encouraged and permitted to attend a university at an early age. It was argued here that the traditional school grade system must be made more flexible if this is to be accomplished. In another book, *Excellence, Can We Be Equal and Excellent Too?* (New York, 1961), John W. Gardner discussed the difficulties involved in the pursuit of excellence and included a chapter on who should go to college.

Among the general works on teaching, two stand out as particularly stimulating and provocative. Gilbert Highet's *The Art of Teaching* (New York, 1950), is based on the author's experiences as a teacher rather than on any specific educational theory. Highet argues that teaching is an art, not a science. The book is very different from educational textbooks in that it has no statistics or conclusions based on research. His analysis goes beyond the traditional examination of the qualities and abilities that a teacher should have and includes an analysis of great teachers of the past and their methods. Highet maintains that teaching is not limited to the schoolroom. It takes place in a variety of face-to-face relationships—the doctor and his patient, the clergyman and congregation, etc. Undoubtedly Highet's book is one of the best contemporary works on teaching in its broadest sense.

An equally stimulating work is Jacques Barzun's *Teacher In America* (6th ed.; New York, 1958). The fact that this book has gone through several editions testifies to its popularity. In Barzun's words, "the advantage of 'teaching' is that in using it you must recognize practical limits exist." Only some subjects are teachable, but as a result of good teaching "priceless by-products, leading possibly to democratic or marital bliss, come from their study." The book consists of twenty-one chapters directed at different facets of the teaching process. While some of the topics discussed concern non-university education, Barzun's ideas on the "gifted" student, how to write, the use of the classics, and his comments on the intellectual life in general are particularly appealing to a university audience.

Houston Peterson's *Great Teachers* (New Brunswick, 1946) supplements Highet's book by describing twenty-two famous college teachers as seen by their former students. Woodrow Wilson is the only political scientist in the group, but many of the others, especially those in the social sciences, were dealing with teaching situations similar to those facing political scientists. The purpose of the book is summarized in the editor's comment that "we of moderate abilities can get a distinct *lift* from a consideration of the exceptional teacher, and rise imperceptibly to new planes of energy and value."

Several other less well-known works provide additional insight into the problems of purposes of good teaching. *Essays In Teaching* (New York, 1950), edited by Harold Taylor, emphasizes the importance of recognizing the individuality of each student. In *Teaching Tips:*

Guide Book for the Beginning College Teacher (Ann Arbor, 1956, 3rd ed.), Wilbert McKeachie gives a brief description of teaching techniques with some evaluation of their effectiveness. In a series of lectures, *College Teaching and College Learning* (New Haven, 1949), Ordway Tead analyzes the inadequacies of college teaching and suggests several approaches toward improving its quality. A more recent study examining critically the standards of university teaching is *Quality of College Teaching and Staff* (Washington: The Catholic University of America Press, 1961), edited by Roy J. Deferrai. The book is a report of a study group which examined the problems of the quality of instruction and shortage of teachers in Catholic colleges.

Two books on the subject of the learning process by Nathaniel Cantor are especially worth noting, *The Dynamics of Learning* (Buffalo, 1946) and *The Teaching-Learning Process* (New York, 1953). The first is an attempt to analyze the meaning of the term a "highly skilled, professional teacher." The theme of the second is that "if learning is to be significant and useful . . . the learner must want to learn." Since learning is largely a personal experience, the teacher must be conscious of his role in this process.

One can only conclude from this brief bibliographical analysis that the amount of material published by political scientists on college teaching is limited but that these materials can be supplemented by more general works. The problem is to choose from the vast number in this second category. The relative scarcity of materials on teaching by political scientists suggests that the profession has not given the subject as much thought as it should.

Index